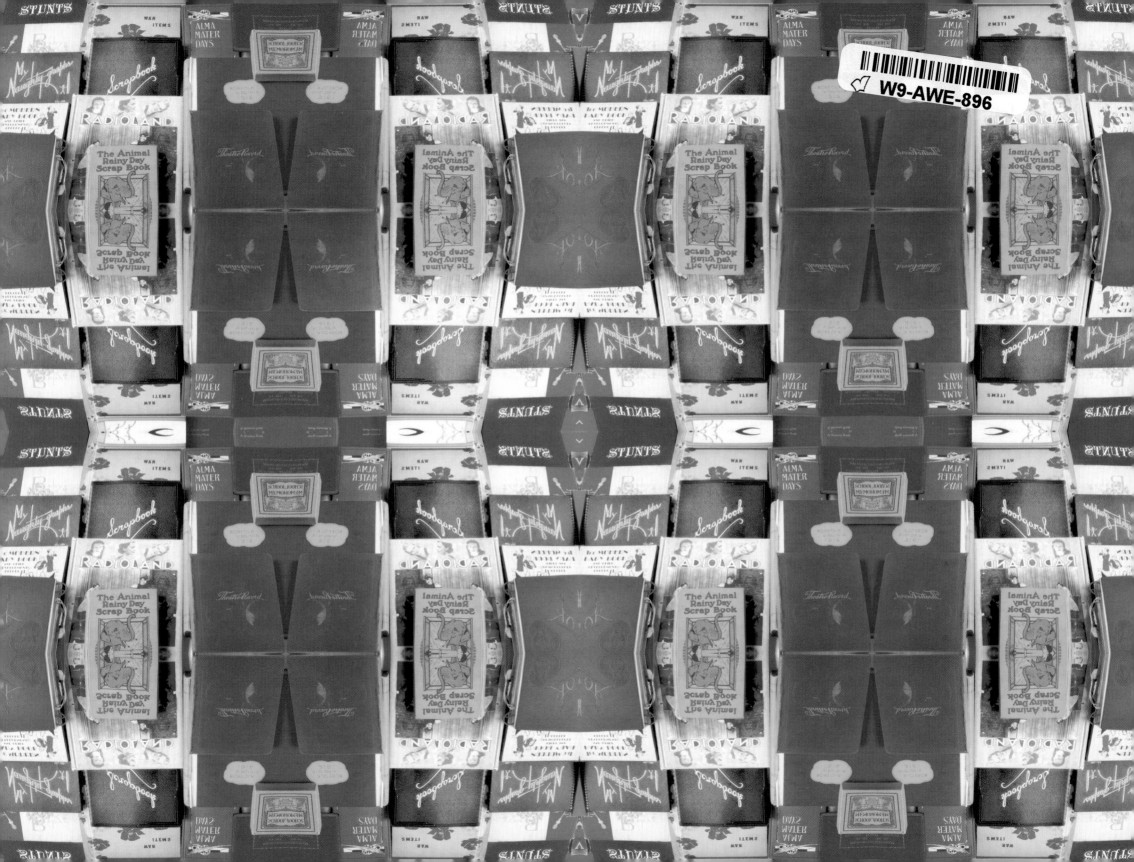

SCRAPBOOKS: AN AMERICAN HISTORY

A WINTERHOUSE EDITION

YALE UNIVERSITY PRESS   NEW HAVEN AND LONDON

JESSICA HELFAND

SCRAPBOOKS: AN AMERICAN HISTORY

Published with assistance from Furthermore:
a program of the J. M. Kaplan Fund.

A catalogue record for this book is available
from the British Library.

Library of Congress Control Number:
2008923233

ISBN 978-0-300-12635-8

10 9 8 7 6 5 4 3 2 1

Portions of this book previously appeared in
Aperture Magazine.

This paper meets the requirements of ANSI/
NISO Z39.48-1992 (Permanence of Paper).
It contains 30 percent postconsumer waste
(PCW) and is certified by the Forest Stewardship
Council (FSC).

Design: WINTERHOUSE.

Set in Electra, Kaufmann, and Rockwell types.
Printed in China.

Cover images: (Front) photograph of young boys, anonymous travel journal,
1912; Fourth of July celebration flag, 1895; Anne Sexton's motel room
key, 1948; anonymous travel journal, 1912; portrait of Minnie Reed, 1919.
(Back, left to right) Broken shovel and bark samples, Kelley Scrapbook,
Briarcliff Manor, New York, 1928; silhouetted friends from school page,
Enloe Scrapbook, Fayette, Missouri, 1923; collaged page from *Delineator*
Scrapbook, ca. 1931; sample page from Radioland Scrapbook, Portland,
Oregon, ca. 1930. (Front flap) Photograph of young boys, anonymous travel
journal, 1912. (Back flap) Anonymous photograph of young boy, Blanchard
Scrapbook, Natchitoches, Louisiana, ca. 1922. Photo of key courtesy of
the Estate of Anne Sexton. Reprinted by permission of SLL /Sterling Lord
Literistic, Inc.

Abraham Scrapbook
Pittsburgh, PA
1927

CONTENTS

FEATURED SCRAPBOOKS

Christine Dobbs
Marietta, Georgia

Marybelle Harn
Cincinnati, Ohio

Kitty Baker
Norfolk, Virginia

Francis Johnson
Waterbury, Connecticut

Candy Jernigan
Travel Journal, India

THIS BOOK DETICATED
TO

HATTIE BRIGGS

BORN 18   DIED 19

HAD BROTHERS AND SISTERS NAMED

CORA, VERNA, ERNEST.

HAD BAD EYES, BAD TEETH, AND BROKE HIP, LEGS.

LIVED IN CENTRAL LAKE, BELLAIRE AND

ON THE FARM. WAS IN ANN ARBOR

HOSPITAL

Hearty
Greetings.

To mrs Briggs
From mr wheeler and
faimly

FOR WILLIAM.

2. With Shanny at 3.
Eastbourne. Sept. 1926.

MINE IS A FAMILY OF OBSESSIVE COLLECTORS. My mother collected portraits—everything from formal paintings to fraternal badges—and my father collected medical ephemera: labels and trade cards, pamphlets and *cartes de visite*, posters and broadsides and illustrated books.

Scrapbooks are their progeny, an ideal hybrid of humanity and paper: ephemeral portraits.

As a graduate student at Yale in the late 1980s, I became interested in the idea of visualizing biography. This was just the beginning of what became a deeper and more comprehensive fascination with first-person stories. Over the years, I have continued to be drawn to visual biographies in general, and to scrapbooks in particular: they seem at once an evocative and a largely overlooked class of artifact. Gradually, I began to amass a fairly sizable collection of scrapbooks of my own, and soon discovered quite a few of them—partic-ularly those produced by, and occasionally for, well-known people—sequestered in public librar-ies and private collections. And it soon became evident that there was something long gone yet still curiously palpable within the pages of these forgotten books—something emotionally vivid and passionate and real. Unauthorized one-offs, cobbled together from common materials, they could hardly be looked upon as valid repositories of social history.

Or could they?

Over the past eighteen months, in preparation for this book, I have traveled the country looking for examples of scrapbooks that met five essential criteria. First, because I am a visual historian, they needed to be beautiful: this was and has remained my primary point of entry. Second, once I was drawn into a beautiful scrapbook, there needed to be a payoff, a *there* there—a story worth telling.

OPPOSITE
Waller-Bridge Scrapbook
Surrey, England
1916

Detail from an early twentieth-century English scrapbook. Here, detailed caption writing introduces the authority of first-person authorship.

The Hair Book
Natchitoches, LA
1733

is made heartbreakingly—and visually—manifest.

There is one final point that deserves mention, and that is the astonishing rise of "scrapbooking" as it is known today—a stunning sociocultural phenomenon that frames the book's final chapter. My initial read on this practice was highly critical: scrapbooking in contemporary culture appears to be driven by a host of cultural issues that have little, if anything, to do with the rich ancestry of this noble diaristic form. In fact, today's scrapbooks might be said to reflect many of our less impressive qualities. (They're also visually homogenous and, not infrequently, historically averse.) In the spring of 2005, I wrote critically about scrapbooking on the blog *Design Observer* and was publicly attacked for being a traitor. It was blithely assumed that as a designer and a woman, I would support the sisterhood. (I didn't.)

I realized then that I had hit a nerve: Why does keeping a scrapbook matter so much to certain people? Did it always matter so much, and if so, how could such a powerful, personal dossier secede from its family and travel the itinerant path that led it astray—to a library, to an eBay auction, to the trash heap?

I decided to find out, and the idea for this book was born.

ONE HAS ONLY TO LOOK AT THESE EXAMPLES of American scrapbooks to realize that history isn't what historians tell us. It happens in fits and starts, marking a journey composed of any number of meaningful individual moments. Hannah Arendt once wrote that to be alive means to live in a world that preceded one's arrival and will survive one's departure. Scrapbooks, immortal vessels that they are, help us steer the course.

JESSICA HELFAND

Third, the scrapbooks selected for inclusion in this book needed to be eclectic: scrapbooks consisting solely of photographs or merely of clippings were rejected, as they lacked the formal complexity that I believed would most convincingly represent a person and the moment in which that individual lived. Fourth, I was convinced from the start that this book needed to include both celebrities *and* civilians. Regarding the scrapbooks of famous people, I chose to include only those which are clearly autobiographical—not produced after the fact by a devoted fan or family member. (On more than one occasion, I've come upon scrapbooks made by famous people *before* they were famous.) Finally, I restricted my research to American scrapbooks. There is no doubt that a different book could be written about scrapbooks made in Britain over the same period, but the U.S.-made scrapbook deserves particular consideration. In its migration from a nineteenth-century parlor activity to a blank canvas for personal expression, the pursuit of a changing, pluralistic cultural identity

X

Harn Scrapbook
Cincinnati, OH
1914

ACKNOWLEDGMENTS

I AM GRATEFUL FOR THE SUPPORT AND COUNSEL of many people whose contributions to this book deserve particular mention.

At Yale University Press, my thanks to Debra Bozzi, Chris Coffin, Laura Davulis, John Donatich, Jenya Weinreb, and especially my editor Chris Rogers. At Winterhouse, I wish to thank Teddy Blanks, Michael Brenner, Jade-Snow Carroll, Joe Freedman, Geoff Halber, Elizabeth Law, and Eileen Schmidt. My agent Steve Wasserman deserves special thanks.

My thanks also to Sean Adams, Kurt Andersen, Andrea Barnet, Georgia Barnhill, Michael Bierut, Cara Bonewitz, Susan Brynteson, Patricia Butler, Lisa Candela, Grady Candler, Allan Chochinov, Lea Cline, Nancy Sharon Collins, Jeri Coppola, John Dolan, Kathy Eldon, Saralyn Ewald, Michael Famighetti, Patricia Fili-Krushel, Armand B. Frasco, David Freund, Jessica Gladstone, Phillip Glass, Hugh Graham, Ric Grefe, Ellen Gruber-Garvey, Shelly Gruendler, Eric Haggard, Melissa Harris, Angela Hayes, Steven Heller, Pamela Hovland, Andrea Immel, Russell Johnson, David Joselit, Carl Kaufman, Barbara Levine, Asher Lipson, Ellen Lupton, Jeffrey Mainville, Itty Matthew, L. Rebecca Johnson Melvin, Russell Johnson, Liza Kirwin, Sandra Markham, Molly McCarthy, Richard McKinstry, Noreen Morioka, Katherine Ott, AnnaLee Pauls, Nicolas Ricketts, Jae Rossman, Davy Rothbart, Brigitte Ruthman, Elizabeth Siegel, Peter Stallybrass, Christine Stansell, Judith Thurman, Emma Tramposch, Susan Tucker, Betsy Vardell, Catherine Whelan, Frank Warren, Kit White, Leon Wieseltier, Richard Workman, Lorraine Wild, Timothy Young, and Michael Zinman.

Finally, to my father, William Helfand, whose appreciation for the social and cultural value of ephemera has been a huge influence in my life; to my husband, William Drenttel, whose many contributions made this book and its author so much better; and to our beautiful children, Malcolm and Fiona, without whom I would have no story of my own to pass along— my deepest thanks.

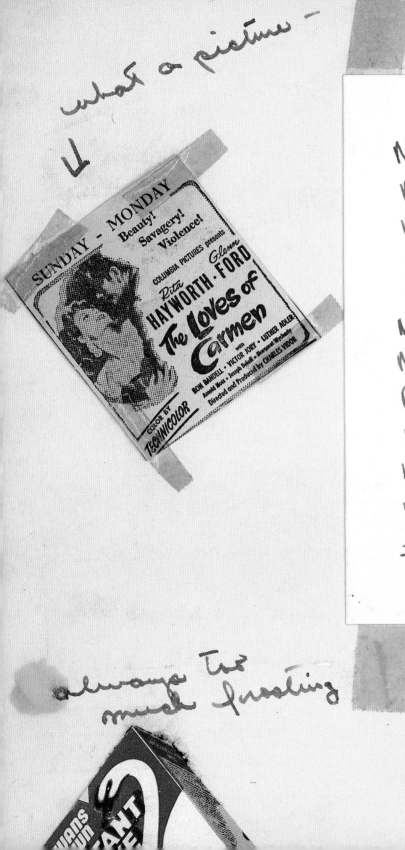

what a picture —
↳

always too
much frosting

↳ soup for lunch

US

Never a night wind sighing low
Never a wild bird's cry
Never raindrop's whispering fall
But you came laughing by.
Never the moon above the trees
Never a falling star....
Never a shadowed winding road
But that is where you are.
Never a silence greets the dawn
Never the rivers glide...
Never again the way alone
For YOU walk by my side.
—

Campbell's

BRIEF ADVICE
TO A YOUNG MAN
CONTEMPLATING
MATRIMONY

a moment her long-
lovely look,
ween her ability
is highly

Stare, pry, listen, eavesdrop.
Die knowing something. You are not here long.

Walker Evans

CAVALIER HOTEL
VIRGINIA BEACH, VA.
326

IF CARRIED AWAY RETURN

the key
to our
room

us

INTRODUCTION

THIS IS OUR STORY

IT IS AUGUST 1948, AND A YOUNG WOMAN IN a small New England town is preparing to leave home. She is nineteen years old and she is hopelessly, desperately in love. Tonight, she is ready, and after weeks of clandestine planning, she is going to elope.

And everything is about to change.

Dreamily, she packs her suitcase, stowing her clothing, her makeshift trousseau, and her few personal belongings. She places her papers in an envelope, tucking a hatpin and a hairbrush into the smallest of purses. Clicking the suitcase shut, she checks her wristwatch, turning, at long last, to leave. But as she reaches the door, she stops short.

Hurrying to the desk in the corner of her bedroom, she pulls the drawer open with an impatient, forceful tug. And there it is, nestled between the handkerchiefs and the stationery with their soon-to-be-obsolete monograms: a long, lean box,

still tightly wrapped in its shiny cellophane skin, which she quickly tears away.

She lifts off the lid to reveal a book—but this is no ordinary book. It is completely empty, page after page of blank, white space. There is nothing there, yet somehow it calls out to her, in that moment, with unspeakable promise.

It is a scrapbook. And it is hers.

IN THE DAYS AND MONTHS THAT FOLLOW, SHE will begin to save things, filling her scrapbook with the countless items that mark her passage into married life: the motel room key from her wedding night; the apology card that follows her first marital quarrel; even a set of miniature firecrackers from an Independence Day fete. She'll add silhouetted cutouts—a drawing of a Campbell's soup can, a photo of Rita Hayworth—and paste in laundry lists, gin rummy tallies and swizzle sticks, a program from an Ice Follies performance and ticket stubs from a Red Sox game. The book will grow thicker and thicker until a year from now, still riding the wave of newlywed bliss, the young bride will look at her masterpiece and grant it the title to which it can only then lay claim: *Yes, We've Been Married Just a Year and This is Our Story.*

Our story: crafted from the material remnants of a couple's first year together. Our story: told through the countless pieces of ephemera that collectively frame a life. Our story: recorded through the eyes and ears and heart of a young bride who, between the recipes and the telegrams, begins ever so tentatively to write poetry—giddy rhyming couplets about love and enchantment, and later, about sadness and despair. To look at her scrapbook now, long after it has been retired from active duty, is to observe at once a deep uncertainty—of herself, of her identity—and a kind of remarkable clarity, an emerging vision pieced together quite literally from scraps of paper, shards of a life.

And through it all, because of it all, she writes. At turns funny and flirtatious, coy and cryptic, a young woman's poetry begins to find form, and with it comes a poet's voice: irrepressible and daring, a firestorm of pathos.

It would be another sixteen years before she would win the Pulitzer Prize, another quarter of a century before she would tragically take her own life. But that one perfect year, Anne Sexton had a story to tell. It was a happy story.

And she recorded it in her scrapbook.

SCRAPBOOKS: FOR OVER A HUNDRED YEARS we've craved them, coveted them, commandeered them as safe havens for those highly subjective, loopy compilations of personal matter. Part personal diary, part cultural stockpile, they've evolved as homespun calendars, enabling us to chronicle the major events and minute details of

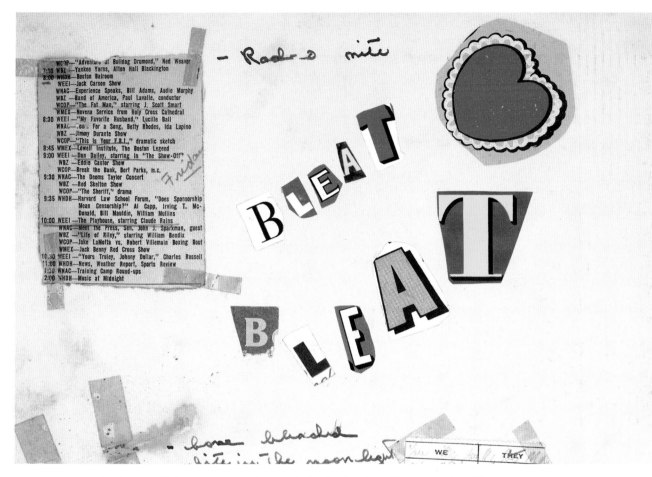

our own personal odysseys. Rich or poor, celebrity or civilian, men, women, and children of all ages kept scrapbooks. Some were ornate, with gilded covers and carefully composed pages of decoupage. Others were retrofitted from second-hand books, with chromolithographs glued sloppily on top of existing texts. Many consisted entirely of clippings, rigorously aligned and chronologically arranged, often around a central theme—pigeons, for instance, or movie stars or, not infrequently, obituaries. There were scrapbooks filled with babies, birds, and baseball statistics; scrapbooks about ice skating, dog breeding,

and the intricacies of boy watching. Fragments of cloth from wedding gowns were included in bridal books, while new mothers included gentle locks from their baby's first haircut. Debutantes saved news clippings, farmers saved weather reports, high school girls saved gum wrappers, and everyone, it seemed, saved greeting cards. Even soldiers kept scrapbooks, pasting in furlough requests, ration cards, and the tattered, beloved photos of their faraway sweethearts. Clumsily folded, haphazardly pasted, randomly annotated with fascinating afterthoughts, the material presence of these personal repositories offers a long-

overlooked glimpse into the American spirit. Why did people feel compelled to save the things they did? What did they value, and question, and believe about themselves and the world around them? And how did the things they saved express what they themselves, for whatever reason, could not say in words?

The scrapbook was the original open-source technology, a unique form of self-expression that celebrated visual sampling, culture mixing, and the appropriation and redistribution of existing media. Over time, it came to mirror the changing pulse of American cultural life—a life of episodic moments, randomly reflected in a news clipping or a silhouetted photograph, a lock of baby hair or a Western Union telegram. As a genre unto themselves, scrapbooks represent a fascinating, yet virtually unexplored visual vernacular, a world of makeshift means and primitive methods, of gestural madness and unruly visions, of piety and poetry and a million private plagiarisms. As author, editor, photographer, curator, and inevitable protagonist, the scrapbook maker engaged in what seems today, in retrospect, a comparatively crude exercise in graphic design. Combining pictures, words, and a wealth of personal ephemera, the resulting works represent amateur yet stunningly authoritative examples of a particular strain of visual autobiography, a genre rich in emotional, pictorial, and sensory detail.

Daniel Boorstin once warned that if we teach history as chronology, the landmarks overshadow the landscape. This, then, is a book about that landscape, and about the individuals who made it their own: the mothers and the children, the suffragettes and the pioneers, the civilians, the dreamers, the unknown heroes of a forgotten era. It is a book that celebrates the soul and the spirit of the American people and, through the unique books they left behind, offers an unprecedented look at an emerging American identity at the birth of the Modern Age.

THE NOTION OF DOCUMENTING ONE'S LIFE through the practice of keeping scrapbooks dates from the Renaissance, when the "commonplace book" first originated. This was an activity in which a reader could reinforce a book's meaning by adding materials including (but not limited to) classical quotations, personal anecdotes, astrological predictions, or devotional texts. Such compilations were not only valuable to their owners but, over time, would come to provide critical cues about the quality and range of intellectual life, showing us how information was both processed and prioritized.

Toward the end of the eighteenth century, the English clergyman James Granger extended this notion with the introduction of a new kind of book that reconsidered scholarship in the context of more varied materials. Books that were "grangerized" were rebound and expanded with the addition of engravings, watercolors, manuscripts, documents, and playbills as well as other miscellaneous items. (Today, such volumes are more commonly known as extra-illustrated books.) Grangerized books persisted throughout the following century at a time when the preponderance of black-and-white printing—coupled with the advent of color lithography—made the acquisition of colored "scraps" something of a novelty. With the introduction of photography in general (and the Brownie Camera in particular) the notion of pairing found matter with personal snapshots came to allow for a new kind of graphic authorship, one that was easily tailored to the interests and budget of each member of the family.

ABOVE AND LEFT
Self-Pasting Scrapbook
Mark Twain
1875

ABOVE
Scraps and Sketches
George Cruikshank
1830

George Cruikshank published this book of miscellaneous images with the intention that they be cut and pasted into homemade albums and scrapbooks.

In 1872, the American writer Mark Twain, himself a devoted scrapbook enthusiast, patented a "self-pasting" version that became an instant success. (According to an item in *The St. Louis Post-Dispatch* on June 8, 1885, he made $200,000 from all his other books and $50,000 from the scrapbook alone.)[1] For those bemoaning the labor in producing their own mucilage, Twain's contribution was significant. In a letter to his friend Daniel Slote,[2] Twain argues that his incentive is "to economise the profanity of this country. You know that when the average man wants to put something in his scrap book he can't find his paste—then he swears; or if he finds it, it is dried so hard that it is only fit to eat—then he swears; if

he uses mucilage it mingles with the ink, & next year he can't read his scrap—the result is barrels & barrels of profanity." By 1900, more than fifty different types of his album were available, and a new obsession was born.

Yet while they would long remain a popular pastime, scrapbooks would gradually begin to provide an unusual psychological outlet, allowing for a kind of personal expression not readily available elsewhere. Although its impact, particularly at a domestic level, would not be recognized for some time, Sigmund Freud's *Interpretation of Dreams*, published in 1900, posited that dreams enabled a kind of expression not achievable during waking hours. Scrapbooks, on some very

basic level, serviced a similar need, frequently abandoning logic in favor of pure whimsy. During the early years of the new century, expectations, social mores, technology, and even hemlines would begin their steady migration, moving away from the exigencies of Victorian restraint toward a new and arguably more pluralistic world order. And so, too, would the scrapbook begin to move away from the decorative, perfunctory symmetry of the nineteenth century toward a more variegated form that recognized—indeed, celebrated—the individual, idiosyncratic, and deeply iconic images of a new era.

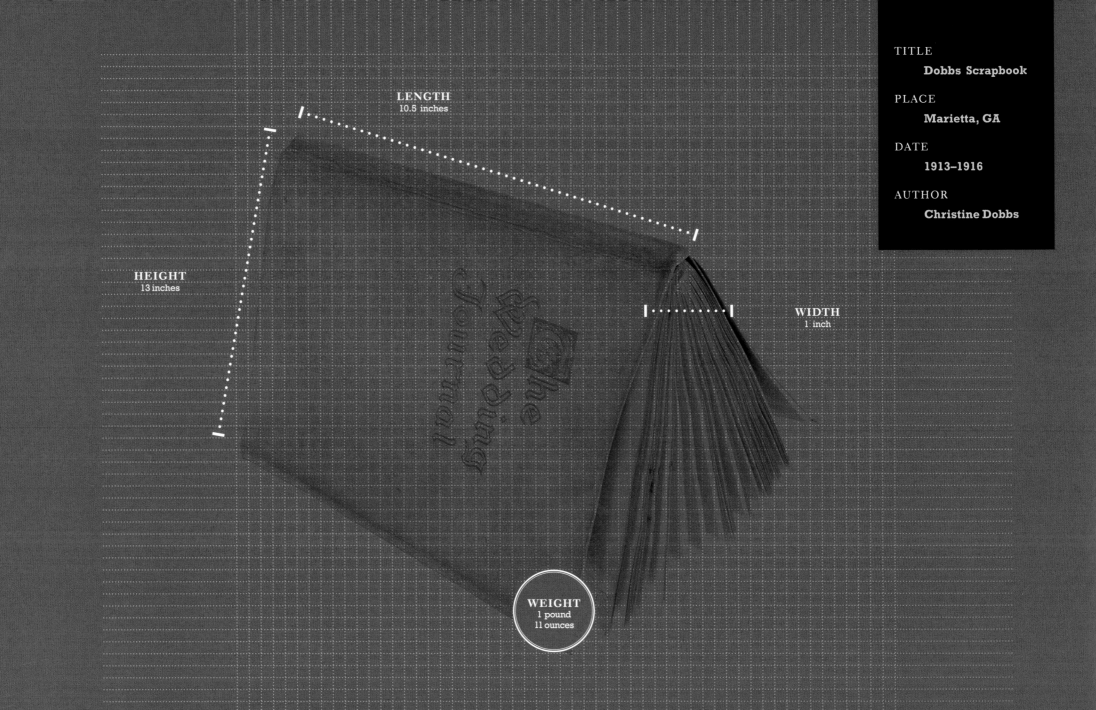

LENGTH
10.5 inches

HEIGHT
13 inches

WIDTH
1 inch

WEIGHT
1 pound
11 ounces

TITLE
Dobbs Scrapbook

PLACE
Marietta, GA

DATE
1913–1916

AUTHOR
Christine Dobbs

DOBBS SCRAPBOOK

MARIETTA, GEORGIA, 1913–1916

George and I did not have
to "meet" we have known each
other since baby-hood —

1913.

Letters

Miss Christine Dobbs.
306. Church St.
Marietta.
Ga.

Miss Christine Dobbs,
306 Church Street,
Marietta,
Ga.

FLOWERS.

Pink Roses.

DOBBS-NICHOLS WEDDING PLANS

Dr. J. H. Patton will conduct the ceremony uniting Miss Charlotte Christine von Scheele Dobbs, daughter and only child of State senator and Mrs. Evan Prothro Dobbs and Mr. George Guernsey Nichols at 8 o'clock Thursday evening June 1st, 1916.

The ushers will be Mr. Tom L. Wallace, Mr. Ralph W. Northcutt, Mr. John F. Hudgins, of Smyrna, and Mr. Alexander Claiborne.

Mr. E dA. Nichols, brother of the bride groom, will be best man. The bride's attendants will be Miss Annie Hahr Dobbs, maid of honor, Mrs. W. J. Milner, Jr., of Atlanta, matron of honor, Miss Sabine Nichols, first brides maid and the other brides maids will be Miss Jean Wallace, Miss Mary Robeson, Miss Lillian Dobbs, Miss Francis Wikle, and Miss Bessie Alderman, of Greensboro.

The grooms men will be Mr. Joseph S. Stewart, Jr., of Athens, Mr. Renick Gregg, Mr. Niles Trammell, Mr. Forman Screven, Mr. Stanton Read, Mr. Ben A. Black and Mr. W. J. Milner, Jr., of Atlanta.

THE MARIETTA JOURNAL AND COURIER

INTERESTING WEDDING PLANS.

A wedding of interest on Thursday evening at Marietta will be that of Miss Charlotte Christine Dobbs, the attractive daughter of Senator and Mrs. E. P. Dobbs, to Mr. George Guernsey Nichols.

The beautiful ceremony will be performed at the First Presbyterian church at 8 o'clock, and the wedding attendants will include: Miss Annie Hahr Dobbs, maid of honor; Mrs. Willis Milner, Jr., of Atlanta, matron of honor; Miss Sabine Nichols, Miss Jean Wallace, Miss Jean Robeson, Miss Lillian Dobbs, Miss Frances Wilkie, Miss Bess Alderman, bridesmaids; Mr. Edgar A. Nichols, best man; Mr. Remick Gregg, of Colorado Springs, Mr. Joseph S. Stewart, of Athens, Mr. Miles Tarmmell, Mr. Forman Screven, Mr. Stanton Read, Mr. Benjamin A. Black, Mr. Willis Milner, Jr., groomsmen, and Mr. T. L. Wallace, Mr. Ralph Northcutt, Mr. John S. Hudgins, and Mr. Alexander Claiborne, ushers. —Atlanta Journal.

Athens Paper

THE BANNER, FRIDAY MORNING, JUNE 2, 1916.

FLOWERS.

Brides Bouquet
was a
shower bouquet of
valley lilies — with center
of bridesmaid roses.
It was always Mudder's
and my wish that I have
a touch of pink in my
flowers.

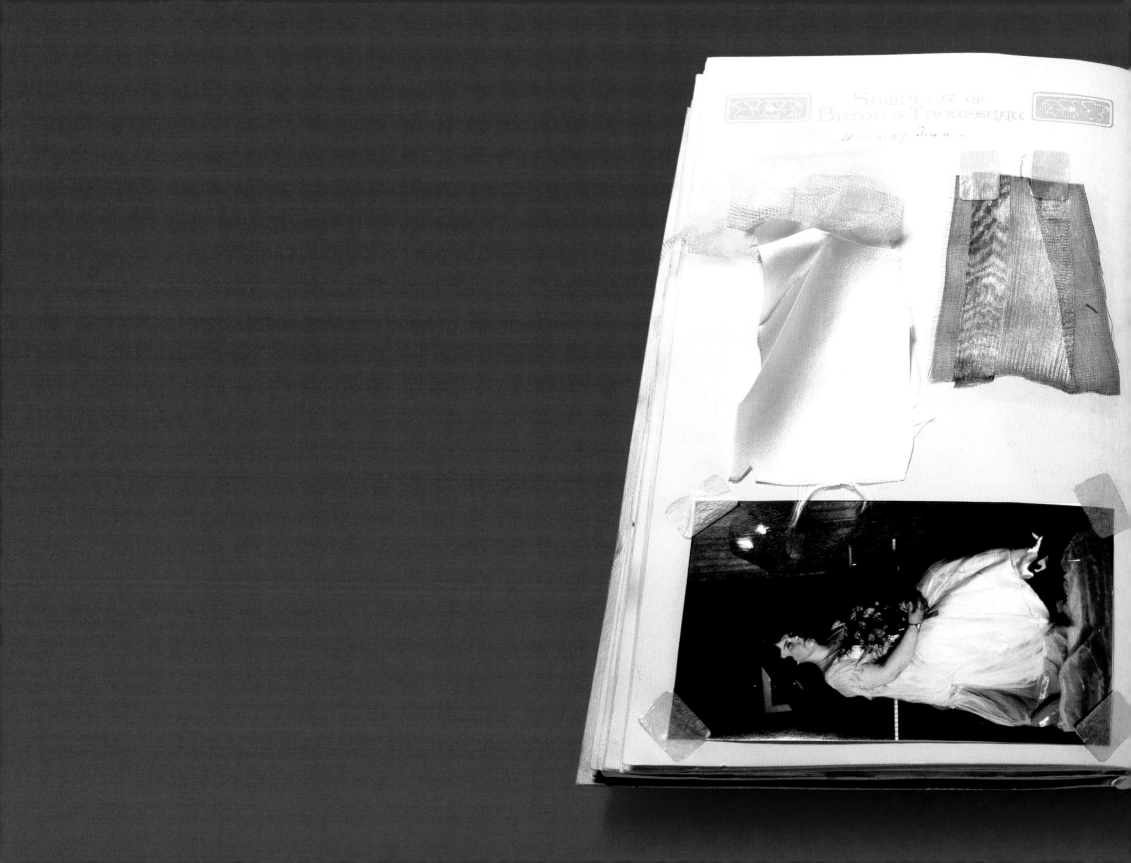

Traveling Suit.

My hat was green straw.
The cream white bird had a
touch of pink about his head,
and was held on with a large
green headed pin and no other
trimming but a band around the crown
of green and gold ribbon, tied in a lovely knot.
The beautiful georgette waist was of a french
lace embroidered in pink and green roses & matched
the lining to my coat, which showed a little in
the front. This touch of pink was on the
skirt pockets embroidered in pinks & greens.
Cream kid gloves, bronze slippers and hose
and a black patent leather pocket book, completed
my going away toilet.

Mrs. Davenport, Modiste.
Atlanta, Ga.

Evening dress of this blue
taffeta. Trimmings of
silver lace, flesh tulle
and bow in the back of
this rose velvet ribbon

Readymade afternoon
dress of ecru net and
lace with taffeta
drapery.

Dinner dress of this blue
with three deep ruffles
of lace edged with the
yellow making the
front. Sleeves are of
the lace.

With this dress I wore a white horse hair hat, with pink wings and narrow pink ribbon on it, and putty colored hose and slippers —

To the left is a ready-made dress of black and white Taffeta —

We do not know the past in chronological sequence.
It may be convenient to lay it out anesthetized
on the table with dates pasted on here and there,
but what we know we know by ripples and spirals
eddying out from us and from our own time.

Ezra Pound, *Guide to Kulchur*

LOVELY BRIDE ELECT

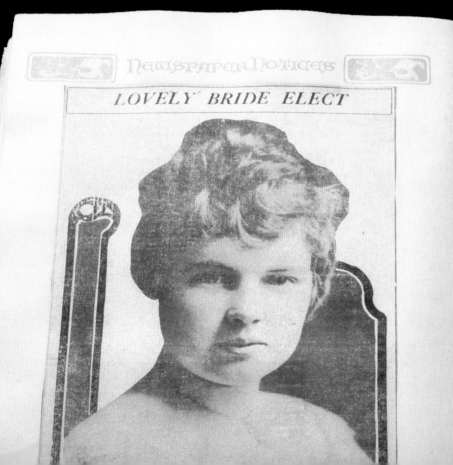

Engagement Presents

The day of our announcement
April the ninth, Rebecca brought me
my first engagement present, a
lovely blue satin powder case for
my dressing bag.

Virginia Cohen Milner made for
me a beautiful green linen
handkerchief.

Mrs. Cohen crocheted a lovely
yoke for both a gown and camisole

CHAPTER ONE   TIME

IN 1870, A PROMINENT NEW YORK SOCIETY couple sued one another for divorce on nearly identical grounds of adultery, insanity, and cruelty. General Egbert Ludovickus Vielé and his wife, Teresa, accused each other of adulterous affairs, and their scandalous accusations were further sensationalized by an extremely public custody battle over their five children.

Throughout this unusually protracted ordeal, Mrs. Vielé kept scrapbooks. In them, she saved correspondence, clippings, and telegrams from attorneys and detectives. She hoarded citations in the press. She even rescued a torn-up letter, placing its fragments in an envelope, which she later glued into her book with an apologetic caption. Finally, she went to considerable effort to include evidence of sympathetic support for her own case, procuring calling cards from her society friends and thereby suggesting that the scrapbook may

well have been entered as evidence (as a sort of silent character witness), in support of her own testimony, in court.

To look at Teresa Vielé's scrapbooks today, well over a century after they were compiled, is to gain particular perspective on the social and cultural customs of urban upper-middle-class life at the end of the nineteenth century. The books themselves originate with a certain formal hand, in which elegant stationery and engraved calling cards are all glued down in neat, straight rows. Precise penmanship graces every letter, note, and invitation. The range of material, too, is abundant, spanning both business and personal items: there are bills and banknotes, receipts from insurance companies, poems and dried plant specimens. And then, gradually—as life itself becomes rapidly unhinged—there are the subtlest visual hints of disorder. Entries become uneven and sloppy, dog-eared or torn up altogether. Over time, Teresa Vielé's scrapbooks come to illuminate the rupture that characterizes her life in general—and her identity in particular. In its stunning shifts of voice, tone, and comparative cultural perspective, hers may just be the one of the earliest "modern" scrapbooks.

A product of the waning antebellum culture in which she had no doubt been raised, Mrs. Vielé was likely to have been deeply preoccupied with the notion of carpe diem ("seize the day"), which translated to leaving one's mark upon the earth. Her scrapbook, great repository of evidence that it was, did precisely this: substantiate her claims, affirm her position, and serve to materially reinforce her presence over time. While her record was somewhat exaggerated (at times even histrionic) in its overall tone, Mrs. Vielé was not alone in her desire to record her life in scrapbook form—nor does her book differ, in many ways, from countless others of its era. A cursory glance reveals the detritus of everyday life, folded and pasted in in a vaguely orderly fashion. But a closer look reveals something quite different—a more open-ended and forgiving canvas upon which to record her own first-person history. Liberated from the obedient formalities which had long framed the conventions of so much Victorian culture, she came to find that her scrapbook held no rules. Here, recollections of time's passage could be rendered as she wished them to be.

At turns boldly outspoken and shell-shocked by fear, hers is a story of full-frontal rupture—the breakdown of a marriage, the implosion of a family, the irrevocable loss of what she had perhaps long imagined to be her implicit destiny. (Teresa Vielé's was by all accounts a temperamental personality: she was described by at least one biographer as "a young woman of beauty, intelligence, fortune, but also an indomitable character.")[1] Yet the recasting of her story in scrapbook form both obliges and enables her to perceive things differently, because

at its core, scrapbook time, unmoored to the demands of the everyday, is characterized perhaps not so much by decorum as by a kind of tacit dislocation. The nature, scope, and relative placement of that information are entirely self-determined, requiring no external approval process—indeed, no apparent formal logic at all—and therein lies its strangely captivating beauty.

It soon appears, too, as if Teresa Vielé's shifting identity benefits greatly from the fragmented

Vielé Scrapbook
New York, NY
1870s

language of scraps, the bits and pieces of her everyday life lyrically recombined to craft a highly personalized narrative. As time passes and she documents the tragic breakdown of her marriage, her scrapbook becomes the ideal vehicle for what emerges as a fairly turbulent emotional journey. For her, the tensions between reality and memory are almost playfully expressed as both timekeeping and truth telling are filtered through her own highly subjective perspective. "Scrapbooks shuffle and recombine the coordinates of time, space, location, voice and memory," observes historian Katherine Ott. "What could be more emblematic of the fractured narratives of modernity than scrapbooks?"[2]

Curiously, the capacity to edit the implicit chronologies of one's own daily life may have been one of the most compelling reasons to keep a scrapbook at the turn of the century—and not only for women. As early as 1895, an article in the *Boston Daily Globe* touted the family scrapbook as a potential "narrative of family skeletons" and urged all public men to keep one. ("How easy to look up the lunacy there has been in the family," it advised, "and perhaps get some degenerate family member therefore quietly put away in a retreat.") Newspapers across the country published articles with suggestions on scrapbook composition, production, and manufacture. The elderly were advised to compile albums of clippings for their families, while volunteers were encouraged to create scrapbooks for the infirm. During both world wars, scrapbook-making volunteers would provide a similar service to soldiers. Collecting and classifying printed matter became a popular pastime for people of all ages, with clippings bureaus available for those too pressed for time to make scrapbooks themselves.

For anyone at the end of the nineteenth century, keeping a scrapbook required little more than a paste pot and a pair of scissors. The popular press lauded scrapbook making as a wholesome occupation for children, offering suggestions on easier, more cost-effective ways to produce memorable albums. There were suggestions for inscriptions ("Dedicate [it] to your best chum," advised a 1903 article in the *Boston Daily Globe*, "in loving memory of the jolly past") and optimistic endorsements ("Women will always be creatures of fads," opined one 1897 editorial in the *Atlanta Constitution*, "and it is well, for any harmless engagement of the mind keeps one out of mischief").

A. T. Stewart & Co.
BROADWAY
New York.

BOSTON   Winthrop Square
PHILADELPHIA   Chestnut Street.
PARIS   Rue Bergère.
LYON   Rue de la Bourse
MANCHESTER   Minshull Street.
NOTTINGHAM   Great Alfred Street.
BELFAST   Wellington Place.
GLASGOW   West Regent Street.
BERLIN   Alte Leipziger Strasse.

New York, May 13th 1871.

Mrs. Teresa Viele,
14 West 28th Street,
City.

Madame:

Mr. Stewart directs me to inform you that after investigation we find the omission in the direction of your parcel was entirely an oversight on the part of the superscribing clerk, which we regret exceedingly should have occurred.

Very Resp'y,

Edward Wood

The New York Times.

NEW-YORK, WEDNESDAY, JUNE 21, 1871.

THE VIELE SCANDAL.

Application of Defendant to Postpone the Trial—The Decision Reserved until Thursday Next—A Scene in Court.

The long-pending cross-action for divorce, on the ground of adultery, between Gen. EGBERT L. VIELE and his wife, TERESA VIELE, was called on for trial at the opening of Part 2, Supreme Court Circuit, yesterday, before Judge VAN BRUNT and a jury. The cause was the only one on the calendar, both parties having answered ready on the day previous, and it being expected to consume one if not two weeks in trial. It will be remembered, as already published in the TIMES, on the decision of the preliminary motion for the custody of the two younger children, Gen. VIELE, the plaintiff, charges his wife with having committed adultery with numerous persons, including several ex-officers of the United States Army, while on the other hand Mrs. VIELE charges her husband with having had illicit intercourse with several women, —mentioning one by name, the charge against whom Judge BARNARD has decided to be groundless.

Both principals were present in Court with their counsel and friends, and a seemingly interested crowd of auditors. Gen. VIELE sat in company with his son and his counsel, IRA SHAFER, BENTON HARRISON and E. L. CALDWELL, while Mrs. VIELE, the defendant, was attended by her counsel, E. DELAFIELD SMITH, FRANK BYRNE and M. W. HAZELTINE, and personal friends. On the case being called counsel for the defendant asked for an adjournment of the trial until the October term. Counsel for Gen. VIELE called the attention of the Court to the fact that counsel for Mrs. VIELE answered "Ready," the day previous, and expressed urgency to proceed with the trial. Counsel for Mrs. VIELE said they considered themselves ready on the previous day, but on that morning had learned from their client that some important witnesses on her behalf were not accessible, and hence a postponement became necessary. Counsel for Mrs. VIELE then read affidavits setting forth that a Mr. DUFF, Mrs. EDWARD COOPER, Dr. BARKER, Mrs. Gen. YATES, Gen. PLEASONTON, and several others, were necessary witnesses on her behalf; that DUFF was in Texas, Mrs. EDWARD COOPER at Long Branch, Dr. BARKER in Europe, and Gen. PLEASONTON in Washington, and that neither of them were accessible in time to go on with the trial.

Mr. IRA SHAFER, on behalf of Gen. VIELE, claimed that the motion was made for mere purposes of delay, as it must be plain to the Court that each and all of the witnesses named could have been subpœnaed with ordinary diligence before their departure for their respective places of present abode ; that it must have been well known, as it was published in all the papers, that Dr. BARKER was about to depart for Europe, and he could have readily have been subpœnaed before his departure. The same would apply to all the others, some of whom it was notorious resided out of the State, and for the examination of whom commissions might have long since been obtained. The defendant, he said, seemed desirous to rest on the temporary triumph, which she seemed to regard as having obtained through the decision of Judge BARNARD awarding her the custody of the two younger children, and hence her wish to postpone the trial until the Fall.

After considerable argument on both sides, Judge VAN BRUNT said he felt much embarrassed in deciding this motion to postpone, as in a case of this character, he was anxious to do complete justice between the parties. It seemed to

3

Nineteenth-century scrapbooks are frequently identified by their excessive inclusion of colored scraps, as if the very access to non-black-and-white ephemera were itself ample cause for celebration. Many nineteenth-century albums were a virtual ode to chromolithography, consisting of pages that basically celebrated the thrill of the colored fragment. Many examples contained trade cards, token-of-affection cards, chromolithographs, and embossed prints, exemplifying the Victorian propensity to create decorative, non-narrative pages. Compared to their predecessors—those staid volumes of black-and-white clippings, poems, and prayers that dominated in the earlier part of the century—books like these are equally notable for their absence of writing.

The scrapbook could also be useful for the politician, for whom it could be "a strong weapon, for in it he can keep a record of his friends and foes." [3] Apparently, however, not all public servants were capable of such shrewd strategy: when Connecticut Selectman Halsey P. Philbrick lost his precious scrapbook in 1904—a scrapbook, it should be noted, consisting exclusively of poems—such was the state of his desperation that the *Hartford Courant* saw fit to report on it on at least two separate occasions.

Throughout this period, journalists covered scrapbooks and scrapbook making as an occasional feature in their cultural reportage. The *New York Times* published a story in 1885 on the ex-president's deathwatch (which had been impeccably chronicled in the scrapbook of the late Mrs. Millard Filmore), while a stoic 1900 editorial in the *New York Observer* praised one album's cathartic appeal as "a consoling refuge many a time when the heart was sorely aching, or the eyes seemed blinded to the 'silver lining behind the cloud.'" There was even a philanthropic appeal to making scrapbooks, with at least one newspaper claiming they made excellent gifts and were "a real boon to the little ones of the very

The Animal Rainy Day Scrap Book

FUN WITH SCRAPS
DESIGNS FOR CRAFTS USING ODDS AND ENDS
Viola Hening

ABOVE
The Animal Rainy Day Scrapbook
1914

Fun With Scraps
1947

Scrapbooks aimed at children were often conceived of as games or toys. Like Colorforms in their modular nature, such books often included sheets of pictures, appealing to a child's love of shapes and puzzles. By midcentury, such projects were decidedly more parent-enabled.

OPPOSITE
Victorian Scrapbook
1880s

AMSTER TESTIFIES OF GIFTS TO WOMAN

Says He Gave Olga Edwards "$10,000 One Year, $8,000 Another and So On."

PHILBRICK'S POEMS.

Mrs. Fay's Tip on Lost Scrapbook Didn't Win.

Selectman Halsey B. Philbrick has been looking for a lost scrapbook of poems for over a year. He has asked all his friends if they had it, he has advertised for it and last fall a description of the book and an account of how it was lost was printed in "The Courant." Mr. Philbrick attended the performance of the Fays at the Parlor Theater last week and he wanted to know if Mrs. Fay could tell him where the missing scrapbook was. He wrote such a question and she said that the book was in the possession of a neighbor of his, who is a Yale man. She also said that if he would write to her she would send the name of the man or such a description of him that there would not be any trouble in locating him.

Mr. Philbrick has been expecting to hear from Mrs. Fay, but up to last night he had not received a reply to his letter. Mr. Philbrick's neighbor who is a Yale man is J. Hanson Coburn, son of Mr. and Mrs. Charles Coburn of No. 105 Edwards street. Mr. Philbrick lives at No. 111 Edwards street. Mr. Coburn has not got the scrapbook. His friends joked with him a good deal

Great Big Policemen Blush Over 20 Tiny Fingerprints

'It's for Their Memory Book,' Announces North Hollywood Mamma of Twin Girl Babies

poor." As early as 1884, a regular column entitled "Mother's Department" featured in *Arthur's Home Magazine* endorsed them as instructional tools and offered suggestions on scrapbook making as a way to teach reading to children. The *Christian Science Monitor* included instructions on teaching the little folks how to make their own paste, while the *Ladies' Home Journal* ran a story proposing a "Sunday" scrapbook, which required nothing more than a blank book, a brush and glue, a Bible, and a Concordance.[4] Just as Teresa Vielé's scrapbook became the preferred space for documenting her legal battles, so too was the Sunday scrapbook made all the more special by restricting its use to one day a week.

Many newspapers across the country covered scrapbooks in their cultural pages. Such public sanctions advocated the value of the scrapbook as a repository of useful reference, appealing to those who perceived organization as a core domestic conceit. Many journalists wrote about the manufacture of the scrapbook—how best to compile found materials, for instance—while more targeted editorials praised their economic, artistic, and historical benefits. An article in the *New York Times* in 1930 shared details of "a mysterious scrapbook" kept by the mistress of a prominent financier, which the defense unsuccessfully attempted to introduce as evidence at trial. A few years later, the *Los Angeles Times* ran a story proving that the urge to record personal history was so great that a new mother carted her infant twins down to police headquarters merely to be fingerprinted. "It's for their memory book," she pleaded, whereupon the "great big policemen" blushed—and happily complied.

NEAR LEFT
Making the Scrapbook
After Juliana Oakley
1868
Chromolithograph

MIDDLE, TOP TO BOTTOM
The New York Times
April 9, 1930

The Hartford Courant
December 26, 1904

The Los Angeles Times
December 20, 1939

Unable to vote until 1920, women played a role during the Great War that was largely symbolic. Wartime propaganda portrayed women as peacekeeping icons—oversized heroines cradling flags or apron-clad domestic goddesses keeping the home fires burning. Far from the front lines, many women participated in local efforts to compile news clippings for their sons, spouses, and brothers overseas. (The Red Cross was one of several organizations that mobilized women as wartime volunteers.) By midcentury, such statistics would change radically: no longer passive observers, more than 150,000 American women served in the Women's Army Corps (WAC) during World War II. Interestingly, by then, scrapbooks were a popular pastime for both men *and* women.

What is perhaps most striking is the degree to which the scrapbook's focus, purpose, and ultimate form would soon begin to diversify. Scrapbooks could be almost anything, and were: heralded as pragmatic repositories of organization one day, stockpiles of filial devotion the next; as useful for documenting funeral notices for the bereaved as for logging wedding gifts for the newlywed. Yet gradually, such duty-bound fidelity to timekeeping would start to shift, and while a market for producing chronologically ordered books would long remain, there emerged a more idiosyncratic sort of scrapbook, one that allowed for more experimental kinds of personal and visual authorship.

It bears mention, too, that toward the end of the nineteenth century, notions of womanhood and identity were undergoing tremendous shifts. Questions regarding how a woman should dress, behave, and even express herself were subject to extraordinary public scrutiny—and not infrequently, they encountered a fair amount of dissent. (Albert Morrow's illustration of a bespectacled working woman was created in 1894—the same year that the United Council for Women's Suffrage was founded in the United States.) At her best, the so-called New Woman was a free thinker, independent of mind and spirit, quite a departure from her previous incarnation as "a tedious echo, or a rigid puppet of propriety."[5] But a more commonly held view, particularly early on, led to more judgmental questions about a woman's place in society. ("As she acquires fresh interest, will she neglect the Church?"[6]) That scrapbooks would, during this period, begin to provide opportunities for exploring this newly minted model of womanhood was evident in a number of albums produced in the years before World War I.

An inside front cover from a 1914 college scrapbook presents a whimsical variation on this theme of picture-only collage. Elizabeth Hildreth's book begins with a blurry snapshot of a kewpie doll surrounded by a whirling constellation of monograms, which were themselves highly collectible by both men and women during this period. (The English writer Evelyn Waugh kept several scrapbooks filled with similar compositions of monograms, fastidiously—and densely—arranged on the page.) Indeed, while many collectors pasted their specimens into an alphabetical taxonomy, young Hildreth operated under no such apparent editorial constraints. Her principal interest seems to have been the creation of pleasing compositions. But at the same time, her pages display none of the polite placements that characterize so many scrapbooks produced during this period. Collaged elements in Hildreth's book are more

playful, and include loose fragments of letter-heads and other typographic miscellany.

Many compositions like these operate from a central image, around which an orbit of smaller images seem to radiate, like a quiet explosion on the page. As picture books, they are almost defiantly decorative: free of personal anecdote and almost predictably symmetrical, they are pretty — and generic. Such books are, from an aesthetic standpoint, the pictorial equivalent of their clippings-only counterparts: both tell us something about the age in which they were produced, but precious little about the person who produced them. But by the turn of the century, books began to contain more than simple collections of pictures, and included more inventive pairings of found matter. With the introduction of chromolithography (color printing), scrapbooks quickly became more colorful and pictorially dense. Collecting images from disparate venues, scrapbookers began to experiment with their own, often fictionalized accounts of their own lives — and even the lives of others.

While many scrapbook makers focused on the family, others considered the broader domestic sphere. During this period, many young girls cut out pictures of home furnishings and people to create scrapbooks of interior settings. Children enjoyed the grown-up posturing of "playing house," while many young women appreciated the chance to "practice" housekeeping and experiment with decor.[7] Others saved pictures of babies, children, and adults and sequenced them in the pages of blank books to create their own stories. Indeed, by adding captions in their own handwriting, they created personalized versions of what were essentially makeshift romance novels. These scrapbooks, sometimes called *Peter and Polly* books, followed a fairly formulaic pattern: boy and girl meet, play as schoolmates, and eventually fall in love and marry. Not infrequently, the last page in a

typical *Peter and Polly* book shows the blissful couple at the altar, or sailing away on their honeymoon, or happily cradling their newborn infant. These sorts of experiments in picture-driven narrative unequivocally privileged romance over conflict and rarely, if ever, challenged the players (let alone the plot). Their significance lay not in exercising dramatic skill so much as in expressing what was, at the time, a fairly radical editorial conceit: rather than focusing on single-page compositions, they relied on page turning to create a kind of sequential yet willfully reconstituted episodic time.[8] Anchored by cheerful milestones (birth, marriage, babies) and impervious to melancholy (death, divorce, war), such books are endearingly primitive as works of composite fiction. And much like their progeny, the serialized dramas on the radio and television that would primarily captivate women in subsequent generations, *Peter and Polly* books are likely to have provided hours of entertainment for their audiences. True, rhyming couplets and metered prose may have been lifted from other sources, but what was different was the fact that the pictures themselves became a kind of natural catalyst for storytelling. Here, editorial

decision making followed a fairly simple trajectory, yet the scrapbook maker had to make the key determination about *when* to turn the page. Such experiments in sequencing demanded a kind of conscientious devotion to shaping a story, and while somewhat obvious, the denouement was further dramatized by the simple and comparatively novel act of page turning.

Yet delightful as they were to look at and admire, such volumes were also implicitly self-limiting. Looking back on them in the *New Orleans Times-Picayune* in 1920, critic Alice Richtor belittles them for their lack of range and their paucity of substance. She defines them as "Pollyanna" books: "Those [scrapbooks] that only mark the hours that shine, and contain not a hint of gloom between their optimistic covers."[9] Yet their introduction, some two decades earlier, marks

perhaps the first instance in which storytelling (and by conjecture, the act of documenting time's passage) is perceived as something potentially discontinuous. A scrapbook, it seemed, did not need to rely solely upon chronological time: it could capture, amplify, even eliminate certain moments altogether. One could even choose to jettison the banal in an effort to create abbreviated, or attenuated, or even—as in the case of *Peter and Polly* books—completely fabricated tales.

As the century progressed, such editorial impulses would find considerable visual reinforcement in the growing popularity of film. Over time, a tolerance for shifting perspectives would become more commonplace, with individual interpretations of episodic time a popular recurring theme. Soon there would be single-topic scrapbooks devoted to movie stars or roller derbies; to camps, clubs, and commencements. Some time later in the century, scrapbook enthusiasts would begin to fill their books exclusively with a lifetime's worth of greeting cards sent from well-wishers. Organized chronologically from celebration to celebration, such scrapbooks parse one's biography by introducing an equally fabricated lens: they leap between happy times (birthdays, holidays) and thereby create their own essentially synthetic storylines. Curiously, the opportunities for delusion may well have increased with the range and abundance of printed matter, intensified against a cultural backdrop of shifting values. It is not uncommon to see scrapbooks that bury the truth or doctor the evidence: scrapbooks, in other words, filled with pretty pictures rather than grim realities. Such editorial gestures differ only slightly from the episodic time lovingly featured (and formulaically crafted) in so many *Peter and Polly* books: yet as the stories themselves evolved and the forms they took grew more varied, scrapbook makers began to experiment with more eclectic materials, telling different kinds of stories,

Scrapbook Houses
1880s–1890s

Writing in the September 1902 issue of *Ladies' Home Journal*, Marion Dudley Richards extolled the virtues of this domestic craft. "These book houses anyone can make, with a slight effort, for any little girl. Fifty or seventy-five cents will buy a large book or album for the purpose, though my first efforts were expended on old report books."

Evening dress of this blue
taffeta. Trimmings of
silver lace, flesh tulle
and bow in the back of
this rose velvet ribbon.

Ready made afternoon
dress of ecru net and
lace with taffeta
drapery.

Dinner dress of this blue
with three deep ruffles
of lace edged with the
yellow making the
front. Sleeves are of
the lace.

With this
dress I
wore a
white horse hair hat
with pink wings
and narrow pink
ribbon on it and
pink colored hose
and slippers.

To the left is a
ready made dress
of black and white
taffeta.

LEFT TO RIGHT
Found Objects

Firecrackers
Woodward Scrapbook
1929

Wooden Spoon
Enloe Scrapbook
1922

ABOVE AND OPPOSITE
Dobbs Scrapbook
Marietta, GA
1916

Christine Dobbs devoted
multiple pages in her
scrapbook to list the
wedding gifts she and her
new husband received.
Equally well documented
is the bride's trousseau,
which includes fabric
swatches from all of her
gowns, like those shown
here. Seven filled pages of
gifts are included in her
scrapbook, including this
journal, given to her by a
Mr. and Mrs. Cohen.

Lock of Hair
Goller Scrapbook
1925

Ticket Stubs
Pearman Scrapbook
1921

Coonskin Tail
Patterson Scrapbook
1954

Sugar Cube
Goller Scrapbook
1925

Foreign Currency
Johnson Scrapbook
1940s

Peanut Shell
Bailey Scrapbook
1907

Golden Bell
Row Scrapbook
1914

Decorative Feather
Sutterfield Scrapbook
1927

Pocket Watch
Bailey Scrapbook
1933

Gum and Cigarettes
Row Scrapbook
1914

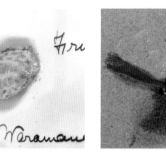

and often pairing and sequencing found matter in more unusual ways.

In the early years of the twentieth century, glue remained the primary bond of choice: cellophane tape wouldn't be introduced until 1930, thereby limiting, to some degree, the extent to which one might choose to include certain odd and extraneous objects. Nevertheless, by World War I there emerged a great preponderance of scrapbooks in which the physical memento was the principal focus. With an accompanying date and caption, these objets trouvés were treasured for their indelible mnemonic associations, amplifying the notion of episodic time by featuring things (and not just paper) with which to instantly prompt the nostalgic recollection of a particular event. This was the purview of memory books—a unique genre of scrapbook that grew steadily in popularity both during and between the wars.

In Richtor's review, she characterizes the act of keeping a memory book as one which is "as contagious as measles, infectious as diphtheria" for young women. "That assortment of unrelated objects affords tangible—and often tastable or smellable—evidence of the human instinct for collecting," she notes, adding that "such things as bon-bon wrappers, gobs of candle grease, ice cream cones, empty bottles, grass, leaves and cotton batting are the most frequently requested souvenirs." As a contemplative note, the critic wonders if psychologists might one day "trace brain connections in the emotions called forth by various (apparently meaningless) objects" and, softening somewhat, poses a rhetorical query. "What can there be in a toothpick to incite spasms of mirth," she muses, "or in a cigar band to move almost to tears? What can there be in a very dirty shoe lace to cause a dreamy, far-away look, or in a single blond hair to cause a vicious flap-over of the page?" [10] Curiously, just as happy events can be captured for posterity, so, too, can a book recall times of pain and suffering. (One scrapbooker

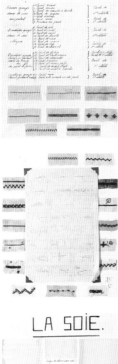

LA SOIE.

Mouyard Scrapbook
France
1936

Thérèse Mouyard studied
briefly at a convent in
France, where her
Saturdays were spent
doing all sorts of
handiwork. Embroidery,
tatting, and sewing
were all documented
in her notebook,
marked in red pencil
by the nuns who
supervised her work.

chose to preserve an actual blister from her ankle—material proof, one can only conclude, of her own extraordinary fortitude.)

This obsession with evidence would become a particularly modern conceit,[11] and one that would become increasingly manifest through the visual choices made in the pages of scrapbooks. Throughout the early years of the new century, books were filled with seemingly extraneous items. Fledgling memoirists saved feathers and firecrackers, cigarette butts and shards of chalk, ribbons and flags, and swatches of fabric snipped from hems or tablecloths. Educated briefly in a convent in France, Thérèse Mouyard meticulously documents in her scrapbook her progress over the course of a few months as she studied sewing, stiching, and embroidery. Samples of silk are accompanied by careful descriptions—some are crèpe, others georgette—but the placement of colored rectangles on the gridded page has a decidedly modern quality. Pages like these hint at a kind of clumsy, yet endearing kind of formal abstraction: they soon cease to be fragments of fabric, dissolving into simple color blocks floating above a picture plane.

In a series of exquisite compositions that recall the work of the German artist Joseph Beuys, one young woman compiled an obsessively detailed book of stains, composed four to a page and accompanied by captions revealing their chemical antidotes. Mary Shultz's *Home Study Scrapbooks*, which probably began in a home economics class, include notes from readings, clippings from the newspaper, and pages and pages of stains: ink and chocolate, fruit and tea, coffee and chewing gum—each of them reenacted, like miniature crime scenes, on square swatches of linen and pasted into her scrapbook. Books like Shultz's celebrate a kind of glorious, wasteful repetition—yet they also typify the notion of the scrapbook as a totem of domestic integrity, an evocation of a kind of "waste not, want not" puritanical thinking that

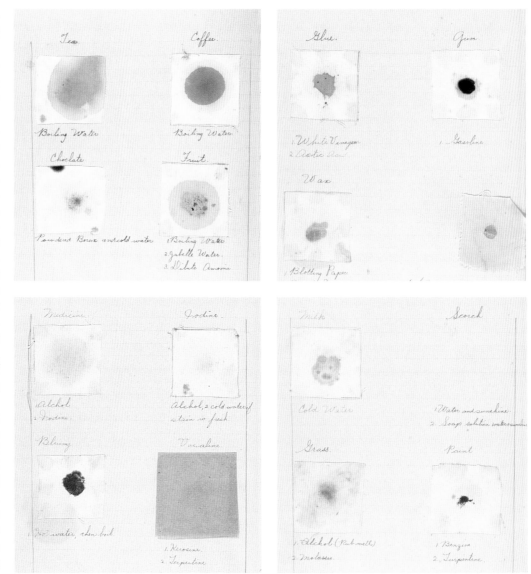

reinforced the importance of hygiene, organization, and thrift.

Another scrapbook made by a Girl Scout during approximately the same period creates a similar composition using twigs and tape. Like so many young girls, Molly Kelley spent a summer at Girl Scout camp that included bonfires and hikes and swimming in the lake, but her scrapbook —pasted onto the lined pages of a school composition book—also includes many of the material fragments that circumscribed her holiday odyssey. She recombines a collection of mundane

Ink.

1. Milk
2. Oxolic acid +
3. Dilate amonia + Lemon juice + salt.

Purple Ink.

1. Alchol + glycserne equal parts.

Red Ink.

1. Cold water and amonia
2. jabelle water

Calla.

1. Amonia

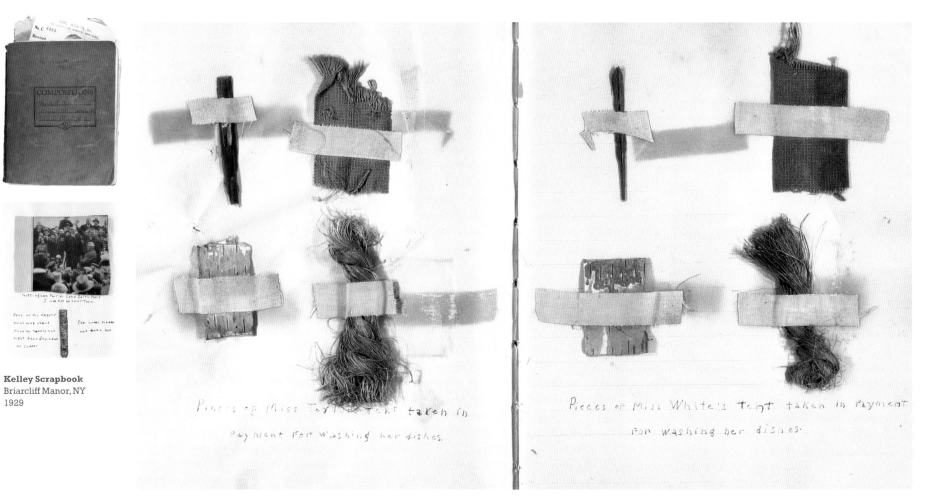

Kelley Scrapbook
Briarcliff Manor, NY
1929

Pieces of Miss Taylor's tent taken in payment for washing her dishes.

Pieces of Miss White's tent taken in payment for washing her dishes.

Please Do Not Throw Paper !In The drain!
Picture the pathetic result →
Be Kind!!!!!!!!!!

artifacts to tell her own particular tale, a story of one girl, at one camp, over the course of one summertime sojourn. With clear, blocky handwriting and dogged intentionality, Kelley unfolds her chronicle over the pages of her book so that the passage of time is carefully orchestrated: there are drawings, collages, certificates, and posters; artifacts rescued from a hike; diary entries recording special dinners with Aunt Jessie; even a fragment from a broken shovel. Today, eighty years later, the ghosted impressions of cloth tape add an additional layer of withered beauty to these pages, once carefully composed, with limited means, by a thoughtful young diarist.

While Kelley's offers an inclusive example, many scrapbooks from this period are just as conspicuous for their omissions. The wife of a prominent Boston lawyer, Jessie Southard Parker kept a scrapbook filled with pictures and stories about her family and their life in Belmont, Massachusetts, just before World War I. There are ink drawings, family crests, Bible records, calling cards, and advertisements; letters, leases, deeds, diplomas, and receipts; poems, announcements,

Piece of shovel broken by
Pearl Brand on the Highway to the World.

Piece of lead   Harriette
foil which   Kuhlman for
was wrapped   the Angels last
around   meeting. August
crackers   28, 1929
Donated by

Twigs from one of the International Trees of
the Highway to the World, came Edith

portraits, lyrics, and news clippings. In fact, given the copious amount of clippings in her book, there is little doubt that Mrs. Parker would have read the newspaper, and one can easily assume she would have been alert to the changes beyond her own parochial doings in a quiet Boston suburb. Yet her entries in April 1912 make no mention at all of the sinking of the Titanic—a disaster not only notable for its hugely hyped (and tragically failed) technological promise, but one likely to have been of consequence to Parker since it claimed so many people of her own privileged class.

Parker Scrapbook
Belmont, MA
Early 1900s

Parker's travels with her
family are well chronicled
with photographs and
postcards marking the high
points of her journeys.

On Aug 17th I left the house to a strange cook - the children
to Torrance & Miss Cameron, and most thankfully started forth
to join papa at this lovely spot. Had a beautiful week

With him - Judge & Mrs. Bushell were exceedingly kind to us
One day took the trip to Kennebunkport and one day
went to Portsmouth.

Here is where a closer read of the scrapbook begins to exhibit a different and very particular story. Unwittingly, the retention, placement, and omission of certain images and texts reveal a distinct view of the world—and one that is rarely, if ever, objective. Conversely, it is in its deeply biased subjectivity that a single human perspective is unearthed, providing an extremely vivid take on what life must have been like at that particular time. Historians can collectively assess what might have transpired across a wide spectrum of social and political forces, but the individual scrapbook tells a different story: asynchronous, irrational, and flawed it may be, but it is also likely to be intensely factual.

Wife, mother, music-lover, theatergoer, and Christian Scientist, Jessie Parker was—like so many women—the self-appointed archivist of her family. Her scrapbooks lovingly reveal a devout preoccupation with recollecting the many aspects of day-to-day life on her family's behalf. School activities, family vacations, even synopses of books and plays are all included in these albums, revealing a woman who was intelligent, compassionate, and well-read. Rebecca Johnson Melvin, curator at the University of Delaware, also notes the degree of introspection evident in these scrapbooks, remarking that Mrs. Parker's "spiritual reflections express a desire to live with a stronger practice of 'Science' and a greater awareness of efforts to improve her self."[12] Curiously, while news of many world events features prominently throughout these pages, there are equally startling omissions, leading one to consider the possibility that Jessie Parker elected to "compose" a more cheerful version of history for her descendants. Whether intentional or accidental, her accounts of daily life in a quiet enclave of suburban Boston cast a fascinating lens on the customary habits of affluent families at the turn of the century.

Parker was also a capable writer. Her analysis of social events leads in particular to occasional

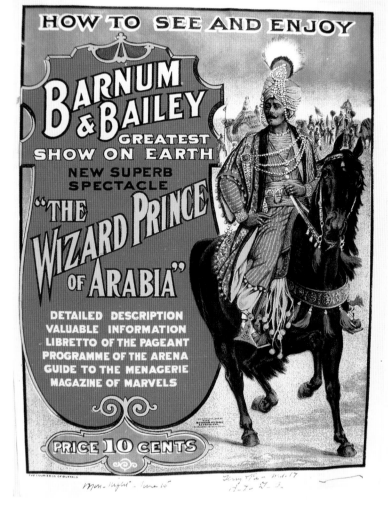

HOW TO SEE AND ENJOY

BARNUM & BAILEY

GREATEST SHOW ON EARTH

NEW SUPERB SPECTACLE

"THE WIZARD PRINCE OF ARABIA"

DETAILED DESCRIPTION
VALUABLE INFORMATION
LIBRETTO OF THE PAGEANT
PROGRAMME OF THE ARENA
GUIDE TO THE MENAGERIE
MAGAZINE OF MARVELS

PRICE 10 CENTS

TREMONT THEATRE

JNO. B. SCHOEFFEL..............Proprietor and Manager
Direction CHAS. FROHMAN and WILLIAM HARRIS

THE SAFEST THEATRE IN BOSTON
Equipped with three celebrated Regan Water Curtains which
are positive in their action. Also an Asbestos Curtain.

FIRE NOTICE

Look around NOW and choose the nearest Exit to your seat. In
case of fire walk (not run) to THAT Exit. Do not try to beat your
neighbor to the street—John B. Schoeffel, Manager.

Every Evening at 8.10, excepting Sunday   Matinees Daily at 2.10

WEEK OF JUNE 14th, 1915

D. W. GRIFFITH Presents

The Birth of a Nation

An Historical Drama in Two Acts,
Founded on Thomas Dixon's Story,
"THE CLANSMAN"

MISS MARY P. REED ENGAGED.

To Marry Edward L. Cutter of Milton.
Mr. and Mrs. Andrew F. Reed of
Somerset street have announced the
engagement of their daughter, Mary
Perry Reed, to Mr. Edward L. Cutter
of Milton. Miss Reed is a graduate
of Miss Baldwin's school, Philadelphia, and the Museum of Fine Arts,
Boston. She is returning home the
last of January from Munich, where
she has been living with Mr. and
Mrs. Rollin M. Gallagher of Middle-
sex school, Concord. Mrs. Gallagher
is a younger sister. Mr. Cutter is a
graduate of Harvard, class 1906, and
is the son of Mr. and Mrs. Frank W.
Cutter of Milton.

Parker Scrapbook
Belmont, MA
Early 1900s

A frequent theatergoer, Jessie Southard Parker saved advertisements, ticket stubs, and programs from her multiple outings. A circus advertisement (*left*) shares space in her scrapbook with a program for the opera *La Gioconda*, which starred the celebrated tenor Enrico Caruso. Parker saw D.W. Griffiths' *Birth of a Nation* at Boston's Tremont Theatre (*above*) just two months after its nationwide premiere in April of 1915. Elsewhere in her scrapbook she saved social notices (*above right*) and wrote in her own commentary.

moments of fascinating reading. Here, she reflects on the somewhat comical tension between her own teetotaling and the social climate at a posh New York restaurant: *Wed. evening we had a little plunge into Bohemian life, which was deeply resented by one of the waiters at Café Martin owing to our temperance principles. In such places they have no use for such modest customers.* On another page, she takes a more reflective view of her efforts. *The pictures & programs interest* [my daughter] *now*, she muses, *but later she will like to read about events & the small happenings in her life.* She adds: *It is also quite a book of reference for me.*

Indeed, Parker's compassion for her children, her appreciation of simple pleasures, even her salvaged memorabilia reveal a woman deeply aware of the passage of time. Curiously, though, she seems to have been completely unaware of certain cultural shifts—the women's suffrage movement, for instance. Nevertheless, it is clear that her scrapbook holds extraordinary meaning and purpose in her life, combining evidence of her cultural interests, recreational pastimes, and spiritual preoccupations. Like a character from an Edith Wharton novel, Jessie Southard Parker displayed a selective obliviousness that likely was not the result of willful ignorance but stemmed from her priorities as a society matron. Hers, then, is not so much a story of social elitism as one of innocent, even somnolent cultural detachment—and in this she was not alone.

Some years earlier, in 1908, Harry Wolfson began a scrapbook to document his college life at Harvard. A gentleman and a scholar, he was also one of a handful of Jewish students. Among his numerous accomplishments, he was president of the Harvard Menorah Society and went on, his junior year, to win one of two coveted travel scholarships in the college. (The other one went to Henry Wadsworth Longfellow's grandson.)

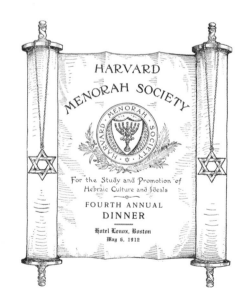

Harry Wolfsbon.
To Whom the Classical Course Honor Was Awarded.

Installed throughout Wolfson's scrapbook are clippings from his hometown newspaper in Scranton, Pennsylvania, as well as numerous entries from several local and national Jewish newspapers. His accomplishments eventually led him back to Harvard, where he would hold a distinguished professorship for nearly half a century. Yet Wolfson's scrapbook is touchingly personal, even narrow. The world is, for the most part, shut out while young Harry concentrates on sports, studies, and making sense of his rich, intellectually expanding world. He was later remembered as a daring and tireless scholar, "studying day and night, resisting presumptive attractions and distractions, honors and chores, with a tenacity which sometimes seemed awkward and antisocial." [13] The degree to which his scrapbook reads like an ordinary college boy's collection of memorabilia adds to its charm, revealing the more human, vulnerable side of this remarkable young man.

School scrapbooks like Wolfson's share a particular view of time in which the demands of the academic year frequently pull focus: classes and schedules, events and celebrations frame the expectations of the group more than they do the needs of the individual. Grace Lloyd Walsh—who graduated in 1913 from high school in Wilmington, Delaware—kept a scrapbook that typifies the dreamy schoolgirl in its portrayal of quintessentially adolescent concerns, with a particular emphasis on the value of amusement. Many books from this period categorize "fun" under such headings as "CLASS YELL," "TEAS AND SOCIAL FUNCTIONS," and "JOKES AND FROLICS." (A more thorough discussion of the lexicon in these and other preformatted books appears in Chapter Four.)

Yet unlike the staid Parker or the studious Wolfson, Walsh begins to reveal through her scrapbook a kind of animated view of the world around her, not so much in content but, more noticeably, in form: she silhouettes (indeed, decapitates) photographs and pairs them with miniature flags and pressed flowers, producing pages that mirror the kind of dynamic visual thinking that was in vogue at salons and galleries all across Europe at the time. It is doubtful that Walsh, who went on to become a prominent businesswoman in Delaware, would have gone anywhere near the New York Armory show that year, where postimpressionism and cubism had made an explosive introductory appearance—yet her playful appreciation of pictorial space suggests that something must have pierced her schoolgirl orbit. Long before the media would begin to transmit messages across far-flung geographic boundaries with ease, Walsh must have been exposed to something—something inventive, daring, and new—in a magazine, perhaps, or in a movie. Serendipitously, rather than intentionally, her world vision began, slowly, to shift. Interestingly, too, she would long retain a fascination with self-expression in general—and writing in particular. Years later, she wrote a short autobiographical story entitled "Mrs. Trobridge Marshall," told from the point of view of a shop owner musing over the success of her business and the social status of her customers. Walsh reportedly sought the assistance of a friend, the author Hortense Calisher, in trying (ultimately without success) to get this story published.

Of course a schoolgirl's world was, in most respects, metered by scholastic obligations. Books like Walsh's deftly preserve the benchmarks of that culture: the report cards, the dance cards, the sports results, and so on. But interstitially, another story begins to emerge: if schooltime was classroom based, what happened outside the classroom tended to be less rigorously monitored, less quantifiable and routine. The absence of the kinds of mediated distractions that have come to characterize twenty-first-century life—the beeps and the bells, the Blackberries and the cell phones—meant that the scrapbook was, in many instances, the primary receptacle for captur-

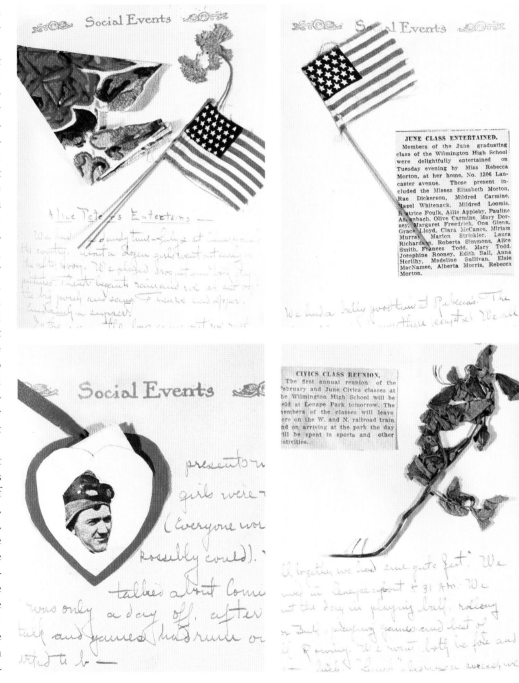

Walsh Scrapbook
Wilmington, DE
1913

Grace Lloyd Walsh's scrapbook includes photographs, autographs, ticket stubs, pressed flowers, and diary entries that describe what life was like for a schoolgirl in Wilmington, Delaware, in 1913. Mostly, though, her scrapbook represents a kind of playful composition at once redolent of a young girl's teenage restlessness and evocative of the more lively kinds of pictorial forms starting to emerge in the popular press.

✚

THE AMERICAN RED CROSS
LANCASTER CHAPTER
521-525 WOOLWORTH BUILDING
LANCASTER, PA.

SOUTHERN BRANCH.

Quarryville, Pa.,
January 8 1920.

$18.50

Received from Elma Reynolds, Treas. Junior
Red Cross of Quarryville, Pa., the sum of Eighteen
Dollars and fifty cents ($18.50) for Red Cross
Christmas seals.

Howard Obold

(1150 stamps ret'd)

Permit me to express my personal appreciation
of the fact that under the direction of your Principal, Mr Ebersole, you so gladly took up the sale
of these seals. You did a good thing, and there
is joy in doing a service that is worth while.
The fight against tuberculosis is a long hard
battle, and the time to realize it is now in your
youth, when you may learn best how to fight against
it. With best wishes to the Quarryville Junior
Red Cross from the Chairman of the Southern Branch
of the Lancaster Chapter A.R.C.

Howard Obold

ing one's observations about the world. The line between private diary and public album makes this a particularly intriguing proposition: in hindsight, it is not always clear whether these books are meant to be shared, and if and when they are created with more public intentions, they risk becoming sensationalistic, even disingenuous as works of autobiography. Where they do succeed —and they succeed brilliantly—is as portraits of social history: at turns comical and confessional,[14] many books are as revealing about teenage curfews and furtive promiscuity as they are about diet, economics, and social class.

Elma Reynolds' scrapbook is endearingly typical of books kept by many girls of her generation. *A Girl's Graduation Days*, published in Chicago in 1921, was one of countless books targeted to young women with vignetted illustrations (here drawn by J. T. Armbrust) and headings designed to help them organize their miscellany. Reynolds' book featured sections for everything from CLASS PROPHECY to INTERCLASS DEBATES, and even included a section for memorable delectations: pages are included for CHAFING DISH and CANDY RECIPES. Interestingly, Reynolds' poetic signoff— *The End of the Rainbow*—appears in the middle of the book, under PLAYS—a gesture that introduces the curious, yet soon-to-be-common editorial tactic of retrofitting content with no apparent regard to the existing page heading.

And this gentlest of interventions highlights what is most revealing, and perhaps of most critical importance: the glimmers of uncertainty. There remains, in so many scrapbooks, the persistent hope that life will always be like this, full of fun and jokes and frolics. Such a blanket disregard for time's inevitable progression is, of course, a basic adolescent conceit—but what's different in these early twentieth-century scrapbooks is the degree to which the advent of great, looming change begins, ever so subtly, to burst the schoolgirl bubble. In one World War I–era album, the

ABOVE AND OPPOSITE
Reynolds Scrapbook
Quarryville, PA
1913–1920

RIGHT
Anonymous Scrapbook
Kansas City, MO
1915–1920

Brevity in caption writing can also lead to a certain amount of ambiguity. For instance, *Taken in France* can mean several things: Was the picture taken in France? Was he taken prisoner in France? Or was the soldier's life taken from him in France?

steadily diminishing numbers of photographs of young men (from the beginning of the book to the end) graphically underscores the impact that the draft would have had on a young girl's social life. In another, a young woman saves public health appeals from the American Red Cross about joining the terrifying fight against the rise of tuberculosis. And yet another book, from a busy California debutante, includes a formal letter from *The Fatherless Children of France*, alongside a photograph of a little girl who has clearly been orphaned by the war.[15] Even after the war,

a growing sense of impending loss is evident in many of these scrapbooks. *Maybe it was for the better,* writes Reynolds in the spring of 1922, *but our hearts grow sad, nevertheless, when we think of what might have been.* If time was on their side, it wouldn't be for long.

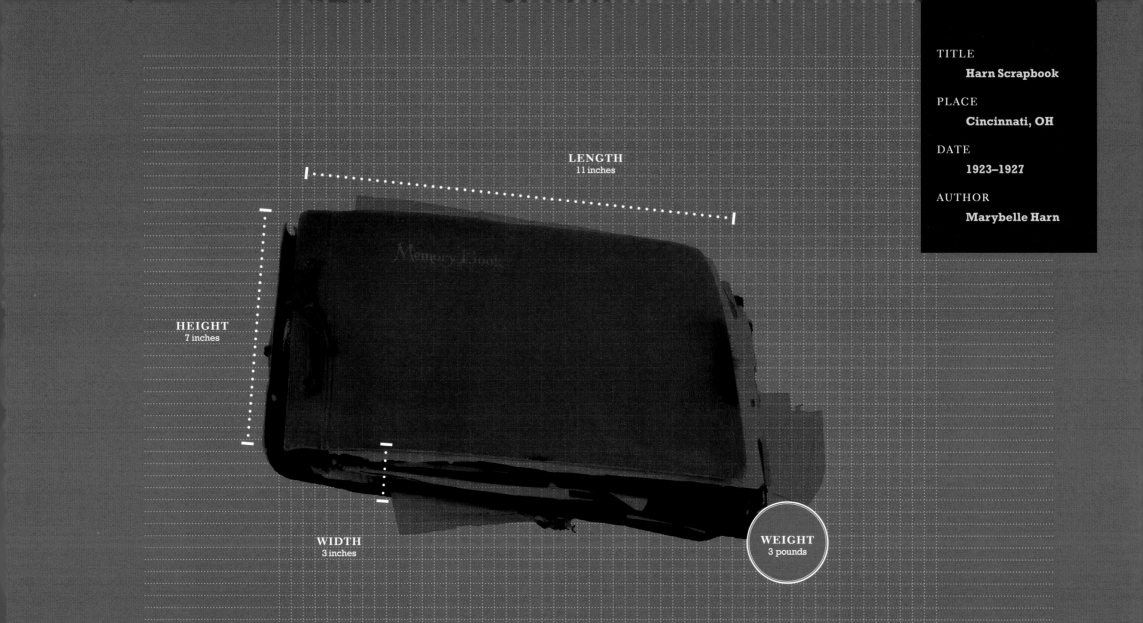

LENGTH
11 inches

HEIGHT
7 inches

WIDTH
3 inches

WEIGHT
3 pounds

TITLE
Harn Scrapbook

PLACE
Cincinnati, OH

DATE
1923–1927

AUTHOR
Marybelle Harn

HARN SCRAPBOOK

CINCINNATI, OHIO, 1923–1927

Mr. Ary Van Leeuwen

"Incomparable Butterfly"

TAMAKI MIURA

Emil Heermann

Burnett C. Tuthill

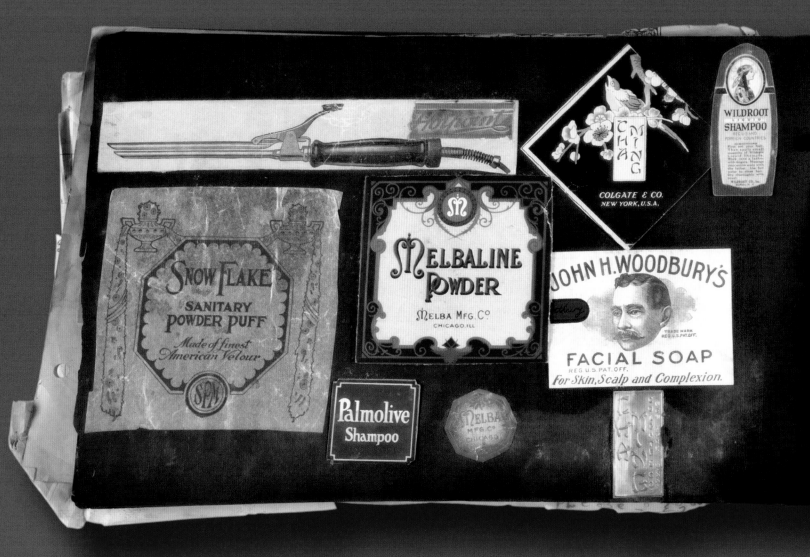

Flowers
gathered
on the
Hike

"Swiped"

SPECIAL DELIVERY

MISS MARYBELLE HARN
CINCINNATI CONSERVATORY OF MUSIC
CINCINNATI, OHIO.

Miss Marybelle Harn
Cincinnati Conservatory of Music,
CINCINNATI, OHIO.

THE VERSAILL
W. F. MOOR
VERSAILLES

P.O. Box 96, Versailles, Ohio.

Flet's visit to the Conservatory.

Cincinnati Conservatory of Music from Park.

If I could do it, I'd do no writing at all here.
It would be photographs; the rest would be fragments of cloth,
bits of cotton, lumps of earth, records of speech, pieces of wood
and iron …

James Agee, *Let Us Now Praise Famous Men*

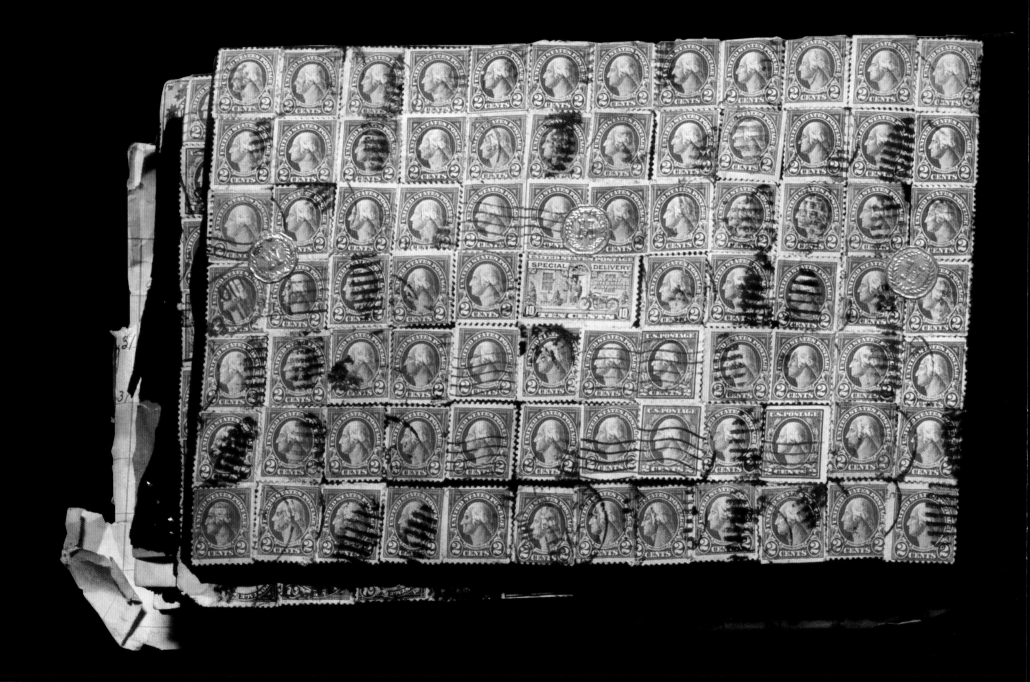

CHAPTER TWO

SPACE

VICTORIAN SCRAPBOOKS, LIKE THE DOMESTIC spaces in which they were produced, took a classic and somewhat reserved formal approach to managing two-dimensional space. Most of these books favored a kind of balanced, bilateral symmetry, in which a large image was pasted onto the center of the page, flanked by a chorus of smaller pictures, often tilted at jaunty angles. Words, if and when they were included, existed as part of the printed matter itself—advertising copy, trade card typography, or news clippings—making for albums far more ornamental than informative.

In an era that solemnly praised the virtues of good social conduct, samples of handwriting and monograms soon became a collectible favorite. Ambrose Horton's self-titled *Commenced Collection of Monograms, Crests and Trademarks* from 1875 offers a pictorial narrative of one man's love of the printed word, with initials gathered alpha-

betically and selected lettering grouped ransom-letter style to re-create new phrases. The design of this book is extraordinary, offering a striking (and relatively early) illustration of ornate typography and lavish penmanship, an example of the kind of graphic extravagance that would begin to diminish in the early years of the new century, soon to be supplanted by more eclectic media.

Later, the word itself would emerge as a visual component in its own right. Lydia Blanchard's 1922 scrapbook combines snapshots, letters, and her own drawings punctuated by the occasional typographic collage. Here, disenfranchised words are shuffled to create new phrases: on one page, the words *Love, Memories,* and *Bride* form a visual spine, with peculiarly brief sentence fragments (*Civilization Masquerade, Complexion Wedding, Classification Advantages*) emerging interstitially on either side. While Blanchard's typographic

OPPOSITE
Harn Scrapbook
Cincinnati, OH
1920s

The scrapbook made by Marybelle Harn, a college student at the Cincinnati Conservatory of Music, included a dense yet rather artfully composed series of collages made from printed and eclectic materials—including (but not limited to) copious numbers of ticket stubs. She was also a capable hand-letterer.

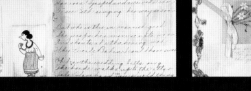

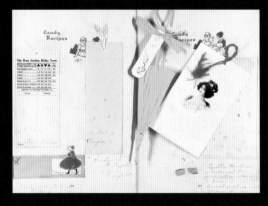

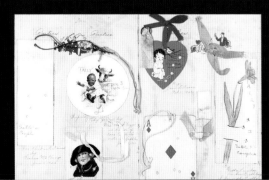

LEFT, ABOVE, AND OPPOSITE
Blanchard Scrapbook
Natchitoches, LA
1922

The Blanchards were a
prominent family in
Natchitoches—the oldest
permanent settlement in
the Louisiana Purchase
Territory. Lydia Blanchard
was her class historian
and appears, too, to have
been a rather accom-
plished artist. Among the
many pictures of friends
in Blanchard's scrapbook
are numerous photos of the
artist Mary Belle de Vargas
(*above, far right*) who rose
to national prominence
because she was born
without arms: a book about
her, *The Armless Marvel*,
was published in 1949.

collages bear a certain formal resemblance to their pictorial predecessors (the collages are all meticulously centered on the page), they simultaneously hint at a more modern appreciation of two-dimensional space. Here, the tension between balanced symmetry and fractured logic offers a snapshot of one woman's struggle to reconcile feeling with form. Interestingly, too, by choosing to work with preexisting words, Blanchard shields herself from too much direct emotional exposure. (Rare was the young girl willing to reveal actual details of her own life.) The language of collage offered the ideal imaginative outlet: it was at once playful and self-protective.

Rare too, in the days in which scrapbooking was a parlor activity, was the idea of using cut paper to produce any kind of first-person narrative. Scrapbooks instead were formal and, in a sense, generic, organized around a central theme (birds or flowers, children or cherubs) or collection (flags, labels, playing cards, or cigar bands), and when completed would be revisited often to admire and share with family and friends. Sentiment books, sometimes called friendship or gift books, remained popular among women in particular and tended to include poems and sayings, aphorisms, biblical quotations, and autographs from friends and colleagues.

Lillie Marsh's Floral Album of 1890 consists of handwritten well-wishes and embellished drawings from her students in Pioneer, Ohio, and was presented to her as a gift at the time of her marriage. Lillie's brother, Clyde, includes his own wish for *Sister Lillie,* and writes: *This world is full of beauty, like other worlds above, and if we'd do our duty — it would be full of love.* In Marsh's album, her students address her as *Friend Lillie*, suggesting the likelihood that hers was a Quaker school.[1]

Despite their sentimental intent, such books reflected a kind of steadfast Victorian propriety and maintained a respectful, almost deferential tone: they were polite, even punctilious—and

were consequently far from personal. As a genre, sentiment books led quite naturally to autograph books, which have more or less continued (albeit in looser incarnations) to the present day. A closer read of autograph books reveals a visible shift in social values, particularly in books kept by women. Many inscriptions refer to marriage (*When you get married and your husband gets cross, come to my house and make applesauce*), for which there was at least one alternative (*Take up the poker and show him who's boss!*), while autographs surfacing later in the century are, quite simply, resplendent in their sarcasm. (*In your slide down the banister of life, regard me as a splinter in your career.*)[2]

Beauty in general—and handwork in particular—was an essential part of nineteenth-century culture, and most middle-class women were well versed in such skills as needlepoint and embroidery. Similarly, scrapbooks not only required manual dexterity but demanded, too, a kind of keen attention to formal discipline and aesthetic detail. There are scrapbooks dating as far back as the eighteenth century that showcase everything from tatting samples to fragments of hair, featuring pages (like their paper counterparts) carefully arranged according to a kind of pristine geometric order. Such order reinforced what were, at the time, certain basic Victorian values—an abiding sense of historical deference and an utter devotion to one's family, for example—and nowhere is this more evident than in the pages that memorialized loved ones.

Documenting ancestry through artistry would have been, undoubtedly, an enormously therapeutic exercise, merging the duty of mourning with the act of making something. Equally formal in their compositional impulses, these memento mori would begin, over time, to merge objective matter (dates of birth and death, for instance) with sentimental captions: "Gone but not forgotten" and "Loving wife and mother" were common refrains. The resultant form was

a kind of static pictorial shrine, captured and, in a sense, ennobled in paper and paste. Here, again, the Victorian scrapbook was nothing if not principled: even when it grew to include waxed wreaths, jewelry, hair samples, or seashells, the memorial was conceived of as a delicate reliquary whose harmonious orchestration of words and pictures was but a humble gesture of obeisance to God and devotion to the lost loved one.

In truth, Victorians were fascinated not so much with life as with death, as one midwestern obituary scrapbook, from 1895, amply demonstrates. Its collector saved death notices graced by particularly gruesome details: *Hid Their Victim in a Ditch*; *Drunken Man Seared With Hot Poker*; and the particularly spooky *Two Weeks With A Corpse: A Senile Mother Alone in a Farm House With Her Daughter's Remains* are just a few of the hundreds of clippings, all of them neatly pasted on top of the pages of a school geometry primer, a practice often found in households whose mildly compromised economic circumstances demanded reuse of an existing text.[3] The resulting palimpsest-like volumes are gloriously, if occasionally paradoxically, dense. It is possible, even likely, that such compilations provided their owners with a kind of inverted twist on the notion of carpe diem: in this context, written evidence of someone else's death was also a tacit reminder of your own blessed life.

The late nineteenth century also witnessed a surge in scrapbooks devoted to travel, enabled, no doubt, by increasing industrial inroads that permitted easier access to faraway places. A good decade before the Titanic sank and the Hindenburg crashed, a brief period of prewar prosperity enabled a culture of unbridled luxury, and from 1900 to 1917, as tourism reigned supreme, so too did the opportunities for lush creature comforts.

The scrapbook kept by Frederick Nixon-Nirdlinger, a theater manager from Philadelphia, chronicles a grand tour in 1909 that took him

Assembly Badges
1890s

Dating from 1851, the
Rebekah Assembly is
the women's auxiliary to
the fraternal lodge,
Independent Order of
Odd Fellows. While
none of the jewelry here
appears to be emblematic
(the Rebekahs recognize
specific symbolic imagery
in their regalia, including
the dove for peace, the
white lily for purity, and
the beehive to represent
the coordination of effort),
this particular assemblage
of beads, hatpins, and
daguerreotype is framed
with black beads and
an onyx cameo.

The Floral Album
1890s

This album was presented
to a young teacher, Lillie
Marsh Rubenstein, by her
students when she left to go
get married.

Death Scrapbook
Rural Ohio
1895

ISOTTA GRAND HÔTEL
GÊNES

L U N C H

Hors d' Oeuvres variés

Asperges à la Milanaise

Rumsteaks grillés
Pommes chips

Fromage   Fruits

VARIÉTÉS

POLTRONCINA
№ 8

VARIÉTÉS

POLTRONCINA
№ 10

ISOTTA GRAND HÔTEL
GÊNES
Dejeuner de 7 à 10 heures

Dejeuner cpl. (Café - The - Chocolat) Lire	1.50
Oeufs à la coque . . . . »	—.25
» sur le plat (2 p.) . . . . »	—.75
» frits ou pochés (2 p.) . . . »	—.75
» sur le plat au jambon . . . »	1.—
» sur le plat au lard . . . . »	1.—
Omelette naturelle . . . . . . »	1.—
» au jambon (ou lard) . . »	1.25
Oeufs à la turque . . . . . . »	1.25
Lard grillé (ou jambon) . . . . »	1.—
Rognons . . . . »	1.50
Sole frite au grillée . . . . . »	2.—
Merlan . . . . »	1.50
Lunch – de 11 ¹/₂ à 2 heures Lire	3,50
Diner – . 7 . 9 . »	5,—

TIP. MARITTIMA
Barcelona

from western Europe to Egypt and Greece. Most of these travels were by train, and the wagon-lit menus and itineraries are all featured chronologically, punctuated by the requisite telegrams and ticket stubs that collectively mark his journey—a journey he made accompanied by his wife, whose presence in this album is negligible. (This omission may well have been a likely foreshadowing of what would prove to be the imminent collapse of their eighteen-year marriage.) There are advertisements for Moorish lace, elaborate steel-engraved letterheads, and an unusual little receipt from the purchase of a helmet in Gibraltar. The graphic variety here provides an apt metaphor for what must have been an embarrassment of riches; yet at the same time, there's something oddly incomplete about this book. The lack of personal details (handwriting, captions, personal observations of any kind) testifies to what was perhaps equally commonplace at the time—that is, the degree to which a beautiful scrapbook, if only made of scraps, ultimately rendered one's extravagant experience devoid of any overt emotional vitality.

Nixon-Nirdlinger's travel scrapbook perfectly captures this paradox: at once a relic of turn-of-the-century material grandeur, it is also a symbol of the emotional repression of the age and its upper class. (One might even speculate that it was a symbol of one man's emotional paralysis.) Bizarrely, the tide would soon turn for poor Fred-

erick, for whom there was a much more turbulent personal destiny in store.

Following their grand tour, the couple divorced, and Frederick married Miss St. Louis of 1923—the young Charlotte Nash, some twenty years his junior—who bore him two children and murdered him, less than a decade later, in their home on the French Riviera. In a highly publicized trial, a French court and a jury of seven bachelors later acquitted the beautiful widow, whose lawyers held she'd acted in self-defense. Indeed, scars on Charlotte's neck revealed that her husband had tried to strangle her.

In retrospect, the fact that the deceased was a Jew during a period of growing anti-Semitism in France may have had a considerable impact upon the verdict. Nevertheless, poor Frederick ended up having the last laugh: in his will, he bequeathed his nearly one-million-dollar

fortune to his two young children, leaving his widow virtually penniless.[4]

Scrapbooks like these remind us that creating an album from saved matter does not necessarily provide an accurate self-portrait. In the end, Frederick's is an essentially decorative volume, and while the wealth of ephemera helps to amplify and dramatize the thrill of his exotic voyage, there is little here to reveal much of his own internal journey. Charting that course would prove to be a rather different task, and one to which the scrapbook would, over time, become ideally suited.

The travel journals of the prolific Welsh novelist Berta Ruck include pressed flowers, photographs, press clippings, and letters from her fans and her publisher. She pasted in theater programs, saved obituaries, collected sheet music, and hoarded all her ticket stubs. Here, the line between factual evidence and fictional experimentation is often blurred: it is clear that she took her cue from the very world she inhabited, and helped herself without reservation to anecdotes as she found them. (Ruck—who published more than a hundred books over the course of her life—was primarily a fictional chronicler of jazz-age romance, and her scrapbook reflects what was clearly both a vivid and a varied imagination.) On one page, she glues the calling card from the British Minister and Lady Phipps: her observations of a late-afternoon visit to their home in June 1928 include the sorts of char-

Nixon-Nirdlinger Travel Scrapbook 1909

One of the most exquisite details in this scrapbook is the series of menus taken from the restaurant on board the train. While the layout remains constant across the journey, the language does not: Cyrillic characters replace Latin ones, and prices are reflected in local currencies. The trip was a long one with many stops, and the scrapbook includes receipts from a series of hotel letterheads and from many shopping expeditions along the way.

Ruck Scrapbooks
Europe
1928–1937

Berta Ruck used her scrapbooks to try out plot ideas and experiment with characters. The line between fiction and reality is not always clear; nor was it, perhaps, when Ruck's friend, the English writer Virginia Woolf, named a character after her in *Jacob's Room* — and killed her off. Ruck's husband took particular umbrage, but the writers remained friends nevertheless.

JUNE 1928.

10g
Österreich

Nr. 56649
AUSSTELLUNG
„FRAU UND KIND"
Gültig zum einmaligen Eintritte
am Tage der Ausgabe.
Sichtbar zu tragen!
Ohne Kontrollkupon ungültig!
Bei Verlust der Karte wird kein
Ersatz geleistet.

Direktion: ERICH MÜLLER
Johann Strauß-Theater
Balkonsitz Rechts 7
Nur gültig für die Vorstellung am
Samstag, 2. Juni 928 Sitz Nr.
Reihe

encored 4 times!

Theater- und Kunstnachrichten.

...rgtheater gelangt morgen Samstag die
...ar und Kleopatra" von Bernard Shaw,
...Siegfried Trebitsch, zur Aufführung. Anfang
...Montag den 4. d. wird das Schauspiel „Neit-
...Gneisenau" von Wolfgang Goetz aufgeführt.
...e, Serie B, blaue Mitgliedskarten, beschränkter
...Anfang 1/28 Uhr. — Dienstag den 5. d. wird
...thardt von Gneisenau" gegeben. Theater-
...ie C, rote Mitgliedskarten, beschränkter Karten-
...ng 1/28 Uhr. — Mittwoch den 6. d., geht die
...ar und Kleopatra" in Szene. Im Abonne-
...ruppe. Anfang 1/28 Uhr. — Donnerstag den 7. d.
...hardt von Gneisenau" aufgeführt. Im
...zweite Gruppe. Anfang 1/28 Uhr.
...ademietheater gelangt morgen Samstag das
...e Fahrt ins Blaue" von Caillavet, Flers
...Aufführung. Anfang 1/28 Uhr. — Montag den
...Dienstag den 5. d. wird die Komödie „Oster-
...Romain Coolus aufgeführt. Beide Vorstellungen
...1/28 Uhr. — Mittwoch den 6. d. wird die Komödie
...ame Tenor" gegeben. Im Abonnement dritte
...ng 1/28 Uhr. — Donnerstag den 7. d. geht bei
...Abonnement die Komödie „Osterferien" in
...1/28 Uhr.
...erntheater gelangt Samstag den 2. d. im
...ie Oper „Tosca" von Puccini zur Aufführung
...en Vera Schwarz, Kittel und den Herren Pataky,
...n, Wolken, Arnold, Ettl, Muzzarelli, Winter.
...r Reichenberger. Anfang 1/28 Uhr.
...Volksoper wurde der starke Erfolg von Julius
...und Ernst Decseys „Der unsterbliche
...der fünfundzwanzigsten Aufführung neuerdings be-
...reizende Biedermeiermilieu, das einen stimmungs-
...für Schuberts Musik bildet, übte wieder seinen

The Town as fascinating
as I remember it. Grey
stately buildings against
skies blue as a childs
eyes —
Profuse lespage in
this place.
Went up up to a
suburb LAINZ
tree-bordered streets
& all so much
cleaner & gayer
than either France

acterizations one might sooner find in a novel: *The Ambassador—a short, pleasant, moustached man,* and later, *Up three flights of stairs, thick red carpet, into a really stately drawing room.* Ruck's personal annotations here are particularly engaging: flanking a newspaper article with the headline "Woman Who Posed for Years as a Man Said To Be Wife of An Australian Named Smith," Ruck scribbles: *I would give much to know the REAL story!* More than mere compilations of ephemera, her scrapbooks, too, reflect both the financial hardships and the romantic strains she experienced during the early years of the Depression, and even offer brief glimpses of the growing anti-Semitism she witnessed during her long stay in Austria.[5]

As Victorian notions of cultural propriety began to wane in the late nineteenth and early twentieth centuries, scrapbooks would begin to disclose different preoccupations—about family, about society, and, most critically in terms of modernity, about self. And in many cases, the spatial manifestations of this shift are unusually striking: from perfunctory clippings to annotated images, the materials sequestered in the pages of these books would grow more varied, and their placement would begin to suggest a more dynamically nuanced relationship to the picture plane. Physical space, once rigid, would achieve a new authenticity as something decidedly more abstract, and with the advent of film, would come to reshape our visual perceptions of chronology, sequence, memory, even reality itself. Pages in scrapbooks would begin to exhibit new and unusual variations in texture and voice, mannerism and inflection. Soon, scrapbooks would migrate away from the realm of the domestic, toward a new, often socially alienated and arguably more internalized sense of self.

Many historians have noted the connection between modernization and social alienation, and it is likely that a more lively internal dialogue with one's own view of the world emerged as a consequence of this tension. In this context, scrapbooks

may well have met a critical emotional need at a time when the country was undergoing massive internal as well as cultural change. Art historian Sarah O'Brian-Twohig has observed that just as President Wilson called on Americans to make the world safe for democracy, many Americans felt not the least bit safe. "There was a huge awareness that what was happening to us was actually changing the parameters of what it meant to be a human being."[6] It is this shift in visual identity perhaps more than anything else that so aptly characterizes the early twentieth-century scrapbook: a fascinating study in pictorial assemblage in which less is *never* more.

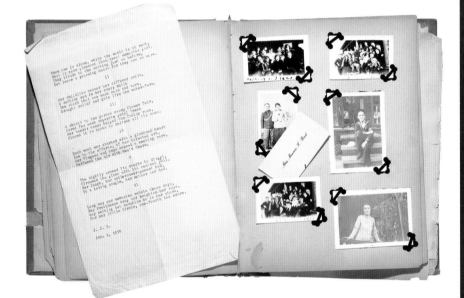

Reed Scrapbook
Philadelphia, PA
1919

Minnie Reed's high school scrapbook typifies the kinds of activities framing a schoolgirl's days: parties and field trips. Featured are pictures of the man she would later marry: she met him on a boat ride, even though her mother warned her that "nice girls don't take boat rides."

ON SATURDAY, MAY 25, 1918, MINNIE HAZEL Reed started a scrapbook. In it, she put anything that meant something to her: dance cards, a pressed flower, ticket stubs and party invitations, postcards, calling cards—and lots of photographs. She kept poems and letters, and documented her class trip to Washington in the fall of 1919 and the proud celebration of her high school graduation the following winter. There are clippings from the local paper, snapshots of her dearest friends, and the inevitable, if occasionally indecipherable, handwritten annotations and subjective jottings. To reconstruct the events of Minnie's life now, more than eighty-five years later, is to piece together a social history of an era long gone, yet what emerges is not so much a serious chronology

Effie Davis Putnam was a Michigan harpist who traveled to Paris to study music around 1900. She remained there until her death in 1943, and appears to have impressed several notable men along the way, among them Auguste Rodin, Mark Twain, and Victor Hugo, as well as this suitor, who mistook Davis for Douglas.

While autographs were captured for future viewing, some scrapbook makers, like Elizabeth Bailey, kept meticulous (if cryptic) accounts of their own lives. Love letters, like this one (*below*), were frequently sequestered in envelopes, often glued addressee-side down to further ensure one's privacy.

as a selective portrait of a particular time and place: of a young girl and her friends, of the clothes they wore, the cars they drove, and the dance cards that linked them, if only for an instant, in a state of exuberant romantic anticipation.

That photos play a central role in Minnie's book is only half the story: the other half lies in the memorabilia that circumscribes, and to a considerable extent amplifies, the story of a young girl at the beginning of her adult life.

Like so many girls of her generation, Minnie produced her scrapbook in a kind of postadolescent bubble. There is no mention of war casualties, of the famous Jack Dempsey fight in 1918, or, for that matter, of the flu epidemic that would go on to kill nearly 22 million by 1920. (In a nation whose 1918 census reported a population of nearly 104 million, this would be a significant tally.) In scrapbooks like these, the larger preoccupations dogging the nation were seldom, if ever, revealed; yet in countless and formidable ways, the pulse of the country is strikingly apparent. The same tensions that would emerge in American cultural life—in the slow and progressive move away from patriarchal order, away from moralistic reserve, away from authoritative hierarchy and pious historicism—would begin to make themselves evident in painting, in music, in literature, in dance. And there, in that fundamentally untethered space that straddled the conscious and unconscious, the scrapbook would offer new and unusual opportunities for self-discovery.

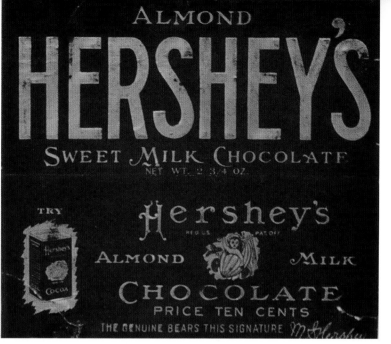

Marybelle Harn was a student at the Cincinnati Conservatory of Music, and the early pages of her scrapbook are filled with the lyricism one might expect: *And may you wield a mighty baton when you become that which you are striving for.* But in addition to her musical aptitude, Harn was also something of a virtuoso hand-letterer: with white ink, she captioned all her photographs, adding spot illustrations when appropriate— *Invitations, Press Notices, Frolics, For My Sweet Tooth*—and varying her penmanship to suit what she obviously believed was the occasional need: a publicity still for Tamaki Miura, an early twentieth-century Japanese opera singer famous for her performances as Cio-Cio-San in Puccini's *Madame Butterfly*, features her name written out in faux Japanese letterforms.

There are notes from friends: *Dear Marybelle, at your convenience would you let me have the dollar you owe me for the coaching lesson before xmas. It's embarrassing to have to ask but I need the money and you probably have forgotten about it. Sincerely, Grace.* A suitor of Harn's, who lived in her hometown of Versailles, Ohio, and was also a skilled typographer, sent her numerous letters, each hand-addressed in a different style. (In a letter to *My Sweetheart* dated November 18, 1923, his sign-off gestures accordingly: *Yours as a Printing Press, Flet.*) A letter postmarked from Versailles two days later—in a completely different hand— to *My Darling* is signed *Au Revoir—Willard*, and turns out to be Willard E. Moore. Perhaps he was known as Flet. (Or perhaps not.)

And then there's the candy, pages and pages of it: Hickok's Nut Butter Kisses, Necco Wafers, Penn-Mar Chocolate Coated Caramels, Badger's Milwaukee Distinctive Sweets, Hunny Munch, Cretors' Tosty Rosty Delicious Pop Corn, Beech-Nut Brand, Hershey's Mint and Clarks Teaberry Chewing Gums, Collins Honey Scotch, Planters See-Thru Virginia Bar, Puritan Googie Juniors Chocolate Peanut, Cap'n Pat the Chocolate Mint Patty, Planters Nut Confections, Crest Choco-

Allied Nations Speak to Rotarians Through Lips of Montgomery Maids

Local Rotary Club Stages Remarkably Interesting Patriotic Meeting Last Night

With dozens of visitors as guests, the Montgomery Rotary Club held the largest and most enthusiastic patriotic meeting in its history on Wednesday night at the Exchange Hotel. The management of the hotel tendered the club the use of its main dining room for the event and it was filled with Rotarians and those they brought as their guests.

The Allies There.

America, Roumania, Serbia, Italy, Belgium, England and France spoke to the throng with the lips of charming Montgomery girls, each gowned to represent the country she spoke for. The costumes of the Allied countries were planned by Mrs. C. A. Thigpen, who has always taken keen interest in the work of the Rotary Club.

The young ladies and the countries they represented were:

Miss Janice Weil, Roumania; Miss Theodosia Lee, Serbia; Miss Mary Rushton, Italy; Miss Jean MacDonald, Belgium; Miss Zelda Sayre, England; Miss Elizabeth Thigpen, France; Miss Ruby Page Ferguson, America.

England's Declaration.

England (Miss Zelda Sayre), after summing up her efforts for civilization, asked America for assistance in these staunch words:

[Interrupted in these benevolent pursuits] for over three years I have been engaged in bloody warfare and the end is not yet. O, America, young republic of the West, blood of my blood and faith of my faith, for humanity's sake together we fight! The Stars and Stripes on the battle lines of glorious France have strengthened my hand and filled my heart with cheer. You have been the hope and the inspiration of oppressed peoples and the generous friend of starving nations. In this hour of great peril, the young manhood of your great republic is needed in all of its strength. Prussian militarism must be crushed to earth. To this task I have dedicated my life, confident that the God of nations is on the side of truth and righteousness

Brilliant Ball of Alpha Tau Omega Men.

One of the most delightful events of the week was enjoyed by a large number of the members of the younger set when on Tuesday evening the Alpha Tau Omega Fraternity entertained most lavishly at a ball at the Exchange Hotel. The hosts of the happy occasion had spared no efforts in the making for perfection in every detail of music, decoration and all appointments for the evening.

The grand march with which the festivities opened was led by Mr. Charles Woolfolk with Misses Torrence Reid of Birmingham and Mr. Paul Le Grand with Miss Zelda Sayre.

Miss Reid wore an exquisite toilette of pink velvet and lace with pink chrysanthemums and Miss Sayre's own was of Rose pall velvet with ... she carried pink roses.

Hail to the Queen!!!!

Zelda

There once was a bird named Zelda
On Perry she skated — and — fell-da
A man passing by — Lost his right eye
When starting to gaze he beheld-a

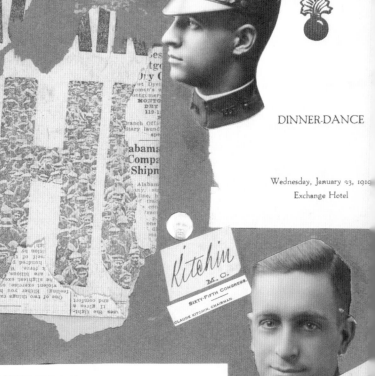

Ordnance Detachm
P. S. & T. Division

DINNER-DANCE

Wednesday, January 23, 1919
Exchange Hotel

Kitchin
M. C.
SIXTY-FIFTH CONGRESS
CLAUDE KITCHIN, CHAIRMAN

OFFICIAL PROGRAM

Fourth Alabama State-Wide Welcome-Home Celebration

167th Infantry, Rainbow Division, U. S. A.

MONTGOMERY, ALABAMA

MAY 12, 1919

lates, Johnston's Chocolate Nougat Bar, Banta's Shimme Waffle, Oh, Johnnie! Milk Nut Roll, and the *Oh MaMa* Pine Appa Roll Milk Chocolate. *For My Sweet Tooth,* notes Harn, alongside a drawing of an oversized tooth.

Like Marybelle Harn's compendium of sweets, scrapbooks from the early years of the new century are primarily joyous. Yet they can be secretive at the same time, leading to albums at once playful and bold, cryptic and contradictory. Zelda Fitzgerald's scrapbook hints at the volatile rhythm of life between 1917 and 1926, a period during which she would meet and marry F. Scott Fitzgerald. What followed for the high-flying couple was a peripatetic era of globetrotting that included the birth of their only child, financial struggles, at least one extramarital affair, the outbreak of World War I, and what appears, by all accounts, to have been a rather excessive amount of drinking. A closer look at her scrapbook reveals some, though certainly not all, of the high points: yet so, too, does it hint at other emotions—anger and uncertainty, fury and regret. Torn from several of the pages are images previously deemed admissible, with shards of clippings surfacing as partially sanctioned narratives. What remains is a series of marvelous makeshift collages that combine found matter with drawing and writing.

The scrapbook itself is a compendium of letters, photographs, clippings, reviews, invitations, gossip, and idle chatter. Some of the pages have an almost Dada-esque quality, with selections of text cut out in rounded shapes, amoeba-like and loosely dancing across the page. Others are more straightforward and didactic, often self-congratulatory and generally flattering. There are many, many pictures of Zelda herself, press photos of Scott, and snapshots from their American and European travels. Throughout, there are hints of their progressively codependent relationship, intimations that his successes were her successes and that their failures were equally shared. (In a letter

Fitzgerald Scrapbook
Auburn, AL
1919

Filled with photographs of herself, her friends, and her family members, Zelda Fitzgerald's scrapbook also includes magazine covers and reviews. The tone is playful, even giddy: one has the impression that Zelda Fitzgerald was always in some kind of flurry of activity—dancing, painting, writing, playing. Even her captions read as though they were intended for dramatic effect, which they probably were.

to her husband in December 1931, Zelda writes *I realize more completely than ever how much I live in you and how sweet and good and kind you are to such a dependent appendage.*) A photograph of a painfully young-looking Zelda—almost a child herself—holding baby Scottie reveals precisely the kind of uneasiness that is everywhere in her writing, a sentiment expressed in countless ways throughout her richly dense scrapbook.

Zelda's compositional instincts owe much to her artistic training (in dance and writing as well as in art), resulting in page compositions that celebrate a kind of random chaos—a fact that nods perhaps equally to her anxieties, to her protracted struggle for an identity separate from her husband's, and to a perpetual yearning for a degree of self-knowledge that somehow lay just beyond her grasp. *I don't want to live,* she wrote in another letter to her husband. *I want to love first, and live incidentally.*[7]

Zelda Fitzgerald's scrapbook was produced during some of her liveliest and most productive years, but these were also the years in which the tension between her professed wish to be a "new" woman and the fact that her efforts were essentially dwarfed by her husband's career made for extraordinary personal (and interpersonal) conflict. She was hospitalized following a breakdown in 1930, and spent the remainder of her life in and out of psychiatric hospitals. While it is unclear whether she continued to contribute to her scrapbook during these later and difficult years, it is easy to imagine the degree to which she benefited along the way from the incomplete, fragmented nature of scraps. In her album, her life materializes in fits and starts, through juxtaposition, eradication, dislocation—and no shortage of hyperbole.

F. Scott Fitzgerald made no secret of the fact that he modeled many of his more impetuous female characters on his wife, which occasionally led him to appropriate her diaries and scrapbooks for his own creative need. Yet while exhibitionism long remained an intrinsic part of Zelda's persona (she loved an audience and craved public attention), she was clearly unsure about Scott's helping himself to her private jottings for his own "material." In a review of his second novel, *The Beautiful and the Damned*, she managed to poke fun at this odd family dynamic: "It seems to me that on one page I recognized an old diary of mine which mysteriously disappeared shortly after my marriage, and also scraps of letters which, though considerably edited, sound to me vaguely familiar," she wrote. "In fact Mr. Fitzgerald—I believe that is how he spells his name—seems to believe that plagiarism begins at home."[8]

One of the psychological benefits for those who kept scrapbooks, in the postwar years and throughout the twentieth century, is that they enabled a particular kind of playacting: the domain of the scrapbook itself was an essentially protected space, offering a private forum for trying on different personalities and experimenting with one's self-image. Scrapbooks became, in a sense, the ultimate laboratories for postmodern experiments in self-conceptualization, and were likely to have been particularly appealing to those who struggled to reconcile different aspects of their lives and personal interests.

There is some evidence to suggest that such experimentation had revealed itself even earlier in the albums of public figures: this was particularly true for those whose self-image benefited from a kind of release that the scrapbook so freely provided. Even Thomas Jefferson (whose scrapbooks loosely mirrored the basic cultural purview of his generation) kept materials that were somewhat at odds with his more public persona. In addition, the president's scrapbooks reveal an abundance of poems and songs praising precisely the life Jefferson did not lead.[9]

For Jefferson the polymath, the scrapbook was therefore likely to have been enormously gratifying. And for Zelda Fitzgerald (whose mental

instability was later attributed to bipolar tendencies, and eventually to schizophrenia) it must have been hugely reassuring. Such open-ended fragmentation was at turns entertaining and liberating—and for Zelda, whose own imagination and visual curiosity were considerable, so were the spirited promises of cubism. Indeed, the very instability of the newly "modern" picture plane was, perhaps on some very tangible level, an ideal model for Zelda's conflicting personal, physical, and creative needs. As a writer, dancer, and artist, she struggled with form (and in particular with finishing things), yet her scrapbook remained, by its very nature, an improvisational endeavor: it was a story requiring no plot, a dance needing no choreography. As such, it may well have been Zelda's ideal medium: a virtual celebration of the indefinite. Here, released from public scrutiny, she could play out different scenarios and probe the boundaries of her various—and at times contradictory—selves. In one heartbreaking verse of self-doubt, a character in her novel perfectly articulates the pain of such dichotomies. "Why am I this way, why am I that? Why do myself and I constantly spat? Which is the reasonable, logical me? Which is the one who must will it to be?"[10]

While less outwardly plagued by such demons, the American imagist poet Hilda Doolittle (known as H.D.) was perhaps equally inspired by experimenting with her own self-image in the pages of her album. She kept a scrapbook that merged her interest in ancient Greece with a kind of deliberate musicality, quite possibly derived from the imagist principles that informed many of her early poetic pursuits.[11] Her book also embodies a kind of willful incongruity, with pages that are at turns symbolic and surreal. There are nudes; a snake; photographs of buildings and ruins; a roulette wheel. Many pages include collaged items—often photos of H.D. herself cut out and superimposed onto landscapes or friezes—and there is at least one

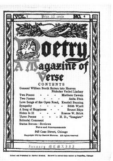

page of silhouetted images intermingled with Greek statuary. H.D.'s life and career were likely more mercurial than the pages in this scrapbook would attest, but there remains something fascinating about the experimental nature of these pages. Shifting scale, flexible space, and a kind of willful approach to depth of field make her collages oddly disturbing, reserved—even bleak. Sitting flatly on black oversized pages, they nevertheless possess a kind of poetic charm, sequenced without captions and thereby revealing little autobiographical information about the poet herself. Because this book is undated, it is difficult to place it precisely within the chronology of H.D.'s work, but the enduring attention to formal rhythm suggests it is likely to have been produced earlier rather than later, when her outspoken views on feminism, her association with Freud, and her eccentric lifestyle (she shared a Bauhaus home with her companion and her daughter, as well as numerous cats and monkeys) are likely to have led to more radical page compositions—and expositions of self.

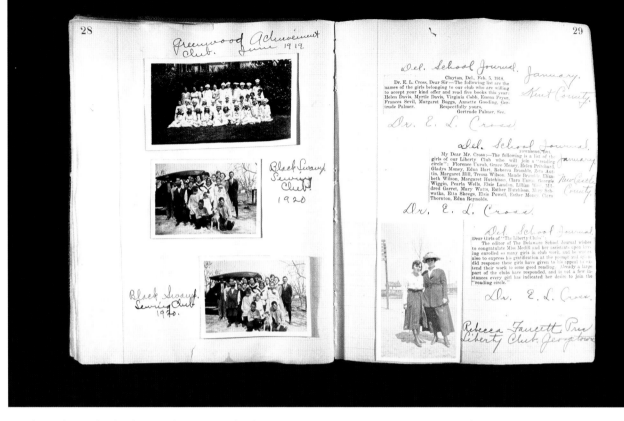

Throughout the book, too, there are indeed hints of other preoccupations—some sexual, others political—that would surface over the years in H.D.'s work. (One page simply shows a naked Doolittle gazing up at a silhouetted clipping of a Greek ruin.) It is also interesting to note the degree to which this scrapbook, belonging to a writer, in fact contains a scarcity of words. In this view, the abstract placement of disparate images allows the scrapbook page to become its own kind of experimental canvas: image driven, playfully cryptic, and open to multiple interpretations.

Such experimentation, when informed by autobiographical reportage, frequently leads to scrapbooks brimming with odd juxtapositions—a wrapped toothpick next to an obituary, for example, or a gum wrapper next to a college diploma. Scrapbooks like these offer material proof of a kind of puzzling ambiguity, highlighting that unique precipice between youth and maturity that passes

Medill Scrapbook
Wilmington, DE
1918–1922

Agnes Medill's scrapbook is filled with photographs captioned in her own hand, and a robust assortment of news clippings reveals what appears to have been a sustained interest in reform, efficiency, and modernization. (She was also partial to domestic science.)

in an instant but seems, at the time, to last an eternity. Often there are bold shifts in scale, reordered sequences of snapshots, silhouetted cartoons, and foldout additions—books within books—which further animate the stories being unfurled. Storytelling, in the context of such graphic mayhem, becomes increasingly discordant (at times frustratingly incomplete) yet remains extraordinarily vivid in its depiction of a particular time and place, of one person's incontestable point of view.

To the extent that life rarely mirrors the timeline we superimpose upon it, such scrapbooks reveal more than mere photographic evidence: they introduce sensory variables including touch, smell, and a kind of physicality that collectively produce a third, or even a fourth, dimension. The early twentieth-century scrapbook is made all the more poignant by the way images are reconsidered in the presence of such ephemera. It is in this context—framed by and interwoven with

the physical proof of lived experience—that the scrapbook retains its enduring vitality, eliciting in the reader a kind of emotional response that the simple photo album, bereft of such riches, does not in fact possess.

There is, for instance, the inadvertent yet delicate folding necessitated by the inclusion of letters or cards, requiring the reader to open each folded portion, to breathe in the smell of the paper, to register the feel of its weight in the hand and experience an implied veil of intimacy being pierced as one opens, and later refolds, each missive. There are the dog-eared pages; the compositional montages; the tiny pencil dangling from a silk thread, still sewn to its dance card from a long-forgotten sorority ball. There are the forgotten envelopes with their canceled stamps (do those addresses even still exist?), the torn invitations and thank-you notes, all of them participants in this singular orchestration, a poignant choreographic swirl of frayed letters and fractured ribbons and a flurry of snapshots suspended in time.

Increasingly and to some extent unwittingly, scrapbooks would thus begin to reveal more than mere first-person narratives, and nowhere is this more evident than in books profiling communities and clubs. As early as 1831, Alexis de Tocqueville wrote that it was a particularly American conceit to form social associations, and indeed, the history of fraternal orders in America can be traced back as far as the seventeenth century. By World War I, groups like these had extended their reach to children (the Boy Scouts, the Girl Scouts, Boys and Girls Clubs, and the Camp Fire Girls, among others) at the local and, later, the national level. Agnes Medill's scrapbook, begun in 1918, includes photographs, newspaper clippings, programs, correspondence, and song lyrics that collectively paint a picture of this enthusiastic group dynamic. During that year alone, Medill organized more than fifteen Boys and

Abraham Scrapbook
Pittsburgh, PA
1927–1928

Dorothy Abraham kept valentines, paper napkins, and the plastic cellophane from a sweetheart's box of chocolates. She saved ticket stubs from football games, school concerts, and Stunt Day at her school. She collected autographs, telegrams, invitations, and calling cards, and pasted in the portraits of each of her classmates and teachers. Included here too are the results from her driving test, a piece of school chalk, and a sample of her expert shorthand. But what is most compelling are the many pages of letters, each of them folded neatly, one next to the other, with the addressee side face down. The envelopes, like paper cocoons, are gently positioned alongside other saved matter, making the page look like an unusual experiment in origami.

ABOVE AND OPPOSITE
Camp Fire Girls Album
Lenape, NJ
1915

The Camp Fire Girls was founded in 1910 by Dr. Luther Halsey Gulick (and his wife, Charlotte) as a nonsectarian club for young women. They placed great value on wholesome play in an increasingly modernized world, and founded the Camp Fire Girls in part to help prepare women for work outside the home.

Reed Scrapbook
Philadelphia, PA
1918

Minnie Reed, Leopold Helfand (the man she would later marry), and (eventually) William Helfand, my father.

Girls Clubs in schools throughout her mid-Atlantic area. Her dedication to her country was deeply felt on a local level, but it was through the organization of these clubs that she mobilized efforts to effect greater and longer change. Medill was active in some of the first 4H Clubs in the State of Delaware, and was an early advocate for sustainable farming practices: working with the United States Department of Agriculture, she lobbied on the importance of food conservation for the war effort. Her scrapbook is as much a testament to her organizational skills as it is a symbol of her dedication to the people she mentored.

While allegedly "modern" in their acknowledgment of what were, at the time, issues of broader cultural consequence, these organizations still maintained a sense of almost tribal deference, and their scrapbooks testify to what was, in essence, a fascinating duality between the demands of public service and the duties of ancient ritual. Five years after the founding of

the Camp Fire Girls, the Lenape Camp Fire Girls Scrapbook of 1915 includes entire pages of colorful hieroglyphic code.[12] (Such marks would come to be designated, later in the century, by patches sewn onto the felt sashes of scout uniforms.) Laws and bylaws are reverently included, along with portraits of the membership outfitted in full Camp Fire regalia. Still, there is a hint of malaise in these photographs of young girls with feather headbands, a hint of mischief barely noticeable in their gaze, as if they are wondering what lay ahead—beyond the campfire, beyond the group.

I do not know what became of Marybelle Harn or of Lydia Blanchard, or what led their scrapbooks to travel the itinerant route that led them to my library. As for Minnie Reed, I do know this much: she went on to marry, to raise a family, and to live to the impressive age of 101. She did not share the scrapbook with me—her granddaughter—but left it to be discovered in a closet by a cousin of mine after she died. We knew some, though by no

means all, of the story of her early life: she had shared many of these photographs with us (proud, I now realize, that she had been so pretty and photogenic), but we knew nothing of the ancillary details. She went to Washington? She went to parties? There were men who danced with her besides Grandpop? Scrapbooks, it seems, derive their meaning (and their grace) from a long gestational cycle, one that demands patience and persistence, and perhaps as little rational intention as possible. Paradoxical as it may seem, the scrapbook would come to thrive on a curious blend of insider knowledge and outsider art. And it is in this tension—between personal sentiment and public space—that a modern biographical odyssey would begin to emerge. Everything was about to change. Even scrapbooks.

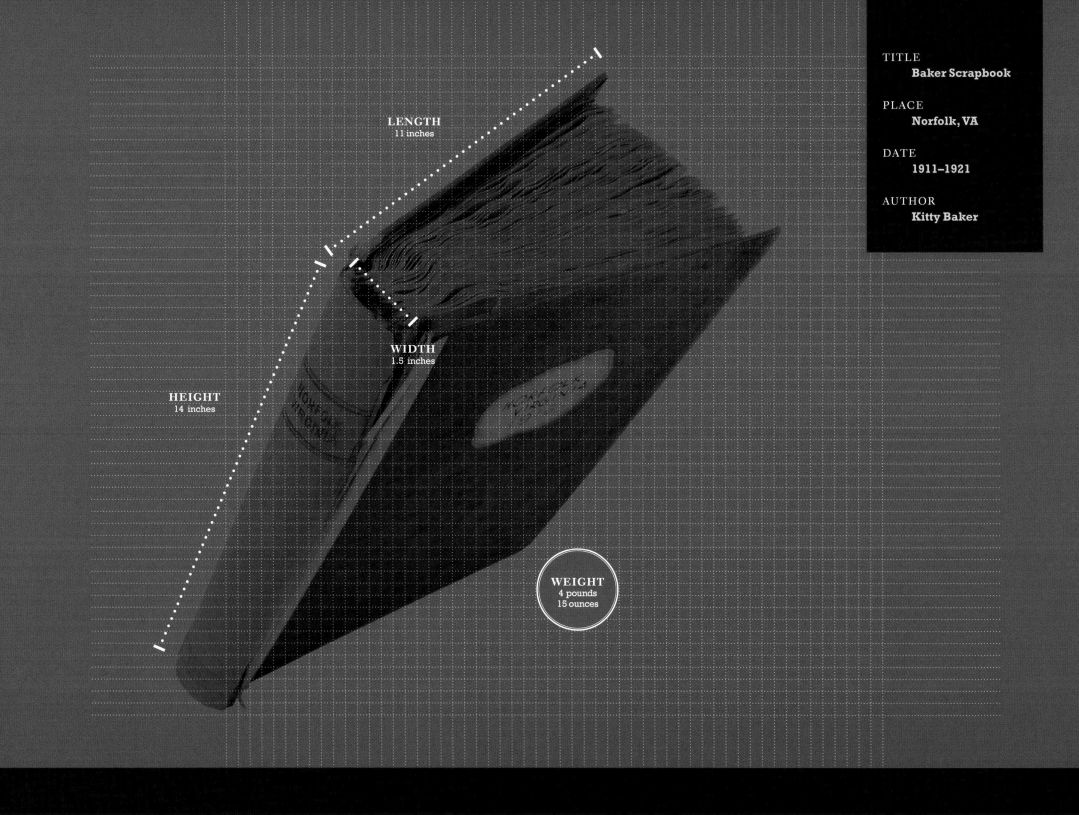

LENGTH
11 inches

WIDTH
1.5 inches

HEIGHT
14 inches

WEIGHT
4 pounds
15 ounces

TITLE
Baker Scrapbook

PLACE
Norfolk, VA

DATE
1911–1921

AUTHOR
Kitty Baker

BAKER SCRAPBOOK

NORFOLK, VIRGINIA, 1911–1921

18

Gay Crowd at Virginia Beach on Easter, 1916

This picture, taken during a house party at Kenilworth Cottage at Virginia Beach during the Easter holidays, 1916, may bridge the gap between then and now for many Norfolk area residents. Identified in the photo, which belongs to Wythe Lee, of Norfolk, are first row (left to right), Lee; Virginia Driver (now the wife of Marine Gen. Lemuel C. Shepherd); Junius Peake, of New York City, and Lydia Taylor (now Mrs. Charles Nash, of Charlottesville); second row, Reginald Whitehurst and Louise Bolton, of Washington; standing, Harry L. Gilliam, of New York City; C. Woodson Pollard, of Norfolk; Mary Faree and Carter H. Coupland, of Virginia Beach; Alice Herbert Webster (now Mrs. Marshall Speight, of Richmond); Dr. Walter P. Adams, of Norfolk; Ellen Maury (now Mrs. J. Randolph Coupland, Jr., of Virginia Beach); unidentified; Elizabeth Bull (now Mrs. E. Bull Maury, of Richmond); J. Randolph Coupland, Jr., of Virginia Beach; Dorothea Randolph (now Mrs. Norborne Berkeley, of Bethlehem, Pa.); an unidentified member of the party, and two unidentified children.

Great dancer Jack Donohue graced the 1921 Follies, finest of Ziegfeld's shows.

Something of an Institution, as Many Will Recall

Easter Week-End House Parties of Yesteryear Made Virginia Beach Fashion Center of Day

Holiday Scene of 1916 Brought into Focus Through Photographs

Easter week-end . . . house parties at Virginia Beach . . . long dresses and picture hats . . . pegged trousers and celluloid collars . . . Galilee Church.

These may freshen the memories of many present and former Norfolk residents of the days when Virginia Beach house parties over the long Easter holidays were quite the vogue.

An Easter scene of 1916 comes into clear focus today in photographs dug from the snapshot album of Wythe Lee, of Norfolk, one of a party of about two dozen at the Kenilworth Cottage that breezy, sunny week-end.

The latest 1916 fashions, which may bring a shudder to the womenfolk who recognize themselves in these pictures, went on display after the party attended services at the Galilee Church, only place of worship at the beach then.

Recorded for posterity were the day's supreme styles — for the women, high shoes, long skirts and wide-brimmed hats; for the men, narrow-legged trousers, high, stiff collars and black homburg hats.

The Easter holiday house party was something of an institution in that era, long-time residents of this area recall.

Parties in the late 'teens and early 20's would rent a cottage for the holidays, arrange for a chaperone and move in, the girls on the second floor and the boys on the first.

Look carefully at the pictures, if you were around in 1916. You may recognize an old friend or even yourself.

High style is on Easter morning exhibit in this photograph taken in 1916 at a Virginia Beach house party of Norfolk area youths and their guests. Left to right are Alfred Van Patten, Lawrence Wrenn (behind Van Patten), Carter H. Coupland, Dorothea Randolph and James E. Etheridge.

The competition for Follies laughs was sharpened by Eddie Cantor's presence.

KITTY BAKER

Name   Kitty Baker

Address + Phone no The Boiserain — 6133 Norfolk

Age 15 yrs 8 mos.   6 Feb, 1900.

Favorite school Annapolis, V.M.I. — M.H.S.

Favorite dance Lame duck, foxtrot.

Best girl dancer Browne, H.W., K. Rain.

Best boy dancer (Angus) Jimmy, ~~Spotie~~ Wyp Dave

Best looking girl Kathleen. Taylor.

Best looking boy Jimmie Jordan, T.B.P.

Best boy friend ~~J.R. one~~ ~~none at all~~ (A. Avery.)

Best girl friend Iquatp. Balour, ~~Kathleen~~ Browne.

Favorite actor Bruce McRae

Favorite actress Maude Adams. Billie Burke

Favorite (movie) actor Wallace Reid, Warren K., Harold Lockwood

Favorite (movie) actress Clara K. Young, Norma Talmadge, Mary Pickford.

Favorite picture Any of the Castles.

Who has the prettiest — you know? Jinx and Ethel.

Favorite play Moloch

Favorite color Blue and gold — red, white and orange - rose. turquoise.

Biggest flirt

Bozzuette — K. Dain. E. Tilton.

Favorite color eyes (boy)   Blue, Hazel.

"   "   " (girl)   Gray, blue, and black.

"   "   hair (boy)   Golden, and brown

"   "   " (girl)   Scarlet. Sable. best of all. dark brown (curly!)

What type of boy do you like best? Not afraid to say what he thinks, or mean what he says!

" " " girl " " " "? Ditto; also impulsive, but rather reasonable.

Favorite rag   Castle Walk; Alabama Jubilee; Araby; Sailor's Jest Stand.

"   foxtrot Ragging the Scale; Georgia Friend; I'm Crazy 'Bout You; Clingville Rag.

"   waltz. Geraldine; Sari; Avec Moi?; Drinking Song.

Nicknames. Kitty, Kit, Miss Puss, Phoebe, Bake, Little Devil, "Kitty-Dear".

TO DOROTHY FROM CONTESSE

ANITA STEWART: Marie Antoinette in a trolley car, Bernhardt, born in St. Louis and working as a stenographer; Juliet living in Brooklyn.

CHARLES RAY

CAUTION
The Products of this company are genuine only when put up in our special watermarked wrapper

Fifi D'Orsay, Will Rogers (1929)

Even with two guns, William S. Hart waited for the villain to start shooting.

The pioneer West of stagecoach hold-ups and two-gun men was passing, but it lived robustly on in motion-picture melodramas. Its most popular hero in these thrillers was William S. Hart, whose implacable and sinewy virtue triumphed over innumerable desperadoes of the screen.

Culver Service

WILLIAM S. HART

William S. Hart was hard-bitten star of Hollywood's early Western movies.

WILLIAM S. HART   1946

William S. Hart Famous Hero of Movies Dead

Los Angeles, June 24. (AP)—William S. Hart, eastern-born "wild west" movie actor of a quarter of a century ago, died late last night of a lingering infirmity which had called his son home from Washington, D. C., last month to enter a court fight over the dying man's affairs.

The iron-faced hero of many a movie gun battle died peacefully in a hospital. His physician, Dr. H. D. Van Fleet, issued a statement saying "death came without a struggle, just as though he were asleep." Hospital records gave Hart's age as 83. Movie press agents earlier had given his age as 76.

At the bedside was his son, William S. Hart, Jr., 24, who last Thursday was appointed co-guardian, with George Frost, of the actor's person. He had charged in court that his father was being improperly cared for and was incapable of managing his own affairs. Frost, who said he was a long-time friend of the actor, was appointed sole guardian of Hart's estate, estimated at nearly a million dollars.

Young Hart's mother, Winifred Westover, from whom the actor was divorced 20 years ago, had been almost constantly at Hart's side during the recent, critical stage of his illness, but was not present when death came. Hart suffered a stroke last May.

Hart had been ill frequently during the last five years and his sickness took their toll of his gaunt frame and slender body. He lived in contentment until his sister, Mary, whom he always referred to as "my darling sister," died in 1943. After her death he suffered spells of melancholy which were broken only when old friends occasionally dropped in.

He lived on his 80 acre ranch in Newhall, 30 miles from the scenes of his triumphs in Hollywood, after his retirement in 1925. The 15-room house, white, rambling and in Spanish style, looks like a cluster of mushrooms huddling on a hill. Every room was overflowing with mementos of his active days—silver saddles, bear rugs, dozens of buffalo robes, guns, Indian headdress, paintings by Remington and Will James and the originals of paintings by James Montgomery Flagg for the several books Hart wrote.

Mary Hart left $150,000 for an animal shelter in Westport, Conn., and $100,000 for a William S. Hart memorial in Newhall. This fund, it is believed, was intended to keep up horseshoe ranch and the Hart home, which he valued at $300,000, if the State or some governmental agency accepts them for public use.

"To give this place to the public," Hart said one time, "is the least I can bequest to show my appreciation for the support they gave me during my long movie career."

WILLIAM S. HART stood for Two-Gun Virtue to a generation of Western fans. He now lives quietly on a ranch at Newhall, north of Hollywood.

Charlie Chaplin and Camera Crew
On location for "The Gold Rush," 1925

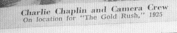

1919

—1919

J. L. Nichols, of the Norfolk Health Department, who was a leader in the campaign to kill 1,000,000 rats in Norfolk, reported that 200,000 had been exterminated. Dr. P. S. Schenck, health commissioner, said that for the campaign to be a success it was necessary for every family in Norfolk to cooperate.

Among movies playing in Portsmouth theaters that week were Douglas Fairbanks in "The Knickerbocker Buckaroo" at the New Orpheum; Clara Kimball Young in "The Better Wife" at the Olympic, and Bessie Barriscale in "The Woman Michael Married" at the Rialto.

—1919

Lt. Preston B. Wilkes Jr., of Norfolk, who for the previous 18 months has been identified with the United States military signal service at Washington, left for San Francisco, Calif., en route to Russia where he had been assigned to duty with the railway corps of that country.

Phoenix Council, No. 152, Junior Order United America Mechanics, Portsmouth, installed J. L. Pollard, councilor; W. E. Smith, warden; R. D. Smith, conductor; O. R. Ivey, outside sentine; W. E. Franklin, chaplain, and J. P. Brooks Jr., trustee. The installing officer was H. R. Pollard, past councilor.

John S. Manley, who had been in charge for a year of the Norfolk office of the National City Co., a department of the National City Bank of New York, was transferred to Detroit, Mich. He was to be succeeded by Kenneth S. Miller from the company's Washington office.

HENRY WALTHALL

Our Folks   By Goshorn

Frederic Gilbert

SWINK

RISING YOUNG ATTORNEY WHOSE OFF DUTY HOBBY IS SAILING HIS 30-FOOT SLOOP *TRIVET*.

IN 1947 HE WON THE CRUISING CLASS CHAMPIONSHIP OF CHESAPEAKE BAY...

A LT. COMMANDER IN THE COAST GUARD RESERVE, FRED SERVED ON CONVOY DUTY AND ANTI-SUB PATROL IN THE ATLANTIC AND PACIFIC.

HE IS TRAINING OFFICER IN C.G. AUX. FLOTILLA 52.

BY GOSH

Valentine

1919

A. P. Wirephoto
CHARLES CHAPLIN

CHARLIE CHAPLIN

CHARLES CHAPLIN

New York Maze of Early Daze
New York's lower Broadway in the early 1880's was a maze of overhead telephone and telegraph wires before they were replaced by underground facilities.

—1918

The Junior Auxiliary to the Board of Missions of Christ Episcopal Church, Norfolk, elected Mrs. A. L. Walker director; Miss C. Alley, assistant director; Miss Ann Jordan, president; Miss Elizabeth Jones, vice president; Miss Hattie Bridges, secretary, and Miss Thelma Nixdorf, treasurer.

Charles E. Ashburner, city manager of Norfolk, was to address the Baraca Class of Freemason Street Baptist Church the following Sunday.

Walter Sykes, for many years a member of the Portsmouth Police Department and for the previous six years traffic policeman at the Portsmouth ferry terminal, left the department to become traffic supervisor under the new ferry management with jurisdiction in Norfolk and Berkley as well as in Portsmouth. His old assignment was given to Policeman C. E. Porter.

MAURY HIGH SCHOOL
M. H. S.—107—C. P. Co.
Norfolk, Va., *March 7,* 1916.
The *work in German of*
Miss Kattarine Baker
has not been satisfactory. Your earnest co-operation is asked to secure immediate and continued improvement.
Of course she can do the work required, but irregular attendance prevents her from doing so.
Very respectfully, *E. M. Mary* Teacher.
Please Sign ....

Irene Castle

—1919

Lt. Cmdr. Patrick N. L. Bellinger, USN, commander of the Norfolk Naval Air Station, was relieved of his command and assigned to special duty with the Navy Department at Washington. It was understood that Lt. Cmdr. Bellinger was to pilot an American naval seaplane across the Atlantic Ocean.

Portsmouth residents acted to place a team in the Virginia League in the approaching baseball season. At a mass meeting to discuss baseball possibilities, a steering committee was formed. The committee was composed of W. H. Colein, chairman; E. P. Packett, Charles F. Harper, S. T. Montague, Earl H. Wright, A. J. Talbot, Mayor J. T. Hanvey, City Manager W. B. Bates, Charles H. Myers and Henry L. Hudgins.

The Virginia Corporation Commission chartered the Central Wire and Iron Co., Inc., of Norfolk. E. J. Nallis was president; Charles M. Smith, secretary, and R. L. Walker, treasurer.

Mrs. D. Lawrence Groner was hostess at her home in Graydon Ave., Norfolk, at a card party in compliment to Mrs. George Riddell, of Baltimore, Md., who was the guest of Mrs. James Iredell Jenkins.

Billie Burke

MAURY HIGH SCHOOL
M. H. S.—107
Norfolk, Va., *Mar 4,* 1916.
The *work of Mrs. K. Baker in everything*
has been below zero and therefore
has not been satisfactory. Your earnest co-operation is asked to secure immediate and continued improvement.
Please notice this and make her attend school more regularly.
Very respectfully,
All the Teachers
re Sign here — *L. W. Baker.*

Happy Days
spent in this
fun. Not a both-
er in the
world except
Dick to me.
and crabs.

A typical   41
morning, with reluctant first—
July. 1912.   Etcetra!

Virginia Beach

Kit (N.C.W.) and Salone.

Annus Cordis Meae.

Utinam reverteretur

In Memoriam
Of my first

Suffrage Parade.
1912.

HITCHING GROUNDS   RICHMOND CHAUTAUQUA   1912

Monticello Hotel, Norfolk, Va.

How many more times will you remember
a certain afternoon of your childhood,
some afternoon that's so deeply a part of your being
that you can't even conceive of your life without it?
Perhaps four or five times more, perhaps not even that.
How many more times will you watch the full moon rise?
Perhaps twenty. And yet it all seems limitless.

Paul Bowles, *The Sheltering Sky*

Annus Cordis Meae.   Utinam reverteretur

In Memoriam
Of my first

Suffrage Parade.
1912.

1912 August 1912

1916

to secure

Teacher S

HITCHING GROUNDS RICHMOND CHAUTAUQUA. 1912

CHAPTER THREE   SENTIMENT

BY WORLD WAR I, THE PASTIME THAT HAD for generations been housed in the family parlor became a more individual, and arguably more private, pursuit. Over time, the diversity of approaches, the capacity for introspection, and the awareness of new possibilities for expression resulted in books that began to reflect altogether new and different sorts of social, cultural, and emotional preoccupations. The scrapbook came to be seen as a kind of time capsule, an archive of printed miscellany, personal anecdotes, and material remnants that filled a private need, yet at the same time reflected a tacit awareness of certain public values. To view these volumes today is to witness the emerging and often contradictory sensibilities of a newly modern age, to see firsthand how Americans embraced adversity and ambition, fear and faith, the self and society. At turns dutiful and daring, the scrapbook came to

mirror the changing pulse of American cultural life—documenting its celebrations and its mournings, its epic struggles and its fleeting glories.

And soon, the very notion of the treasured memento begins to change. The pressed flowers wither and turn brown, casting mirrored, ghostlike impressions on their facing pages. Letters are dog-eared from years of folding in and out. The glue fails, the photo corners unhinge, and the once-fastidious chronologies migrate across the page, creating new, unintentional compositions. Annotations are added in a more controlled hand, lending the wisdom of hindsight, the objectivity that inevitably comes with maturity and distance. And there is more: more time passing, more unexpected discovery, more things added that shed a new and curious light on life as it bears witness to an unprecedented age of technological progress. Soon, the faded recollections are coupled with

OPPOSITE
Baker Scrapbook
Norfolk, VA
1911–1921

Pages from Kitty Baker's lifelong repository of words and pictures reveal a young woman with a spirited take on life. Baker openly mourned the passing of the Nineteenth Amendment, which must have represented an end to her days of youthful protest; meanwhile, she spent considerable time saving candy wrappers and pictures of her favorite film stars, and made a point of including her poor conduct reports from school.

other matter: train timetables, ration cards, letters bearing strange postmarks and exotic stamps—evidence of a new, increasingly mysterious world.

With wartime apprehension a daily reality, it is no wonder that tokens of religious sentiment come to play a significant role. Prayer cards, church announcements, and press clippings profiling religious leaders provide what would have undoubtedly been perceived as a kind of psychological reinforcement during times of heightened self-doubt. For one young doctor in Seattle, the scrapbook became a kind of personal Bible, densely crafted with articles on science and religion, education, and, somewhat asynchronously, the virtues of motherhood. Dr. Rodolfo Acena was a Filipino American doctor whose enormous scrapbook—which he diligently maintained for well over a decade—includes clippings and personal memorabilia united in elaborate, hand-drawn frames. In some instances, Acena used a typewriter to add on to newspaper articles pasted in his book: his page compositions are highly detailed and include many examples of exquisite penmanship and calligraphy. While such handmade page embellishments were not uncommon in scrapbooks, they were rare in books kept by men, and still more unusual for the scrapbook of a physician.

Conflicting perspectives are recast here in one giant, coordinated effort, produced with extraordinary care and craftsmanship. Portraits of American presidents as well as pictures of the pope appear with greater frequency than any personal family photographs (suggesting that Dr. Acena may well have derived a reinforced sense of well-being not so much from religious worship as from hero worship). At the same time, the conflation of piety and patriotism here is significant in that it testifies to what may have seemed, for many, a plausible method for making sense of war. Dr. Acena clearly valued his Catholic faith, yet his album also reflects an almost deferential respect

for his profession, more than an occasional nod to his political leanings, and perhaps most of all, an enthusiastic embrace of his newly adopted country. Dr. Acena's scrapbook becomes, consequently, a kind of self-initiated primer for good citizenship. Devotion, in this context, is essentially fungible—whether it is to one's mother, school, church, or country.

Acena Scrapbook
Seattle, WA
1930–1943

Dr. Rodolfo Acena saved everything he could get his hands on that reinforced his patriotism for his newly adopted country—even his school rejection letters. (One reference described him as a good little Filipino boy.) Weighing 11 pounds, the book is dominated by newspaper clippings, all meticulously laid out and framed by the author's spectacular penmanship. Dr. Acena was especially fond of drawing circles around favorite photos.

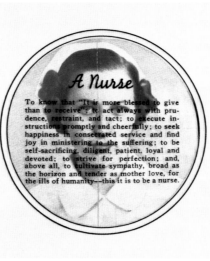

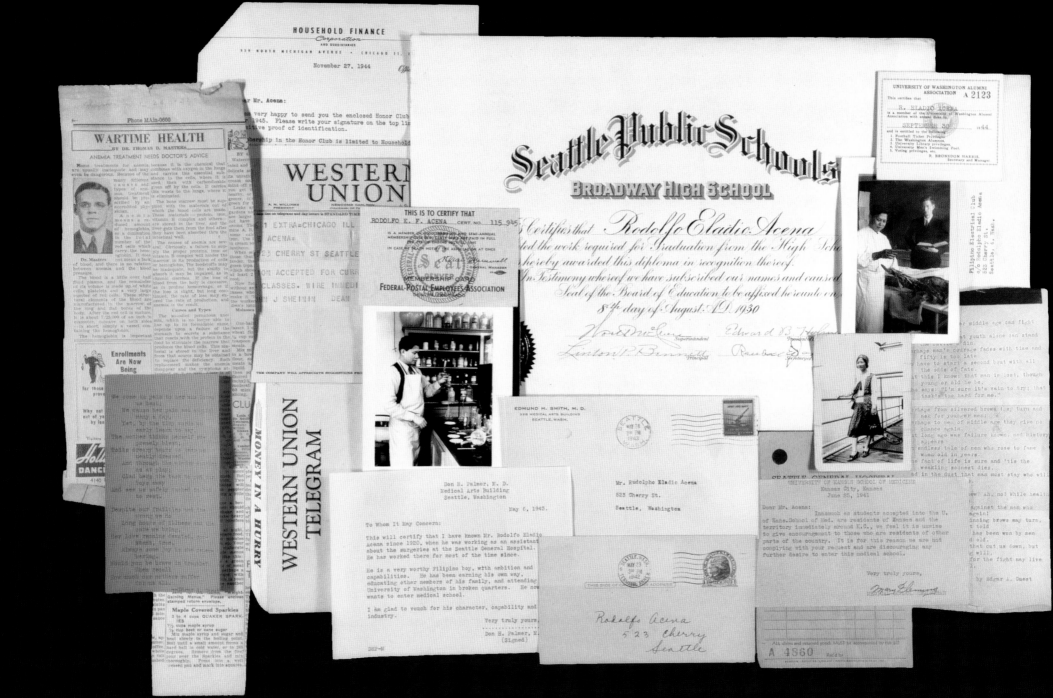

dent might invite what official character,
members of Congress, strangers or citizens

The President on levee days to give in-
formal invitations to family dinners; not
more than six or eight to be asked at a

of departments should, of
access to the President on
eign ministers of some de-
ld also be entitled to it.
am informed," writes Ham-
adors only have direct ac-
ef magistrate. Something
at prevails there would, in
right. The distinction of
diplomatic characters re-
, and the door of access
e too wide to that class of
ve thought that the mem-
ate should also have a right
ccess on matters relative
administration. In En-
ce peers of the realm have
e have none such in this
believe it will be satisfac-
ple to know that there is
en in the state who have a
al communication with the
will be considered a sa'
secret combinations to

Hamilton for g
this privilege, not the
that in the constitu-
are coupled with the
rtain executive functions
pointments. This makes
constitutional coun-
them a peculiar claim to
the right of access."

ance with France and that of the definitive
treaty with Great Britain to be added.

These are the only written replies that

* Jefferson's Works, ix. 97.   * Hamilton's Works vol. iv., p. 3.

Scene — Depart B
Time : 10 . A.M.
Character : Edith

The bright green
red electric bulbs
threw an
iridescent glow
over our heroine
~~dark and~~
dark beauty.

A look of scornful
fury flashed in
her black eyes &
a red fire of rage
burned in her
olive cheeks
Pepperel she

explains with
a stamp of
her tiny foot
Pepperel I
won't descend
again to that
unbearable stuffy
room

"Topsy Turvy."
Three act comedy
A Laugh, a Scream.
Full of "Pep."
At Bayfield Opera House.
In June.
* * *

For so many Americans, the very notion of faith was itself called into question: How could war be waged in the name of freedom if it could claim so many innocent lives? To look back at one's treasured scrapbook was to be reminded of the discrepancies between yesterday and today, to wonder if innocence had forever been extinguished in the name of progress. Curiously, such fundamental anxieties are less prevalent in scrapbooks produced during World War I: brutal though it was, America's entry into battle came late, and the psychological ramifications of loss were consequently delayed, even minimized in many scrapbooks. In one poignant exception, a photographic scrapbook kept between 1917 and 1922 is meticulously captioned, and laid out with a fastidious eye to chronology. One cannot help but notice a distinct attrition, from beginning to end, with fewer and fewer men appearing in its pages.

By America's second entry into war, however, the tone had evolved into something distinctly

patriotic, reminding us that scrapbooks were the place to record, remember, and even revive our imperiled optimism. "Nothing is too great a price to pay for all of the things we have taken for granted for such a long time," writes one essayist in the *Washington Post*: "for church bells ringing on a Sunday; for the Easter parade; for walks under the stars, holding a loved one's hand; for romps on the beach; for hot dogs, and ice cream cones, and pop; for chats with the peanut vender on the corner, a good American too, although he bears a foreign name… for movies on Saturday nights—bike rides on Sunday; for smoke from a chimney beckoning you home; for arguments between friends; for Kate Smith singing, "God Bless America."[1]

The scrapbook now not only becomes a space for reflection but offers, too, the opportunity to engage in a kind of deliberate material reconsideration. Newspaper clippings, for instance, offer the illusion of factual evidence, yet are often bril-

liantly discredited by more private ruminations. Edith DuTeau was by all indications obsessed with the well-publicized 1931 divorce betweeen Cynthia (née Wyatt) Kleinmeyer and her husband, Ted, who had, as a boy, inherited a substantial trust fund. The Kleinmeyers, who had married only seven years earlier, had two girls who were apparently friends of the DuTeau children, and Edith used her scrapbook to reckon with her connection to this glamorous, if infamous man: the reuse of an existing book suggests that Edith's family's financial resources may have been limited, even though her children frolicked with this wealthy family.

DuTeau Scrapbook
Los Angeles, CA
1914–1923

Edith DuTeau collected poems and clippings, mostly about celebrities and often about scandal. Her scrapbook includes numerous references to one person in particular: the scion of a well-known Southern California family, Ted Kleinmeyer was dubbed the "poor little rich boy" by the press, who delighted in recording his many public mishaps, which included an "orgy of spending" and a highly publicized bounced check for $400 that resulted in a one-year prison sentence.

Though perhaps unintentionally, the authoritative language of the press is challenged by the very inclusion of personal matter—the saved correspondence, crumpled notes, and weathered postcards, for example—that bear witness to public events with an unparalleled candor. The abbreviated lexicon of the telegram introduces yet another contradictory rhythm. An unusually trenchant vehicle for personal communication (*8 lb 4oz baby boy born 4:45a* STOP), the laconic prose that came to be the telegram's most distinguishing characteristic was frequently at odds with its underlying sentiment. (*Mother and baby doing well* STOP *Father over the Moon* STOP.) Such tensions are everywhere in scrapbooks where such asynchronous gestures are formally obliged to coexist—graceful penmanship alongside militant abbreviations, personal anecdotes alongside public proclamations—a microcosmic view of history writ large, and its impact on humanity, writ small—one scrapbook at a time.

The twentieth century brings with it a host of new idioms, unprecedented consumer habits, and shifting social expectations, and scrapbooks from this period aptly reflect what were, undoubtedly, certain dissonant changes in popular culture. While it is easy in retrospect to rationalize the incipient growth of industry and its effects on society as a whole, it is likely that the impact of such change was extremely difficult to comprehend, particularly at a human scale, particularly while it was happening. A great deal of this uncertainty was expressed through odd juxtapositions: people saved news clippings whose headlines proclaimed extraordinary events, pasting them into scrapbooks alongside eminently forgettable items. There are prayer cards next to gum wrappers, flattened cookie boxes next to college diplomas. A native of Brockton, Massachusetts, Verna Leonard boarded at Hyannis Normal School (which became Hyannis Teachers College while she was there) from 1931 to 1934, during which

time she maintained a two-volume, tour-de-force example of scrapbook chronology. (On one page that typifies Verna's compositional style she pastes her laundry receipt next to an advertisement for a steamy movie.) Handwritten captions and personal annotations try to explain her logic, which is sometimes peculiar: later in the book, Verna proudly saves the "Listed Wrong" label from the school laundry, with a caption explaining that she did it on purpose *so that I could get one of these for my mem book.*

Some of this comparatively new approach to page composition was revealed through an eclectic new vernacular: people saved rapturous song lyrics, militant speeches, and the most plaintive of love letters. And some of it was

expressed, firsthand, through their own writing—anecdotal, expository, sometimes witty, often shrewd. Through the ephemera retained, the clippings added, the memorabilia excavated, and the personal writing comes an additional dimension, providing a layer of sentimental meaning that emerges with its own distinct voice: a voice of deep curiosity, growing self-awareness—and no shortage of healthy skepticism. Here, feelings are expressed through language but also through typography, through penmanship, and through the gesture of the hand, which bespeaks its own deeply human touch.

Calling cards, too, reflect peculiar shifts in certain social conventions over the years. The etiquette of nineteenth- and early twentieth-

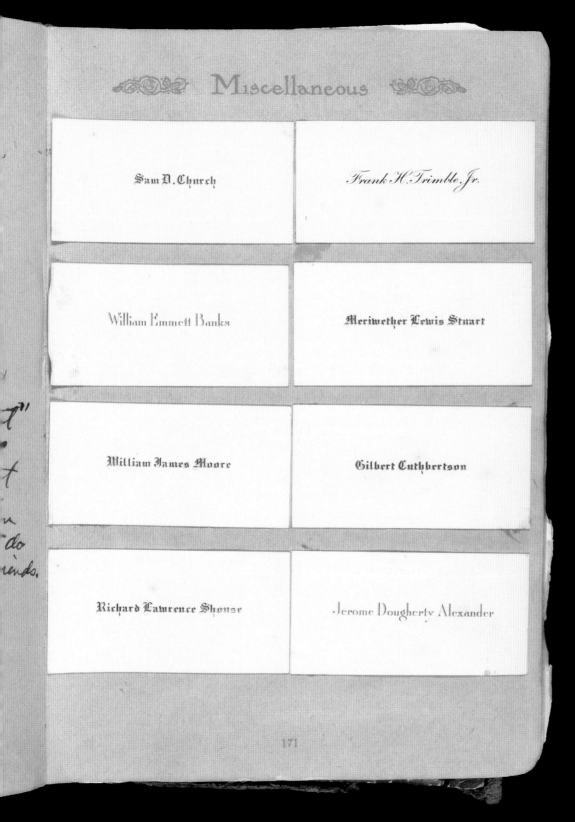

Miscellaneous

Sam D. Church

Frank H. Trimble, Jr.

William Emmett Banks

Meriwether Lewis Stuart

William James Moore

Gilbert Cuthbertson

Richard Lawrence Shouse

Jerome Dougherty Alexander

I HAVE NO ASSISTANTS
[But Deliver The Goods Myself]

JOHN VOWELL

DEALER IN

LOVE, KISSES & UP-TO-DATE HUGS

SINGLE · OUT FOR A GOOD TIME · BUT LONESOME

MY CAPITAL, $9,999,999
[IN MY DREAMS]

HOURS:
ONE UNTIL WON

ABOVE AND LEFT
Donovan Scrapbook
St. Louis, MO
1921

TOP RIGHT
Enloe Scrapbook
Fayette, MO
1922

By the 1920s, the notion of a calling card grew outmoded, even quaint: some, like John Vowell, chose instead to market their own more playful personalities.

RIGHT
Abraham Scrapbook
Pittsburgh, PA
1918

century card culture was complex, and while only the name was typically used, the fonts, weights, placements, and sizes of the cards often varied greatly. Cards of condolence and mourning were typically framed in black (a custom that survives today, especially in certain Latin cultures), while other customs were observed for wedding, greeting, visiting, and calling cards. True calling cards bore nothing on them but the name of the caller: it was considered inappropriate to include one's residence, particularly for women. Those concerned about the importance of good breeding were also advised to opt for smaller rather than larger typefaces, which were disparaged as commonplace. [2]

The increasing availability of the camera enabled an unprecedented kind of pictorial documentation in the years just before World War I, and credit was initially given to the company that produced the Brownie. The idea that photography in general—and photographic portraiture in particular—no longer required the formalities of the equipment-laden studio was itself a significant shift, especially for women, who would prove to be the primary documentarians of their own lives as well as the lives of their loved ones.[3]

Today we went Kodaking out on the lawn, writes Ellen Donovan in her memory book, where she includes detailed descriptions of her outings, her numerous graduation gifts, and her remarkably complex wardrobe. *The dress which I wore to the banquet was a party dress made very simply of light blue and silver changeable taffeta,* she reports in the spring of 1922. *It was made in quaint style with a tight basque waist, corded and with little sleeves slit up the center.* Her detailed sartorial study concludes with a rundown of the accessories she chose for the occasion: *My shoes were white kid and I wore white silk hose,* she writes; *tulle around my shoulders and a wreath of silver leaves on my head.* Ellen's female friends—with names like Sadie and Daisy, Olive and Pearl—penned their autographs with snippets of rhyming verse, while the boys signed their names with the formality characteristic of the aspiring American gentleman: included too are signatures from a *"G. Cuthbertson," "L. H. Milligan,"* and an imperious-sounding *"Meriwether L. Stuart."* All are represented with autographs and photographs, as well as a robust collection of calling cards: seen together, these artifacts collectively bridge the cultural etiquette of late nineteenth- and early twentieth-century youth culture.

The pressures of middle-class social conduct notwithstanding, the prevailing sentiment in many adolescent-produced scrapbooks from this period is fun, and nowhere is this demon-

Mrs. Cecil Blount de Mille

Undated portrait of Elinor Moses (*above*) and photo of the Marlborough School for Girls in Los Angeles (*right*). A calling card from Mrs. Cecil B. DeMille appears on a nearby page (*far right*).

BELOW AND OPPOSITE
Moses "Stunt" Book
Los Angeles, CA
1919–1922

It is 1920, and from the Hotel Virginia in Long Beach, California, comes a scene worthy of *The Great Gatsby.* The page consists of a pressed rose, a dance tally, and the calling cards of no fewer than three men. Who sent the roses that Valentine's Day: Was it Frederick? Harold? Or even Edward? The reader is left to guess, as there is little here to indicate a preference: none of the names on the dance tally match the cards. On the far side of the page lies a napkin, and on it, scrawled hastily in a man's hand, is a message titled simply: *What Elinor Ate For Dinner, 7/6/20: 1/2 cocktail, 3 olives, All My Chicken Salad. 4 cherries.* Unsigned, it nevertheless illuminates a scene between a young woman and her male companion, one summer evening by the sea.

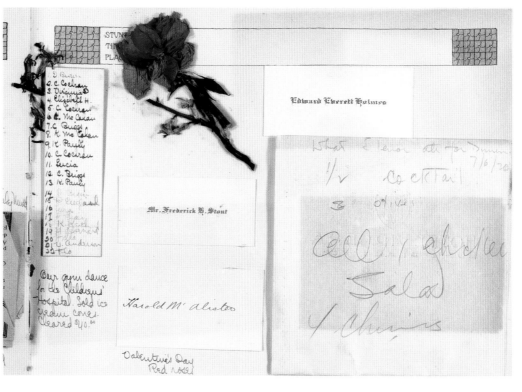

MEMENTOES·OF·FRIENDSHIP

CARDS--PRESSED FLOWERS--CLIPPINGS--NOTES

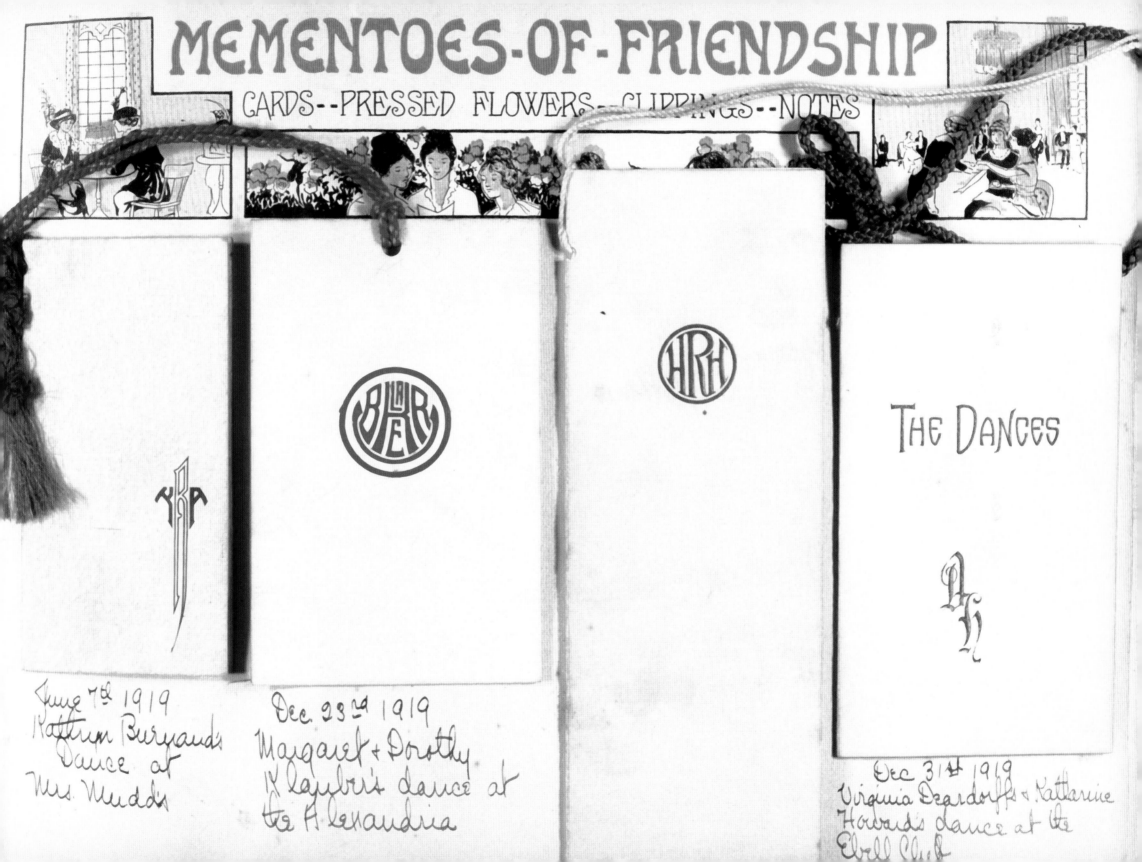

THE DANCES

June 7th 1919
Kathryn Bryant's
dance at
Mrs. Mudds

Dec. 23rd 1919
Margaret & Dorothy
Klaybri's dance at
the Alexandria

Dec. 31st 1919
Virginia Deardorff & Katharine
Howard's dance at the
Ebell Club

BURGLARS RAID WEDDING PARTY AND SHOOT GROOM

Best Man and Brother of Bride Also Wounded in Desperate Battle in South Oxford Street Mansion.

Bridegroom, best man and the brother of the bride-to-be were shot by two young masked bandits who sought to hold up the assembled guests at an ante-nuptial banquet being given in the home of W. A. Moses, capitalist, at 426 South Oxford street, last night. The festivities were in honor of Edward W. Moses, his nephew, from Kansas City, and Miss Virginia Holmes of 6710 Franklin avenue, Hollywood, who are to be married tonight at the Oxford-street address.

Hardly had the seventeen guests seated themselves at the gaily decorated table when the bandits entered the dining-room from the butler's pantry with revolvers leveled. Edward Moses, Robert Lester, his best man, a merchant of Kansas City, 26 years of age, and Everett Holmes, 17-year-old High School student, brother of Miss Holmes, grappled with the two men. In the battle the highwaymen shot all three youths and then fled.

The wounded trio were rushed to the Receiving Hospital where it was learned that none was fatally hurt. Then it was announced that the wedding would take place tonight, as scheduled, even though the bridegroom is confined to his bed. He was shot through the shoulder, his best man between the thumb and first finger of his left hand, where he had grabbed a bandit's gun, and young Holmes through the chest. The latter was the most seriously wounded, but the police surgeons say he will recover.

After the shooting, which occurred about 8.30 p.m., Mr. Moses tried to telephone the police, only to find that the wires had been cut. From a neighbor's house, Detective Sergeants King, Oaks and Ballestero were summoned. Chief Home ordered that every available man be dispatched to the scene of the crime to form a dragnet for the criminals.

WOMAN DRIVES BANDIT CAR.

The only clew to the bandits was furnished by Mrs. Estella C. Dowling of 357 South Oxford street. She told the detectives that while she was sitting on her front porch, shortly before the shooting, she saw a Chandler touring car drive up before her house and stop a short distance away. A woman was driving. She got out and walked rapidly the length of the block, past the Moses home and surveyed the lighted house. Then she returned to the car and waited with the motor running. She was hatless and excited, Mrs. Dowling said. At this point Mrs. Dowling became alarmed and retired into her house. Detectives believe that this was the bandits'

SHOTS AT A BRIDAL PARTY

EDWARD MOSES AND ROBERT LESTER HIT BY BANDITS.

Dinner Was Given in Los Angeles by Uncle of Kansas City Groom-Elect, Who Is to Wed Miss Virginia Holmes.

LOS ANGELES, June 8.—Two masked bandits forced their way into the home of W. A. Moses, 426 South Oxford street, here last night, and attempted to hold up the guests at a pre-nuptial wedding party given in honor of Edward Moses, son of Lincoln E. Moses of Kansas City and young Moses's fiancee, Miss Virginia Holmes, formerly of Kansas City.

Young Moses, Robert Lester, son of John C. Lester, vice-president of the Ridenour-Baker Grocery company of Kansas City, and Everett Holmes, 17, brother of Miss Holmes, were shot when they refused to obey the command of the bandits to hold up their hands.

BRIDEGROOM SHOT IN THE BACK.

Moses was shot in the neck. Holmes was shot in the back and a bullet severed one of Lester's fingers. The three men were taken to the Good Samaritan hospital. The groom elect

EDWARD MOSES, SHOT BY BANDITS ON THE EVE OF HIS WEDDING DAY.

Piggly Wig

Plenty of

Plenty of

Plenty of

thing in the

Moses Stunt Book
Los Angeles, CA
1920–1922

On June 8, 1920, at a bridal dinner given for cousin Edward, three intruders (allegedly seeking the $15,000 in diamonds worn by the twenty members of the bridal party) broke into the Moses residence, and shot the bridegroom and two other men, including the bride's younger brother. The "Nuptial Bandits" were apprehended several days later. The wedding took place a day later at the hospital, where the groom lay recuperating.

strated more theatrically than in books from late in the second and early in the third decade of the century, quite a few of which were titled not *Scrapbook*, but *Stunt Book*. *Who Am I?* asks the title page in a jolly volume from 1919. *My Name Is Fun … I live on stunts. I can't exist without them. It is the duty of everyone who receives this book to help keep me going.* Initially published in 1914, this book—like so many produced during the early years of the century—formalized scrapbook management with content-specific headings, with various pages allocated for one's autographs, photographs, and clippings and notes. Ironically, the attempt to introduce an organizational system backfires more often than not, thereby reinforc-

ing the frequently illogical paths that such books appear inevitably destined to take. Over time, the tension between compartmentalized time and actual day-to-day time would reveal itself in books that would challenge conventional scrapbook structure, a particular feature that evolved in tandem with preprinted memory books (which are discussed in greater detail in the following chapter).

Moses' *Stunt Book* conjures a Gatsby-like world of parties and dances, a social whirlwind of carefree abandon. The captions identify people and places, the occasional date, sometimes an anecdotal aside, as on July 4, 1919: *Spent most of the day resting and writing letters at Aunt Clare's. Rained hard. Sang all the way home.* The culture of "stunts" was a particular social oddity during the Jazz Age, and included such things as flagpole sitting and dance marathons, though simpler fare (sometimes characterized as jokes and frolics) was also part of this enduring ritual of silliness. Party favors often included fortunes, typically written in rhyming couplets or prose, as in this example: "Oer a long-haired artist, you will lose your heart; you may wish to wed him; he's wedded to his art." Other party favors included trinkets and tricks to be performed. Later in the century, punch cards offered the same service, with rolled-up challenges waiting to be released upon the puncture of a pencil tip—a comparatively early, and goofy, variation on the classic game of charades.

And then, a scene from a different play.

May 22, 1920. The Chairman of the American Committee for Devastated France thanks one Miss Elinor Moses for collecting twenty-three checks totaling more than one thousand dollars. It is, he says, an errand of mercy.

But there's another envelope beside it: a year earlier, another letter from France was also sent in gratitude to the same Miss Elinor Moses, who, it seems, is the American godmother to a little girl. *Thank you very much, Dear Mademoiselle, for your*

Moses Stunt Book
Los Angeles, CA
1920–1922

A studio portrait of Julienne Galinier, the child "adopted" by Elinor Moses after the war. She autographed the back of her photograph. (Photographer unknown.)

kindness and sympathy for our fatherless children of France. Included is a photograph of a small girl of perhaps six or seven, posing beside an oversized hoop, her beautiful little face weary, the expression unusually taciturn. On the reverse, in an adult's shaky hand, is the child's name. Below it is written: *votre fille adoptive.*

Such acts of charity may indeed have been expected of young debutantes with the means to perform them, but the inclusion of these letters still reads as a complete tonal shift from what is otherwise a life of unfettered amusement. It is an astonishing thing to imagine the emotional bond, such as it might have been, between a wealthy young heiress and an orphaned child in France, and this chapter sheds rather a different light on the autobiographical antics of a stunt-seeking debutante. Her name may have been "fun," but she just so happened, too, to have a rather extraordinary heart.

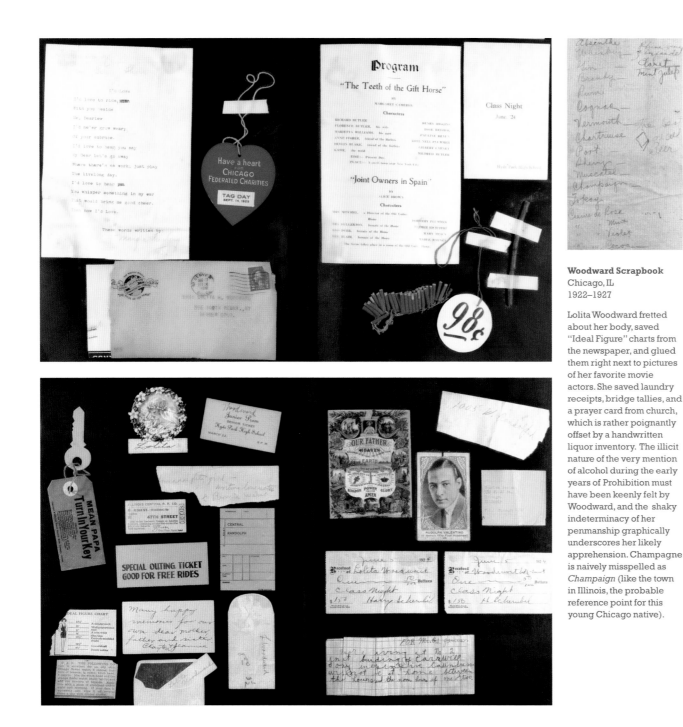

Woodward Scrapbook
Chicago, IL
1922–1927

Lolita Woodward fretted about her body, saved "Ideal Figure" charts from the newspaper, and glued them right next to pictures of her favorite movie actors. She saved laundry receipts, bridge tallies, and a prayer card from church, which is rather poignantly offset by a handwritten liquor inventory. The illicit nature of the very mention of alcohol during the early years of Prohibition must have been keenly felt by Woodward, and the shaky indeterminacy of her penmanship graphically underscores her likely apprehension. Champagne is naively misspelled as *Champaign* (like the town in Illinois, the probable reference point for this young Chicago native).

Naturally, sentiment was not always expressed through such acts of random generosity. The new century brought with it as much trepidation as new opportunity, and there are scrapbooks that aptly reflect this unprecedented shift in social custom and civic expectation, resulting in a kind of fierce attitude, a sort of strident, "come-and-get-me" line of defense. Lolita Woodward's 1920 Chicago scrapbook is a visual study in growing pains. Conflicting interests are revealed here through curious juxtapositions: a photo of Rudy Valentino next to a prayer card; a string of miniature firecrackers next to an anonymous twig; and a tentatively drafted list of cocktails next to a Cracker Jack box. Her book includes no shortage of song lyrics (the refrain from Ida Cox's *Mean Papa, Turn in Your Key* dangles from its own miniature cardboard key), of poems and verses ("The Flapper's Prayer"), and a set of printed instructions for backseat drivers ("Shut UP!"). But it is the sharply worded holiday greeting card that most succinctly captures the emotional tenor of her book: *These are the days of suffragetting, of profiteering, rent hogs, excess taxes and prohibition. If you think life is worth living, we wish you a Happy New Year.*

Life, it seemed, was not only worth living, it was worth capturing in some sort of indelible form. For young women who came of age before the passing of the Nineteenth Amendment, and whose identities and senses of self-worth may very likely have been shaped by promises of domestic sanctity, the scrapbook held enormous comfort. Part security blanket, part safe haven, it shielded its owner from powerlessness, apprehension, and fear. Many women who were active in the suffrage movement kept scrapbooks documenting their efforts.[4] Some, like Lolita Woodward and Kitty Baker, identified with suffrage as a kind of liberating, unifying social act: Baker's memorial for her first suffrage parade reflects her disappointment once votes for women had been legalized and the suffragettes retired from active duty.

Baker's scrapbook begins in 1911 in Norfolk, Virginia, where she later enrolled in high school, though her infrequent attendance there resulted in at least two warning notices—both of which she saved for her scrapbook. (Such gestures indicate her pride in her own capacity for rebellion—which was apparently considerable.) Her scrapbook suggests a young woman deeply preoccupied with gaiety—and remarkably unconcerned with her performance in school. Baker saved aces from any number of card decks, preserved pictures of Buster Keaton and Mary Pickford (adding her own illustrations of Charlie Chaplin), and managed, for reasons not altogether apparent, to rescue no fewer than three different Hershey Bar wrappers during the early years of the century. The assemblages on Baker's pages are extraordinary: she added years in red pen and left few spaces blank. One has the impression she worked very hard to stay busy, and her book reveals a formal density consistent with this effort.

Occasional school warnings are outnumbered not only by dance cards and party invitations, but by numerous pages, in Baker's own handwriting, of questionnaires: citing everything from favorite eye color to favorite pastime, she interviewed all of her friends, creating a robust, if highly unscientific, census of her own perspective on popular culture just before World War I. The book is filled to overflowing with carefully silhouetted photographs of favorite film stars—Norma Talmadge, Douglas Fairbanks, Billie Burke—and includes meticulously scripted captions and dates, some of which may have been added later. Indeed, there is some evidence to suggest that she may have continued to make occasional contributions to her scrapbook until the early 1960s.

Baker positions advertisements for soft drinks next to photographic collages of Charlie Chaplin next to feathers, drawings, and huge amounts of writing, all of it neatly aligned, framed in ink, and captioned with dates. Oddly, certain items from

Baker Scrapbook
Norfolk, VA
1911–1921

later in the century are included at the end of the book, all of them featuring banal things—Main Street traffic in Norfolk, a picturesque cemetery in Richmond—confirming that Baker's heyday was precisely that high-school period that dominates the majority of the pages. Her life was a social whirlwind, and her book reveals an extraordinary compositional mind at work. And what better way to make sense of things than to write them down, even if they still made no apparent sense? Many

scrapbooks became the preferred destination for secreting thoughts that could not, for whatever reason, find expression elsewhere. Indeed, where illicit topics were concerned, sex topped the list.

As suggestive sexual imagery became more available commercially, its acquisition was of particular interest to men, and those men who kept scrapbooks often used their books to conceal (and, one can probably assume, revisit) their findings. The noted writer Carl Van Vechten and

This is the story of a beautiful, sensitive youth, born into that twilight zone so little understood by a world sympathetic alone to virility in its men. It is a strangely tender narrative that will open a new world to the reader, a world which lives in fear and loves in secret.

"An exquisite handling of a delicate subject."

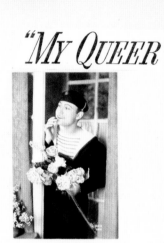

Lover Boy in a New Role: He'll Be Quiet

Safe, But No One's Sane After
Take this precaution!

Play SAFE

Van Vechten Scrapbooks
New York, NY
1940s–1950s

the photographer George Platt Lynes both kept scrapbooks of male pornography, Lynes's being rather formal and artistic, while Van Vechten's was heavily annotated in his own hand, with racy captions and brazen headlines. These scrapbooks, which were probably created during the 1950s, were donated to Yale upon his death in 1969 with the caveat that they not be opened for twenty-five years. Within the twenty scrapbooks he left are photographs, clippings, and reflections on homosexuality and gender roles during the early to mid- twentieth century. (Van Vechten commented on Christine Jorgensen's sex change in 1958, for example, which would have fascinated him on several accounts: not only was Jorgensen one of the first people to have sex reassignment surgery, Jorgensen was also a photographer and writer.) Van Vechten made ample use of found typography to concoct his own headlines, which he frequently juxtaposed with found photographs of nude men. Clearly intended to be provocative, the resulting scrapbooks reveal a particular period in gay history: the overall tone is playful, permissive, at times even sanguine, even though these pages were likely to have been crafted in utter secrecy.

Far more common, however, was the scrapbook whose author did not dare acknowledge having acquired such images but instead wrote tentatively about what he (or, more commonly, she) could not speak of in public. Sandwiched between the varsity track results and the program from a high school commencement ceremony, an entry in one young woman's scrapbook, simply entitled *The Affection Show on Street*, carefully describes a licentious (if marginally titillating) scene late in the spring of 1922. While strolling home with a companion one evening at dusk, Ellen Donovan spots a couple through an open window engaged in what appears to have been a rather visible demonstration of fellatio. As alarming as it must have been to catch a glimpse of the girl's head on

the boy's lap, Donovan seems almost as shaken by certain extraneous details. *The girl's hair was down,* she writes in horror, *and her shoes were off.* She goes on to list all the fraternity boys who congregated to watch from the street corner, and concludes with her record of their overheard critique. *Tommy said the boy was slow,* she solemnly notes, *because the girl did all the loving.*

Love, particularly romantic love, had traditionally been expressed in scrapbooks through tokens of affection, valentines, and other ephemera that gestured (albeit in a rather generic form) to the affairs of the heart. But it soon became evident that the heart faced more critical challenges, harbored deeper secrets, and even engaged in more random acts of emotional wish fulfillment. It bears mention, too, that scrapbooks grew over time to recognize more distant objects of affection—movie stars, for example—and by the late 1920s had become altogether sycophantic. In the days before television became a staple in every American living room, the opportunity to ogle over stars was restricted to print journalism. Keeping star scrapbooks offered the chance to collect pictures and revel in the minutiae of a famous person's civilian life, creating a kind of vicarious thrill for star-obsessed viewers. Scrapbooks featuring movie stars were popular during the 1920s and 1930s and were often made from the simplest materials: in one example, a two-ring notebook holds lined paper which enabled the owner to introduce his or her own captions, of varied length, depending on the level of interest.

A preponderance of scrapbooks that highlight the Lindbergh kidnapping offers a striking example of the kind of emotional release provided by paper and glue. Many of these books combine pictures of the Lindbergh baby with images and inspirational quotes. In one example from 1932, a young girl sketches her own family tree in the midst of several pages of Lindbergh memorabilia: it's as if she's actively trying to cement her own

Donovan Scrapbook
Grand Rapids, MI
1922

Ellen Donovan's scrapbook
is filled with invitations
and dance cards, but she
was also a devoted diarist.
Mostly she describes the
parties she attended her
final year in high school.
But her entry for May 21
describes an unsettling
scene she witnessed: an
intimate encounter spied
through a window.

The Affection Show on
Street.   May 21, 1922.

Never forget that night
Sunday nite May 21. Homer
and I were coming home on

Street and the second house
from the corner had the light on
and the blinds up. We glanced
in which was quite natural. And
what did we see Oh! dear! Some
girl was lying her head on the
boy's lap. The girls hair was
down and her shoes were off.
Homer and I laughed and went
home. I went and got Opal
and she and I went down

thinking there would be no one
else there and who should
we find but nearly all the
Kappa Sigma boys including
Bill Shepherd, Tommy Gregory
Ernest McDonald, Frank
Gumple, David Bywaters, and
many others. Squaw Bell and
his wife came along. We all
enjoyed the show. Tommy said
the boy was slow because the
girl did all the loving. Ha. Ha.
We found out that the girl was
Mary Frances Gill (poor
girl) and the boy was a
college boy named Mr. Foster.

How to Make Your Scrapbook of Movie, Cowboy and Sports Stars

Each cover and page has two holes punched at the side. This is done to make it easy for you to fasten the pages together and make a scrapbook.

You may use a heavy cord, shoe-string or ribbon, to fasten your covers and pages together like illustration A.

Or you may use two long brass fasteners like those at right. Just put them through the two punched holes and bend back the flexible ends like illustration B.

You may want to add to this scrapbook other pictures, magazine articles and stories about your favorite stars. The looseleaf binding makes it easy to do.

Framed or Cut-out Pictures of Your Favorite Stars

Perhaps you would rather have several of these beautiful colored pictures of your favorite stars on your desk or bureau. By simply trimming off the border on the left side you will have a picture entirely suitable for framing.

Or you may wish to have a cut-out picture which would look like that at the left.

To make such a picture, first paste the entire color picture of your favorite star on a piece of light cardboard. The back of a pad will do very nicely. Then draw a line around the picture the way you want it cut out, including extra space at the bottom to use as a stand for the picture. Cut around the outline you have drawn with a strong pair of shears, and then fold the stand torward and put the notched sides in place to hold it firm and steady. Your cut-out picture is now finished and ready for use.

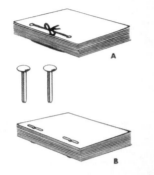

CUT ON HEAVY BLACK LINES
FOLD ON DOTTED LINES

Identify Your Scrapbook

Don't forget to write your name and address plainly in the space provided on the inside front cover. This identifies the book as your property and it can be returned to you if lost.

Now that you have read these suggestions, you may wish to cover this page by pasting a star's picture over it.

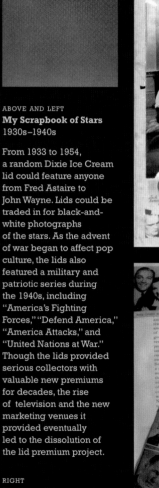

Piglow Scrapbook
Grand Rapids, MI
1921–1922

Edna Piglow constructed careful genealogical charts of her own family in an attempt to try to make sense of the Lindbergh kidnapping: interspersed between her own notes are photos clipped from the newspapers featuring details, as they emerged, of the missing child.

Janet Gaynor

immortality through the act of mapping her family ancestry, juxtaposing her own first-person history with the sensational details of the nation's most famous (and imperiled) baby. Edna Piglow would have been a teenager when the Lindbergh kidnapping occurred, and her scrapbook devotes nearly twelve pages to newspaper articles and photographs of the baby and his family. Pages like hers read almost like rhetorical benedictions, pictorially praising the virtues of motherhood, the magic of infancy, the immeasurable tragedy of loss. Other pages reveal a typical teenager's preoccupation with the media. (Piglow was partcularly taken with Dick Powell and Ruby Keeler.) True to teenage form, preoccupations with fame and mortality are well represented throughout this scrapbook, while shades of shifting concern are also revealed. Early on, Piglow devotes a page to a preferred actress: *My Favorite Comic Star: Marjorie White in Happy Days; Sunny Side Up; Just Imagine; Follies of 1930.* Below it, she later added a sad update in red pencil: *Killed in auto crash in 1935.*

At the other end of the production spectrum were star scrapbooks that were produced by manufacturers, often as premiums, to encourage collecting and sell products—in this case, ice cream. *My Scrapbook of Stars*, which was released in numerous editions during the 1930s, was issued as a cover for the premium photos of movie stars that you could get from sending in Dixie Ice Cream lids. Instructions on the cover's reverse were detailed and included tips on cutting and framing pictures of your favorite stars. Books filled to overflowing with portraits of Shirley Temple, the Dionne Quintuplets, and any number of matinee idols reflected this obsequious desire to sentimentalize public figures, resulting in scrapbooks that were less immediately personal and far less autobiographically expressive. Many scrapbooks filled with the media coverage surrounding certain tragic public figures (the Lindbergh kidnapping, JFK's assassination) lent a twist of arguably innocent schadenfreude to this practice, and became more and more common as the century wore on. The pop-culture bias toward celebrity worship eventually became an integral part of scrapbook culture and has, for that matter, continued to the present day.

Public figures kept scrapbooks too, and while they tend to be perhaps less outwardly intriguing (one expects famous people, after all, to lead interesting lives), a closer look often reveals startling preoccupations. More often than not, celebrities had the funds but lacked the time to make their own albums, and hired assistants to make scrapbooks for them. The idea of a star making his or her own scrapbook was, therefore, something of a novelty: shortly after the release of the film *Top Hat*, Ginger Rogers began compiling her own "pictorial record of scenes from the pictures in which she appears." [5] Even a figure as unsentimental as Lillian Hellman kept scrapbooks, and what she saved shows someone perhaps a bit less resilient than otherwise thought: she appeared to care deeply, for instance, about what others thought of her. In clips that she glued into her scrapbook, one interviewer wrote: "She is the kind of girl who can take the tops off bottles with her teeth." Reported another: "She is genuinely feminine to a degree that borders engagingly on the whacky." And writing of a trip to the Soviet Union in 1944, famed gossip columnist Hedda Hopper mused of Hellman: "Lillian Hellman plans a book, six magazine articles and a play while in Russia... That won't give her much time to get chummy with Stalin, will it?"

Hellman can't be faulted for caring about how she herself was characterized in the press. But what's more intriguing is her public response to it: by far the most fascinating component of her scrapbook is the rough drafts of hate mail she penned to Tallulah Bankhead. (The final letter was printed in *Time Magazine*, which she also saved.) In a press climate of catty one-liners, Hellman's humorous—if venomous—critique of Bankhead may not seem so unusual: after all, it was during this same period that the actress ZaSu Pitts famously compared Hedda Hopper to a ferret. But what's striking is the amount of extraordinary personal effort that went into attacking the actress publicly, and Hellman's apparent glee when her letter was finally published in a national magazine. This portion of her scrapbook seems to

Hellman Scrapbook
Various locations
1944–1946

While filled mainly with correspondence and drafts of her radio broadcasts, Hellman's scrapbook also highlights her deliberate efforts to sustain a long-lasting row with Tallulah Bankhead.

radiate with self-satisfaction: *I think the time has come*, Hellman writes, *to say that hate from Miss Bankhead is a small badge of honor.*

By midcentury, the profile of the scrapbook-keeper had expanded to include journalists, story-tellers, and would-be historians of all ages and, indeed, genders. On one side, the scrapbook was acknowledged as a more serious undertaking (one *Washington Post* reviewer enthusiastically recommended forever removing "the hearts-and-flowers stigma from diaries and diary-keepers"), while the *New York Times* reported on one Ohio man's thirty-year effort (50,000 pages and nearly 500 pounds of paste) to document the world around him starting with the Civil War. A Chicago man's twenty-year obsession led to thirty-five scrapbooks praising the virtues of marriage and the American family. (Such ambitious efforts highlight, however unintentionally, a scrapbooker's capacity to craft a highly skewed reality: the world according to *me*.) Yet as serious as such exhortations could be, others testified to the opposite claim entirely, impressing upon readers the need for even more fictional scrapbooks, and advising children in particular to find pictures "just waiting to be made into scrap-

book chariots to carry needy or lonely children into the glorious Land of Makebelieve." [6] Such a curious blend of fairy-tale fiction (escape) with journalistic due-diligence (reality) reflects the persistent uncertainty that, for many, characterized life between the wars.

Scrapbook production was seen as both a craft and a calling, a creative endeavor and even an act of community service, with scrapbook-of-the-month clubs organized regionally in the United States through such organizations as the USO and the DAR, and internationally through efforts initiated by Beatrice Warde on behalf of the English-Speaking Union. A distinguished American designer and typographer, Warde married an Englishman who took her to Great Britain during World War II, where she was appalled by the parochial biases of both the English and the Americans. She consequently spearheaded efforts to have children of both nationalities make scrapbooks of their experiences: by exchanging their albums, they would share real, first-person perspectives on cultural attitudes toward life on two continents during the war. The idea was seeded in 1941, when Warde "suggested to a woman who

NLT

EDITORS

TIME

TIME LIFE BUILDING

ROCKEFELLER CENTER

NEW YORK NNEW YORK

DECEMBER FOURTH TIME MISQUOTE ME AS SAYING AT MOSCOW RECEPTION THAT
ACTOR DOESN'T MAKE MUCH DIFFERENCE TO THE PLAY STOP AS HUNDRED GUESTS
AND STENOGRPAHIC RECORD WILL TESTIFY I SAID ALTHOUGH MANY ACTORS HAVE
MADE PLAYS SUCCESSFUL NO ACTOR HAS EVER MADE GOOD PLAY INTO BAD PLAY
OR BAD PLAY INTO GOOD PLAY WHICH IS VERY DEFFERENT STATEMENT AND
SHOULD QUIET EXCITABLE MISS BANKHEAD WHO IN TIME ISSUE DECEMBER
ELEVENTH SAYS QUOTE I LOATHE LILLIAN SHE DOESNT KNOW WHAT SHE IS
TALKING ABOUT OF COURSE SHE IS REALLY WONDERFUL PLAYWRIGHT IF LILLIAN
HAD GOOD PLAY RIGHT NOW ID DO IT EVEN THOUGH I HATE HER UNQUOTE
ACCOUSTOMED AS I AM TO YEARLY PUBLIC GREETINGS/THE WELL BRED DAUGHTER
OF OUR PLANTATION SOUTH THINK TIME HAS COME TO SAY THAT HATE FROM
MISS BANKHEAD IS A SMALL BADGE OF HONOR AND PRAISE UNDESIRABLE STOP
MISS BANKHEAD WILL NEVER AGAIN ACT IN PLAY OF MINE ONLY BECAUSE I
WZ I CAN STAND ONLY CERTAIN AMOUNT OF BOREDOM STOP HAPPY NEW YEAR
TO YOU AND HER AND I WILL BE GRATEFUL IF YOU PRINT THIS CABLE IN
FULL

                    LILLIAN HELLMAN

III	IV	MY TEST	VARIATION
132	150		
135	153		
136·	154		
137	155		
139	157		
139	159		
143	161		
144	162		
147			
148			

safe pressure.

ssure.
nary

Major

APPENDICITIS:

Hospital _____

Date of entrance _____ , 19____ . Leaving _____

Surgeon _____

Nurse _____

OPERATION:

Hospital _____

Date of entrance _____ , 19____ . Left _____

Surgeon _____

Nurse _____

OPERATION:

Hospital _____

Date of entrance _____ , 19____ . Left _____

Surgeon _____

Nurse _____

OPERATION:

Hospital _____

Date of entrance _____ , 19____ . Left _____

Surgeon _____

Nurse _____

CSSURE is the force of the blood which may be
or in the temple as it flows through the blood
h or low blood pressure is very apt to indicate
us trouble. In such cases it is always advisable
hysician.
s a very intricate machine and needs care and
y as does any industrial machine. LET US
RKING EFFICIENTLY.

Minor

TONSILS REMOVED: Date of operation _____

Surgeon _____

Nurse _____

ADENOIDS REMOVED: Date of removal _____

Surgeon _____

Nurse _____

hysician at least once a Year

wanted to do something to hurt Dr. Goebbels" that scrapbooks would give the most accurate portrait of what daily life was like in each country. (An initial scrapbook, produced by a group of young women, included "everything from details about maple sugar production to the Sunday School picnic.")[7] Forty schools from across the nation participated in the program's launch, which was sponsored by Books Across the Sea, an organization Warde had founded a year earlier, under the aegis of the English-Speaking Union, to help offset Nazi propaganda among expatriate Americans who had remained in London following the fall of France.

Gesturing to instincts at once domestic and diplomatic, scrapbooks thus retained their fascination as purveyors of all kinds of information. Long before Michel de Certeau would revive our cultural appreciation for the everyday,[8] an article in the *Christian Science Monitor* characterized scrapbook making as a kind of archaeological pursuit, engaged in by those interested in becoming "excavators of the commonplace."[9] Soon, food and drug manufacturers, insurance companies, and advertisers joined with commercial publishers to produce their own scrapbooks. There were books aimed at college girls, at new mothers, at celebrity worshippers (a significant breed) and cigar-band collectors, and at every conceivable kind of traveler and tourist. Endorsed by health professionals, some books were offered as premiums, while others were heavily marketed as gifts. And while an emphasis on the autobiographical scrapbook long remained, at least one World War II–era scrapbook manufacturer marketed its books to the families of soldiers who were, it was believed, less likely to forget if there was a dedicated archivist (usually a wife, mother, or sister) on hand to save the things that mattered. "So many men who were engaged in the World War of 1917–18 have sorely regretted that they did not keep a record of their service with Uncle

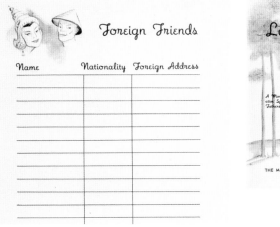

Log O' Life
McMillin-Foley Publishers
1939 and 1946

Pages from the 1939 (*opposite and right*) and 1946 (*above*) editions.

Two separate editions of this book were published within a ten-year period, with pages for everything from dental records to infectious diseases to autographs, photographs, and fingerprints ("in event baby's identity is confused in the hospital, or the child is lost or in a case of lapse of memory later in life"). In both editions, the page for entering personal identification statistics includes four options for listing race—black, white, red, and yellow.

Sam," notes one publisher in 1942, "their affiliations and troop movements, where they went, and what they did, when they returned, together with dates and other interesting data. Their wives and children also regret it."[10]

Capitalizing on the widespread tone of apprehension that prevailed in wartime, many publishers approached the keeping of a scrapbook as a therapeutic activity. Preformatted pages guided the user, and reframed the act of worry into a hopeful and arguably creative activity. It is likely, too, that the culture of rationing that pervaded American society during World War II led to a feeling of patriotic duty where scraps were concerned: rescuing and preserving them were considered prudent and wise. If the soldier in question were to be killed in action, the scrapbook would, arguably, be that much more meaningful as a record of life, love, and loss. A person could be gone but, because of the scrapbook, would not—indeed, could not—be forgotten. Capturing, preserving, and exulting upon such profound yet ultimately fleeting memories would soon fuel an entirely new subindustry, resulting in a new genre of scrapbook that would grow, over time, to serve an oddly pervasive love interest: the love of nostalgia itself.

Scrapbooks Show America to England

Forty high schools throughout the country are doing their best to tell our English allies just what life in America is like by preparing scrapbooks to give complete pictures of their daily lives. The first books that have been completed reveal these collective enterprises are amazing in their scope and depth of perception as to just what things, little and big, make America American.

The books are being prepared and sent to England under sponsorship of "Books Across the Sea," an organization carrying on an exchange of "ambassador books" to give each country an understanding of the other's life and problems.

Suggested in 1941

The forerunner of the school scrapbooks came from Vermont in 1941 when Mrs. Beatrice Warde of the English-Speaking Union, suggested to a woman who "wanted to do something" to hurt Dr. Goebbels, the British would like very much to know what the real America is like. The book was very carefully prepared by a group of women, and included everything from details about maple sugar-making to the Sunday school picnic. Mrs. Warde said it was exactly the right thing for its first audience, an English mother who wanted to know the kind of life her daughter was living with foster-parents in Vermont.

The school scrapbook project was started after 40 other regional books had been prepared and circulated through Great Britain. Both projects were kept more or less quiet until last week for fear of a deluge of scrapbooks that would have taxed the limited shipping space.

The high school plan is stimulating a response. Not only has correspondence started between the American schools making books and British schools receiving them, but the British students in turn are preparing pictures of their daily life to send here. First of these books are expected to arrive in the early fall.

'Ballad for Americans'

Students at Danbury, Conn., prepared a book that was the personification of the "Ballad for Americans." Besides a picture of the school life (including football), there was a tabulation of the nationalities of the students, beginning with the American Indian, and going through all the European nations.

The spirit of America today was shown in the book prepared by Newtown High School, Elmhurst, Queens. The students knew exactly what they wanted to say, and they knew how to say it.

ABOVE
The Washington Post
January 22, 1942

"Not only has correspondence started between the American schools making books and the British students receiving them," noted Beatrice Warde, "but the British students in turn are preparing pictures of their daily life to send here."

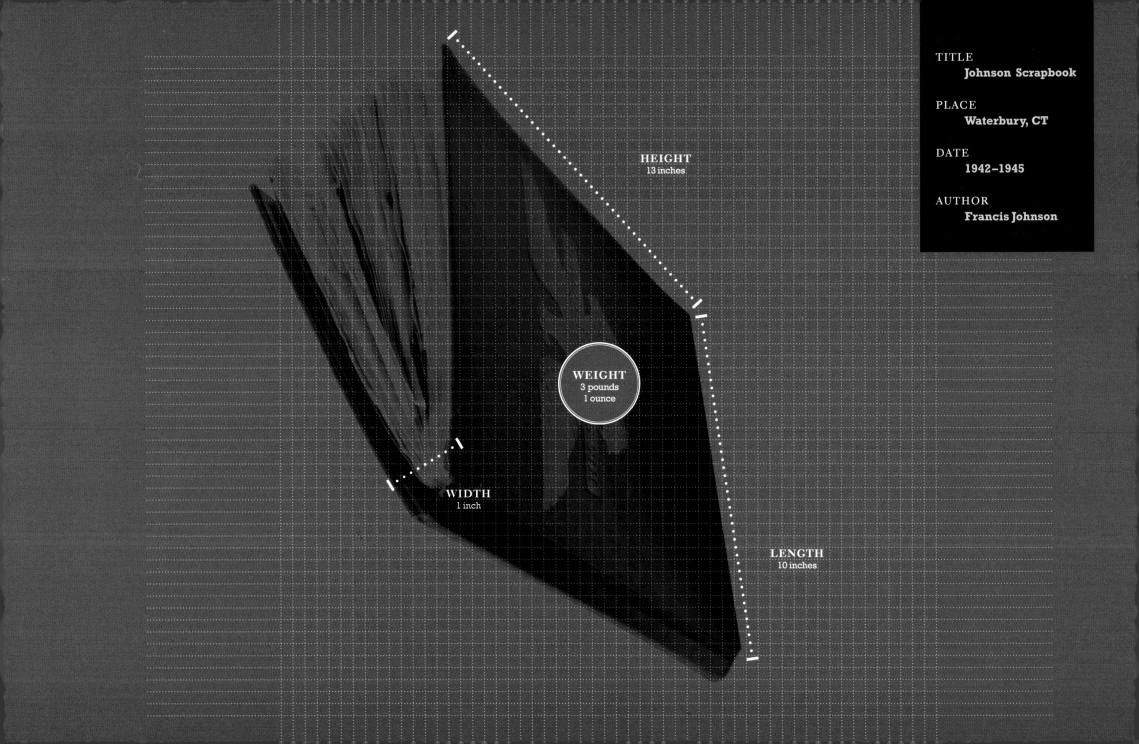

HEIGHT
13 inches

WEIGHT
3 pounds
1 ounce

WIDTH
1 inch

LENGTH
10 inches

JOHNSON SCRAPBOOK
WATERBURY, CONNECTICUT,
1942–1945

PLEDGE

I PLEDGE ALLEGIANCE TO THE
FLAG OF THE UNITED STATES
OF AMERICA * * * AND TO THE
REPUBLIC FOR WHICH IT
STANDS * * * ONE NATION
INDIVISIBLE * * * WITH LIBERTY
AND JUSTICE FOR ALL

E Pluribus Unum

Enlisted August 12th 1942
Taken while at Atlantic City

Francis H. Johnson
NAME

Marine

In Air Force

Edward J. Lynch, 18, of Waterbury is a member of the United States Marine corps. He recently completed training at Parris Island, S. C. Lynch is the son of Mr. and Mrs. Samuel F. Lynch, 344 Farmington avenue. He attended Crosby high school and was a member of the Alpha Hi-Y. His brother, Robert, is serving in the Army Medical corps.

Brother Checking Department ... *in the Air Corps in France* (Pvt.) ... *Johnson. He is son of Rudd* ... *in Wisconsin. Pop was a toolsetter before he joined the Army.*

HOME ON FURLOUGH — PFC. ETHEL A. HEDGES, daughter of Mr. and Mrs. Mark L. Hedges, 221 Willow St., a member of the U. S. Marine Corps Women's Reserve, is home on furlough from her station at San Diego, Calif. She served as a battalion messenger. A graduate of Crosby high school, she was employed by Scovill Mfg. Co. before entering service last December. She received her basic training at Camp Lejeune, N. C.

W. F. Butler, Navy Veteran, Dies At 23

William Francis Butler, 23, 75 Lexington Ave., son of Edmund and Helen (Repka) Butler, died yesterday at his home after a long illness.

Born in Waterbury, Mr. Butler was a student at Crosby High School when he enlisted in the U. S. Navy. He had served 37 months in the Atlantic and Pacific theaters, and was aboard the USS Bristol when it was sunk in the Mediterranean by enemy fire. He also participated in the invasion of Sicily. Discharged in February, 1946, he held the rank of seaman 1/c. At one time, Mr. Butler had been employed by the U. S. Rubber Co. He was a member of the Disabled American Veterans.

Besides his parents, he is survived by a brother, Daniel E. Butler of Waterbury, and a nephew, Wayne Butler.

The funeral will be held Tuesday from his home at 8:15 a. m. to St. Margaret's Church where a solemn high Mass will be celebrated at 9. Burial will be in Calvary Cemetery. Friends may call at the residence, 75 Lexington Ave., after 7 p. m. today.

WILLIAM FRANCIS BUTLER

There was no sounding of taps, no volleys of shots from a firing squad or other military rites at the committal services this week for young Billy Butler, war hero and former Crosby High School student. The ceremonies were brief and marked with a simplicity that was in keeping with Billy's life. He never cherished a yearning for the spotlight. His was a sincere modesty. But for the record let it be written that no military rites or eulogies were necessary to preserve the affectionate regard that hundreds cherished for the youth. From the classroom to one of war's hot spots, the Mediterranean Sea when the Allies were pounding at Salerno and Anzio for a foothold was the quick transition in which Seaman Butler figured. His ship was pounded from all sides. Land batteries hurled shells incessantly at the American naval forces; wave after wave of Nazi planes unloaded their lethal greetings. It was a nightmare. Young Butler in abandoning ship on one occasion was painfully injured, but survived. He came back to join his former associates at Crosby, to enjoy peace again, to enjoy friendly, social contacts and to plan life all over again. But apparently it wasn't in the Divine Plan, for the injuries he suffered in the Italian campaign became aggravated and resulted in his hospitalization. From the start "Billy" realized that he was fighting a losing fight, but he faced it with the fortitude and courage and at times with smiling cheerfulness as when he met some of the "gang" from old Crosby. His passing was inevitable and although his nearest of kin and close friends realized it, they took courage and solace from Billy's attitude. So let his friends proudly write that epitaph that is justly his—"He was a swell kid, a real guy, a man's man, a real hero!"

"We join ourselves to no party that does not carry the flag and keep step to the music of the Union."
— Rufus Choate

Personal History

Frances H. Johnson   1917   Waterbury

Name   *Date Born*   *Place*

34   Colley   Waterbury   New Haven   Conn

Home Address   *Street*   *City or Town*   *County*   *State*

5   120   Blue   Blond   Ruddy   American

Height   *Weight*   *Color of Eyes*   *Color of Hair*   *Complexion*   *Nationality Background*

Russell Grammar 1932   Wilby High 1937

Schooling: Graduation Dates, Schools, Colleges, Place, Date, Degrees

Athletic and Scholastic Achievements

Trade or Profession   *Situations or Positions Held with Names of Firms, Places and Dates*

Catholic

Religious and Church Affiliations

Scovill Mfg Co   048 03 1111

Where Employed when Entered Service   *Social Security Number*

Y. M. C. A.

Fraternal, Social, Professional Club or Labor Organization Affiliations

Favorite Pastime   *Favorite Sport*   *As Spectator*   *Hobby*

Henry   1823   Waterbury   Feb 3, 1943

Name of Father   *Date Born*   *Place*   *If Deceased: Date and Place*

Lucy Knapp Johnson   July 8, 1875   Waterbury

Name of Mother   *Date Born*   *Place*   *If Deceased: Date and Place*

Names and Ages of Brothers and Sisters

Helen, Lucille, Alice, Paul, Ted, Harold,

Name of Wife (if any)   *Date Born*   *Place*   *Married: Place and Date*

Names of Children (if any) Place and Dates of Birth

Additional Information concerning Personal History

Personal History Written by   *Date*

> "Lives there a man with soul so dead,
> Who never to himself hath said
> This is my own, my native land." — SCOTT

And What Was Going On Back Home?

ON THIS PAGE KEEP A RECORD OF ALL IMPORTANT FAMILY EVENTS SUCH AS BIRTHS, DEATHS, MARRIAGES, ACCIDENTS, SICKNESS, ANNIVERSARY CELEBRATIONS, GRADUATIONS, ETC., WHILE HE IS AWAY.

Death of Father, Feb 3rd 1943
Birth of Susan Santoro Nov. 29, 1943
Birth of Margaret ___ Jan 14, 1940
Birth of _ Ed Jr., Jan 7, 1943
Birth of David Champagne
Birth of Henry Jr., Johnson

Betty Johnson, Graduation from
            grammar school
Barbara Johnson, Graduation from
            grammar school
Marjorie Johnson, Graduation from
            grammar school

ON THE FOLLOWING PAGE PASTE CLIPPINGS, PHOTOGRAPHS, OR SOUVENIRS, OF EVENTS IN WHICH THE FAMILY WAS INVOLVED OR ACTIVELY INTERESTED.

"Where's the coward that wouldn't dare
To fight for such a land."
— SCOTT

"In giving freedom to the slave we assure freedom to the free—honorable alike in what we give and what we preserve."
— LINCOLN

THIS IS TO CERTIFY THAT

H. Johnson 11073616 Sgt.

NAME   GRADE   SERIAL NO.

RATING   ORGANIZATION

SERVED HONORABLY AND WELL IN THE
UNITED STATES ARMY AIR FORCES IN
WORLD WAR II.

COMMANDING GENERAL
ARMY AIR FORCES

ARMY AIR FORCES
Certificate of Appreciation
FOR WAR SERVICE

TO

FRANCIS H. JOHNSON

I CANNOT *meet you personally* **to thank you for a job well done; nor can I** *hope to put in written words the* **great hope** *I have for your success in future life.*

Together we built the **striking** *force that swept the Luftwaffe from the skies and broke the* **German power to resist.** *The total might of that striking force was then* **unleashed upon** *the Japanese. Although you no longer play an active military part, the contribution you made to the Air Forces was essential in making us the greatest team in the world.*

The ties that bound us under stress of combat must not be broken in peacetime. Together we share the responsibility for guarding our country in the air. We who stay will never forget the part you have played while in uniform. We know **you will continue to play** *a comparable role as a civilian. As our ways part, let me* **wish you God speed and** *the best of luck on your road in life. Our gratitude and* **respect go with you.**

COMMANDING GENERAL
ARMY AIR FORCES

"With malice toward none, with charity for all, with firmness in the right as God gives us to see the right." — LINCOLN

War He[roes]

PLACE NAMES, PICTURES AND ITEMS CONCERNING PERSONS W[HO]

David P. Healey — Gudacanal
Robert L. McMellis — France
Donald Noonan — Saipian
Harry J. Leonard — France
Donald H. Wigglesworth — France
Edward Meehan — Europe
Billy Callaigan — Europe
Jimmy Gibbons — China

David P. Healy, Marine, Is Killed in Action

War Casualty

PVT. DAVID P. HEALY

20-Year-Old Waterbury Boy Enlisted In Service Jan. 8

Pvt. David P. Healy, 20, son of Patrick Healy of 1367 South Main street, was killed in action recently while serving with a Marine corps unit at an undisclosed combat zone, according to a telegram received here last night.

Pvt. Healy, who enlisted last Jan. 8—just one month after the United States declared war against the Axis powers—is the first Waterbury Marine known to have been killed in action. (Corp. Francis J. Jamele of this city, also of the Marine corps, was killed in an airplane accident last June 20).

Although the telegram of regret, sent by Lieut. Gen. Thomas Holcomb, commandant of the Marine corps, arrived here last night, it was not turned over to the youth's father until this morning.

The message follows: "Deeply regret to inform you that your son, Pvt. David P. Healy, U. S. Marine corps, was killed in action in the performance of his duty and in the service of his country. To prevent possible aid to our enemies please do not divulge the name of his ship or station. Present situation necessitates interment temporarily in the locality where death occurred and you will be notified accordingly. Please accept my heartfelt sympathy. Letter follows."

Besides his father, Pvt. Healy is survived by a brother, Corp. John Healy, former Fordham university student, who is now a surgeon's assistant in the Army Medical corps at Baltimore; two sisters, Marcella, who is now Mrs. James Shea of Forest Hills, L. I., and Lorraine Healy of New York city.

The youthful Marine was a graduate of Wilby high school. While at St. Margaret's parochial school, he played on the school's baseball team. He worked at the Apothecaries Hall Co. store after school hours from 1937 to 1939. Prior to his enlistment, he worked at the American Metal Hose division of the American Brass Co.

Mr. Healy explained today that he and his son lived at 334 Willow street, but after his son enlisted he moved to his present address.

Prayers for Pvt. Healy will be offered at the next meeting of the Corp. Francis J. Jamele detachment, Marine Corps league, it was announced by Edward C. Scholey, commandant. Mr. Scholey said members of the unit will attend a Mass soon at which other prayers will be offered.

"A man who is good enough to shed his blood for his country is good enough to be given a square deal afterwards."
— THEODORE ROOSEVELT

But human beings do not perceive things whole;
we are not gods but wounded creatures,
cracked lenses, capable only of fractured perceptions.
Partial beings, in all the senses of that phrase.
Meaning is a shaky edifice we build out of scraps,
dogmas, childhood injuries, newspaper articles,
chance remarks, old films, small victories,
people hated, people loved; perhaps it is because
our sense of what is the case is constructed from
such inadequate materials that we defend it so fiercely,
even to the death.

Salman Rushdie, *Imaginary Homelands*

No. 91 Imm.   Form C.

CANADA

ORDER FOR DEPORTATION

THE IMMIGRATION ACT, SECTION 33

To ~~U. S. Immigration~~
(Transportation company)

and to *Francis H. Johnson*
(person named)

Port of Entry *Vulsbury*, Province of *U.S.*

THIS IS TO CERTIFY that *Francis H. Johnson*
(name in full)

of *1009 West Main St. Waterbury Conn.*
(last place of residence)

a person seeking to enter Canada at this port, ex *Auto*
(mode of travel)

from *New Haven* which arrived at this port on *July 27/38*

at *7* o'clock has this day been examined by the Board of
Inquiry (or officer in charge) at this port, and has been rejected for
the following reasons:—

Does not come within the ~~classes~~ grant classes mentioned
in Section 7 paragraph H iv. of the Immigration Act.

*Sec 3 SS (J) Liable to become
a public charge
Immig Act s 33*

And the said *person named* is hereby ordered
to be deported to the place from whence he came to Canada or to
the country of his birth or citizenship. Such conveyance shall be by
the transportation company which brought the said
to Canada.

Dated at *Philipsburg* this *7* day of *July* 193*8*

signature
Chairman of the Board of Inquiry
or Immigration Officer in Charge

(SEE OVER)

SCOVILL MANUFACTURING COMPANY

ESTABLISHED 1802

WATERBURY 91, CONNECTICUT

P. O. BOX 1820

EXECUTIVE OFFICES   March 1, 1944

TO THE FAMILY OF ———————— FRANCIS H. JOHNSON

The above left the employ of Scovill Manufacturing
Company to enter the armed forces of our country.
With you, we are proud of him. We are sure he has
and will continue to give a good account of himself
in whatever capacity duty may place him.

We are pleased to present to you, at his request,
this copy of "His Service Record" with the hope that
in years to come, you and he will value this complete
record of his achievements.

Sincerely yours,

SCOVILL MANUFACTURING COMPANY

JMB:MRM   *signature*
Enclosure   President

CHAPTER FOUR   NOSTALGIA

THE CULTURE OF RATIONING THAT PERVADED American society during and between the two world wars shed a uniquely favorable light on the virtues of saving as a way of life. A volatile economy, changing diplomatic policies both at home and abroad, and a sense of protracted vulnerability in the wake of war led, for many, to a renewed appreciation for life itself, making the practice of maintaining a scrapbook an almost existential activity—and most certainly a meditative one. Keeping a scrapbook, it suddenly seemed, might be as close as anyone could get to achieving at least the illusion of immortality. Implicit in this supposition was an increased desire to rescue (and a distinct tendency to embellish) the past: yet it is likely, too, that such an open embrace of nostalgia may have provided a welcome antidote to wartime anxiety. Indeed, the surge in sales of scrapbook supplies in the years immediately following the terrorist attacks of September 11, 2001, eerily reflects this sentiment, suggesting that to keep a diary, journal, or scrapbook is one way to steel oneself against the inevitable tide of uncertainty that surges in the wake of any kind of tragedy. (The relationship between creativity, uncertainty, and the renewed popularity of the American scrapbook is explored in greater depth in the following chapter.)

Although it had been considered in the eighteenth and nineteenth centuries as a disease or ailment to be cured (one doctor described it as a "hypochondria of the heart"),[1] nostalgia in general (and the act of recording memory in particular) was a mere consequence of longing for simpler, happier times—and was, for that matter, the scrapbook's raison d'être. No longer were albums merely the place to save pretty scraps, to collect labels and autographs and pictures from

MEMORIES
OF MY
SCHOOL DAYS

magazines: they became instead the preferred destination for all kinds of personal (and often quite ludicrous) pieces of memorabilia. Scrapbooks were the place to hold loose earrings, gobs of candle grease, long-ago-extinguished cigarette butts and obscure bits of chalk; broken pencil shreds, torn coonskin-cap tails, bits of cellophane, and packages of rusted razor blades. The items people saved became tokens of hope, beacons of meaning, catalysts for remembering what might so easily otherwise be forgotten. Over time, the widespread appeal of such tangible memory keeping would become intrinsically linked to the very practice of keeping a scrapbook—or, as it so happened, a memory book.

Memory books were books whose pages were preformatted, designating where things should go—which often meant segregating word (clippings, correspondence) from image (photographs, drawings) and thereby crafting a more controlled environment for personal storytelling. At least one newspaper praised this practice early on as a worthwhile activity "for young girls" even though it was equally perceived (and somewhat denigrated) as a "fad."[2] There is some evidence to suggest that scrapbooks and memory books were so engaging to young women that educators, seeking to inspire their students, incorporated them into the classroom. In what was, in retrospect, a comparatively interactive experiment for teaching English composition to high school sophomores, one New Haven teacher asked her students to create scrapbooks over the course of the nine-month academic year. "The composition class was motivated," she reported. "The English work was broadened. Pupils knew more of books, magazines and the use of the library." The conflation of paste pots and pedagogy found its way into curricula even at the college level. In 1937, girls at Colby Junior College were asked to make their own scrap-textbooks for a course in contemporary American problems.[3]

Memory Books
Various publishers
1900–1930

Initially, memory books were illustrated with romanticized figures of demure women in caps and gowns. Over the years, gracious living gave way to more giddy, even raucous kinds of merry (and memory) making. A more plaintive expression can be found on the title page from *School-Girl Days: A Memory Book*, which is taken from the writings of the eighteenth-century Irish philosopher George Berkeley, who wrote, "Our youth we can have but today."

The appeal of the memory book loomed large, and soon there were numerous preprinted volumes from which to choose: *Her Memory Book* offered pages for DINNERS, DANCES, and FIVE 'O CLOCK TEAS, while *School-Girl Days: A Memory Book* included space for such things as SPREADS AND ENTERTAINMENTS, CLASS YELL, and KODAK SNAP SHOTS. The advent of consumer photography had a huge impact on the production of visual narratives in scrapbooks. First introduced in 1900, the Brownie camera sold for one dollar, making picture taking hugely affordable to the average citizen, and thereby putting photography within everyone's reach. In an early newspaper advertisement for Macy's department store, Kodak touts the novelty and importance of camera ownership: "Men and women are, more and more, looking upon a Camera as a part of their outing requisites."[4] Suddenly, it seemed, one could capture memories with an astonishingly personal focus. As the material traces of an irrecoverable past,[5] photography enabled the aspiring autobiographer to crystallize memories as they were happening, and was, for that matter, a significant catalyst in the visualization of memory in scrapbook form.

The preprinted memory book soon fostered a climate of subtle editorial management, with pages parsing individual moments at a glance. Segmented by life's major events, *Her Memory Book* concludes with pages for recording one's engagement and subsequent marriage, not only reinforcing the implicit denouement of what were assumed to be any young girl's personal aspirations but also, and more critically with regard to the memory book in general, providing a scalable repository for future memory. Pasting an item into a scrapbook virtually cemented one's memories —essentially locking them in place—and to the degree that nostalgia is dependent on the modern conception of unrepeatable and irreversible time, such gestures were enormously reassuring.[6]

And here is where a significant cultural shift occurs: whereas earlier scrapbooks were often produced from the materials at hand (lending a haphazard and distinctly homespun quality to the resulting books), the anticipation of memory as a core emotional need—and one with a person-

Memory Books
1895–1945

A selection of the many
different varieties of
memory books produced
during the early years of
the twentieth century.
Many of them were geared
to students, and included
rubrics to help guide the
aspiring diarist, journalist,
or scrapbooker.

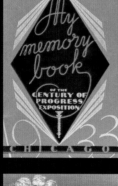

Memories
of my
School Days

Happy
School Days

A Memory Book

GRADUATION
MEMORIES
of
HAZEL

GRADUATION
MEMORIES

Published by
C.M. Sellers & Company
New York City

A Girl's
Graduation
Days

ABOUT
MY SCHOOL
AND ME

The
GIRLS
MEMORY
BOOK

MEMORY
BOOK of my
College Associates
their Expressions
and Biographies.

New York
H. L. MORTON & CO.
47 West 34th St.

SPORTS
Mem
BOOK

School
Friendship
Book

Down
Memory
Lane

School Belles
Illustration and design by
Amelia Winter
1925

alized and highly visual component—was a uniquely twentieth-century conceit. If earlier public sentiment had advocated the joy and thrift of making an album on your own, modern views of practicality, organization, and heightened efficiency privileged these newer editions—commercially produced (and often copiously illustrated) books that classified memorable events in advance of their ever happening.

The rise in production of memory books—often tailored to a particular interest group (brides, Boy Scouts, babies and their fawning parents) greatly facilitated Americans' growing urge not only to save but to document. Such publishers as Barse and Hopkins, G. W. Dilingham, W. C. Horn, Jordan and Company, C. R. Gibson, and Reilly and Lee produced numerous such volumes, many of them geared to young people. *High School Days: A Memory Book* (1908), *School-Girl Days* (1910), *My Golden School Days: A Record Book for Happy Memories* (1911), *School Memories* (1914), and *Happy School Days* (1918) were all produced around World War I and are comparatively innocent in their depiction of memory-worthy events. Later books, particularly those geared to high-school students (many of whom were destined to change from student to soldier almost overnight), are remarkably more poignant as a result.

It is possible—likely even—that these publisher-sanctioned editions lent a tone of welcome credibility to memory keeping. Equally possible is that such a practical structure offered a more forgiving space for even more chaotic recollections. And while seemingly paradoxical, the tension between form (solid, dependable) and content (slippery, incoherent) was perhaps the memory book's great triumph. In an age of increasing mechanization, modernization, and public progress, the personal memory became something of an endangered species: nostalgia, after all, skews experience by prioritizing the romanticized over the real, the idiosyncratic tidbit over the bona fide event. What better way to stay anchored to reality than with a preprinted (and thus predefined) digest of memory's key classifications? Shepherding the scrapbooker through the process of compiling an album was at once a formal and a psychological exercise, and preprinted rubrics were one way to eliminate the organizational guesswork in page composition—which, for all intents and purposes, was based on the simple act of committing memory to paper.

The language in memory books evolves over time, as do the illustration styles,[7] reflecting changes in everything from school slang and contemporary fashion to attitudes about politics, technology, and community service. With vivid color and drawings inspired by John Held, Jr., *School Belles* conjures a spirited era of stunt-seeking students and stern, pickle-faced teachers. Here, clever compositional options were likely intended to make filling out each page an engaging pastime: rubrics include such standards as SCHOOL PENNANTS, SCHOOL CHEER, and SCHOOL SONGS as well as a page simply marked SCANDAL! The illustrated 1944 edition of *My Naughty-Graphs* gestures to a similarly comical view of school and features the magnificent line illustrations and hand-lettering of American cartoonist Charles Forbell. Gradually, too, the market was flooded by a host of "specialty" memory books, many of which were issued as premiums by advertisers; here, the role of memory was enhanced by graphically highlighting its association to a particular product, service, or event.

Along with the prescriptive language introduced by the memory book came a more conscious approach to timekeeping through events.[8] There are scrapbooks that isolate, and consequently celebrate, episodic time—scrapbooks in which Christmas cards, for instance, are used to document a lifetime of family reunions. (While interesting as catalogues tracing the formal genesis

My Naughty-Graphs
Illustration and design by Charles Forbell
1944

A graphic designer, illustrator, and cartoonist, Forbell was a staff artist for the *New York World* as well as a regular contributor to magazines including *Life* and *Judge*, where he created series including "In Ye Goode Old Days" (*Life*) as well as "In Ancient Times" and "Ancient Sources of Modern Inventions" (*Judge*) throughout the first three decades of the twentieth century. Forbell also created the short-lived newspaper comic "Naughty Pete" in 1913.

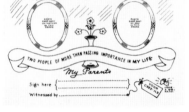

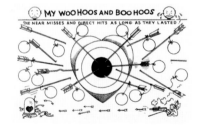

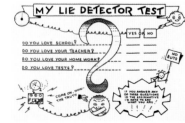

MY SCHOOL DAYS

Precious wisdom, brightest mem'ries,
From thy cloistered halls we bear,
Alma Mater's gifts are legion—
Ours now to do and dare!

ILLUSTRATED BY
FLORENCE WHITE WILLIAMS
PUBLISHED BY
SAALFIELD PUBLISHING COMPANY
AKRON, OHIO

My School Days
Illustrations by
Florence White Williams
1920

The title page for a
typical memory book,
with pages included for
everything from "Class
Year," "Colors," "Pin," and
"Ring" to "Favorite Books
and Authors," "My Chum
and Other Best Friends,"
and "Kodak Snap Shots."

sense of authorship. Such gestures are fascinating precisely because they add an arguably rich layer of opinion—and, not infrequently, of dissent. These crossed-out or covered-over pages reveal much about their authors and their values during the memory-book-making process. Preprinted headings also served to cement certain implicit social values. The book titled *Graduation Days* (published in the early 1930s) includes pages for GIFTS, GREETINGS, and THE GOWN, whereas a decade later, at the onset of World War II, *School Souvenirs* presents rather a different portrait of young women, including a page entitled WE MAKE OURSELVES USEFUL. Other headings, like FOOD FADS AND REFRESHMENTS, offer a reminder that even amid the increasing demands of public service, sometimes a girl just needed a Cherry Coke.

As a genre, memory books achieved a particular kind of organization through compartmentalization, thereby cultivating a keen awareness of distinct moments, individual accomplishments, and personal milestones. Such volumes extoll the virtues of major events (weddings, graduations) or highlight quantifiable details (baby's weight, bridal gifts) rather than urge the maker to seek the more elusive details that might, in fact, constitute a more unique memory. (Here again is where the crossed-out heading introduces a welcome gesture of defiance.) In many books, independently judged value is trumped by a more mediated, public sanctioning of what is deemed memory-worthy, implicitly privileging the public memory over the private moment. [9] In a comparatively early demonstration of the "do-it-yourself" mandate that would come to typify early twenty-first-century culture,[10] memory books were captivating precisely because they were both instructive *and* interactive. They were also, particularly in regard to women, profoundly infantilizing. And nowhere was this more apparent than in memory books targeting the new mother.

of the greeting-card industry, such books tend to provide scarce information about the individuals whose books they were.) Like the photo album, they jump from event to event, focusing on the cards themselves and ignoring the interstitial and arguably more meaningful details along the way.

Preprinted headings also shifted the emphasis by introducing topical subdivisions, which proved useful even when the author chose to bypass, change, or ignore them entirely; curiously, such deviations highlight the degree to which scrapbookers selectively asserted their own

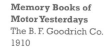

**Memory Books of
Motor Yesterdays**
The B. F. Goodrich Co.
1910

Curiously, the B. F.
Goodrich Company
produced two different
memory books for
motorists in the same
year. "In this little book
keep a record of your
jaunts," one noted. "It will
be an unending source of
pleasure and may often
be of value." Included are
pages for gasoline and
oil records, a road log
for interesting trips, and
advice on how to change
and store tires.

The notion of motherhood as central to a woman's identity was one nineteenth-century legacy that would be slow to change, and while women's roles would begin to evolve and diversify, the fierce internal power of the maternal drive remained (and has remained) essentially unweakened. Throughout the century, mothers would continue to produce ambitious albums documenting everything from baby's first cry to baby's first tooth to baby's first appearance in a place of worship, saving every shower card, every congratulatory telegram, even the occasional note (and, if at all possible, the autograph) from the obstetrician. Not surprisingly, these books tend to be copiously written in before and directly after the birth of a child, with a rather noticeable attrition occurring in the subsequent sleep-deprived months to follow.

One notable exception to this pattern can be found in the scrapbook kept by F. Scott Fitzgerald's mother: in addition to documenting every notable detail of his infancy, her baby book included a page on which to record the child's signature, beginning at the age of five and continuing annually until the age of twenty-five. Remarkably, Fitzgerald obliged: the result is as much an astonishing piece of social history as it is a stunning symbol of mother-son bonding. Mollie McQuillan Fitzgerald was a fastidious keeper of her son's baby book, recording everything from his "cute sayings and sensible remarks" to his first cry, first step, and first prayer—even the program card from his dance school in Buffalo. F. Scott Fitzgerald himself would become a serious diarist: at the age of ten he compiled a twenty-six-page *Thoughtbook* of his doings, and in 1919 he began keeping a record of his career in an accounting ledger. *Mother and I never had anything in common,* he wrote in a letter to his sister some years later, *except a relentless stubborn quality.* [11] Apparently, too, both mother and son shared an abiding interest in recording their memories.

Fitzgerald Baby Book
St. Louis, MO
1890s

Memory books targeting the new mother were published in substantial quantities from the 1890s through the twentieth century and, at least initially, took their cue from the friendship, sentiment, and gift books that had enjoyed such popularity during the eighteenth and nineteenth centuries. [12] Whereas books of friendship and remembrance had long been fashionable among women and were key progenitors of scrapbooks and memory books, the memory book had the potential to be much more. It was simultaneously more personal (like a diary) and more eclectic (like a scrapbook), and because it was intrinsically connected to one's ancestry, it was likely to have been considered far more emotionally resonant. [13] No longer confined to the preservation of scraps for their aesthetic value or pure novelty, memory books were valuable because they were autobiographical, unique, and unquestionably real.

Nevertheless, most early "baby" memory books tend to be highly decorative, filled with lavish illustration and framed by expressive typography; even the text itself is ornamental and flowery, often including prayers and poems, sonnets, snippets, and space specifically earmarked for found materials and other precious, sentimentalized objects—baby's first tooth, for example, or a lock of trimmed hair. Books like *The New Baby's Biography* (1891), *Baby's Kingdom* (1894), *Mother Stork's Baby Book* (1904), *Babyhood Days* (1915), *Our Baby's Biography* (1920), and *Tattle Tales* (1942) figured among numerous titles in this genre, many of which were endorsed by hospitals, drug companies, and health practitioners who saw them as ideal marketing vehicles for their products. Some were given as gifts by obstetricians to their patients, and a few—*Baby Grows in Age and Grace: A Guide for the Catholic Mother* (1951), for instance—were even distributed under the aegis of certain sectarian interest groups. Such a book offered reassurance by enabling the more devout parent to monitor some of the many

MOTHER · STORK'S BABY · BOOK

PUBLISHED IN NEW YORK BY THE DODGE PUBLISHING COMPANY | ILLUSTRATED BY RANDALL WHEELAN

BABY GROWS IN AGE AND GRACE

A Guide and Record for the Catholic Mother

by

SISTER MARY DE LOURDES

Sister of Mercy at Saint Joseph College
East Hartford, Connecticut

Artist Director: John J. Hayes, Census Librarian
Imprimatur: H. Henry, J. O'Brien, D.D., Bishop of Hartford

Attendance at FIRST MASS

Attended first Mass at

with   date

Reaction to service

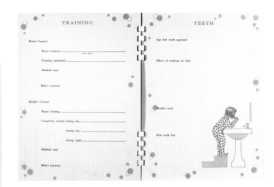

TRAINING   TEETH

ABOVE
Mother Stork's Baby Book
Dodge Publishing Co.
1904

ABOVE RIGHT
Baby Grows in Age and Grace
C. R. Gibson and Co.
1951

RIGHT
Mother's Memory Book
Toledo Metal Wheel Co.
1920

An example of the sorts of premiums offered by advertisers, many of which were pegged to nutritional products for the mother and baby or, as in this case, touting the safety of a baby carriage's wheels.

Mother's Memory Book

ABOVE
Tattle Tales
Givens and Co.
1942

A utilitarian verion of a book for parents bound with a plastic comb, to allow the pages to lie flat when writing.

Tattle Tales

BABYHOOD DAYS

First Laugh
On the .... day of ....
Baby pealed forth .... first
laugh in presence of ....
First Word
Baby's first word was ....
spoken at the age of ....
First Tooth
Baby's first tooth was discovered
on .... day of .... in year
of .... when baby was .... old

Record of Birth

ABOVE AND LEFT
Babyhood Days
Barse and Hopkins
1915

OPPOSITE
The New Baby's Biography
Brentano's
1908

religious milestones in a child's life. An accompanying chapter on motherhood as cooperation with God sets a serious tone for a memory book that allocates areas for marking signs of development (physical, spiritual), record of baptism, world happenings on baby's birthday, and preventative measures for illness—which included such afflictions as diptheria, whooping cough, and scarlet fever. Also earmarked for record keeping are baby's first spontaneous prayer, attendance at first mass, and date on which child first recognizes holy pictures.

By the early 1950s, there was even a baby book for adoptive parents. Billed as the first record book especially for adopted children, *All About You* begins with the day the adopted child formally enters his or her new home. Written by an adoptive parent and featuring an introduction by the executive director of the New England Home for Little Wanderers, the book came packaged with an information booklet with articles addressing "Why, When, and How The Adoption Story Should Be Told."

One of the more delightful examples in the new-mother genre comes from a 1928 book entitled *The Dietary Adventures of Annabil Lee*, which opens with a fictional account of a baby's arrival, by stork, to the arms of its waiting mother. Written by Gertrude I. Thomas, an instructor in dietetics at the University of Minnesota, the account was an attempt to portray the epicurian experiences of a fictional baby "to present the food problems of the young mother in the order in which they arrive." The book also includes a page for baptism details (or, as in the case of the book pictured here, the bris); room for baby's footprints, thumbprints, and handprints; a weight and height chart; pages for dental records; and plenty of space for photographs. In chapter after chapter, the book offers nutritional guidelines for the nursing mother and, upon the introduction of solid food, menu suggestions for baby. Along

RIGHT
All About You
C. R. Gibson and Co.
1959

BELOW
Baby's Memory Book
Libby's, Inc.
1945

A premium given to new mothers, this pamphlet included pages for immunization records.

BELOW AND LEFT
Baby's First Seven Years
The Chicago Lying-In Hospital
1941

Described as a kind of sentimental storehouse, a scrapbook is touted here as something of "real value to the inner life of a child."

Foreword

IN PRESENTING this delightfully illustrated Scrapbook we make possible an orderly collection of those priceless mementoes that too frequently are lost or damaged beyond repair. A small cardboard box, yellow with age, may serve very well as a movie prop but it is a sorry container for the precious and irreplaceable reminders that make up the color and pattern of a child's life. Cherished memories of the past are recalled and lived again as you turn the pages of this Scrapbook. Each event, insignificant or important, recedes into forgetfulness until the Scrapbook is opened and there, before you, your memories leap to life once again. . . . A Scrapbook is a lovely kind of sentimental storehouse. All through life a collection of silly little trinkets, silly to everyone but their owner, will mark days that should always be remembered. Today your child goes to a party. Twenty years from now the only memory of it will be wrapped up in a flimsy paper souvenir or a bit of ribbon. Tomorrow your child will come home with a childish, grotesque scrawl that is his—or her—first venture into the realm of self-expression. . . . A Scrapbook, moreover, is of real value to the inner life of a child. It gives him a feeling of being significant—a feeling which psychologists say is a basic emotional need. It is a truly personal possession, the first and only edition of a life story in the first person. It seems fitting that such a book as this should be sold for the sole benefit of the Chicago Lying-in Hospital and Dispensary of the University of Chicago where so many hundreds of life stories have their beginning every year.

The Mothers' Aid

CHICAGO LYING-IN HOSPITAL AND DISPENSARY • THE UNIVERSITY OF CHICAGO

The Dietary Adventures of Anabil Lee
Thomas

W. CLOVIS CUMMINGS, M.D.
GYNECOLOGY & ABDOMINAL SURGERY
OKLAHOMA CITY, OKLA.

ABOVE AND LEFT
The Dietary Adventures of Anabil Lee
F. A. Davis Co., Publishers
1924

In addition to menus for baby, this book includes suggestions for special diets and convalescent foods, including many varieties of stewed and boiled foods, and no shortage of puddings.

with these items are filled-in portions of delirious prose input by the hand of the owner. (*Nice mouth; good head,* reads one such entry from the mother of a little girl born in 1928. *Chinese eyes. Those ears! So sail-boaty! What a good baby.*) Such books are a tour de force of prescriptive language, offering cues and checklists to ensure a kind of professional polish, and requiring little if any editorial or organizational effort.

Here, too, the tricky line between parenting and propaganda is routinely abused. A book by Mary Hale Martin, a nutritionist for Libby, includes advice, statistics, and space for immunization records along with an advertisement for Libby's Spinach, a gesture that virtually links vegetable intake with disease prevention. Other books were even more earnest: "Because they [the Baby Mine Company] believe in babies and love them," writes a solemn Melcena Burns Denny in *The Book of Baby Mine* (1940). "Because they believe in Quality Advertising as well as quality products and service, you have the enjoyment of this unusual and helpful baby book—their gift to you and Baby." And she's not done. "And we believe that you, in turn, will want them to have the enjoyment of your telling them of your appreciation and of a share of your patronage." Denny's flowery illustrations and hand-drawn type seem a peculiar match for a book that features articles on things like caring for baby's navel, managing tantrums, and dealing with the occasional convulsion. Along with pages allocated for QUAINT LOCKS and FAVORITE TOYS are illustrated fragments of childhood verse, pages for FIRST BANK ACCOUNT, and detailed instructions on how to give an enema.

In general, motherhood tends to be more romanticized in earlier books, while efforts to document baby's progress are, by midcentury, more overtly mechanical: here, nostalgia is not so much framed by a kind of sentimental longing as positioned as an oddly fabricated appeal to novelty.

Issued by the Lincoln
Dairy Company in
Hartford, Connecticut,
this booklet contains
detailed data on all things
dairy. Pages are allocated
for birthstones, flowers,
weights, measures,
and nap schedules for
the milk-fed child.

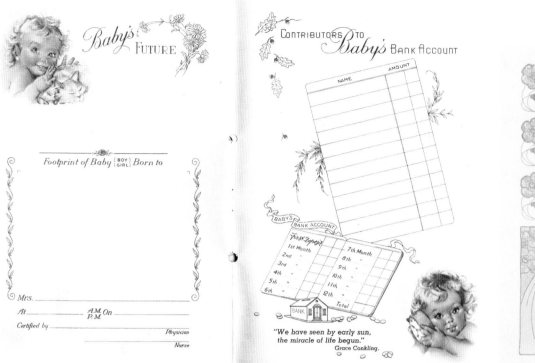

Baby's FUTURE

CONTRIBUTORS TO *Baby's* BANK ACCOUNT

Footprint of Baby { BOY / GIRL } *Born to*

Mrs.

At _____ A.M. On _____ P.M.

Certified by _____

Physician

Nurse

NAME   AMOUNT

BABY'S BANK ACCOUNT

First Deposit
1st Month   7th Month
2nd   8th
3rd   9th
4th   10th
5th   11th
6th   12th
              Total

BANK

"We have seen by early sun,
the miracle of life begun."
Grace Conkling.

Baby Creeps
Date -

Baby Stands Alone
Date -

Baby's First Steps
Date -

Insistent editorial notes were sometimes added to reinforce the value of memory keeping for future generations. "A small cardboard box, yellow with age, may serve very well as a movie prop but it is a sorry container for the precious and irreplaceable reminders that make up the color and patterns of a child's life," notes one. Originally published in 1928 by the Mother's Aid of the Chicago Lying-In Hospital (and revised many times since), a 1941 edition of *Our Baby's First Seven Years* includes saccharine words of encouragement ("Cherished memories of the past are recalled and live again as you turn the pages of this Scrapbook") along with sober warnings ("A baby's book should contain a great deal more than a mere record of worldly events affecting the new candidate for citizenship"). Note the authors: "A record of all the phenomena which transpire during these years will have a value that grows with time, and increases greatly with the number of babies upon whom such observations are made... Books such

as this, carefully filled out, will give valuable information in every department of medicine, will guide the teacher, the physical culturists, the eugenist, and the statesman, in their broad efforts to improve the race, as well as the physician in the treatment of the individual case." There is an air of almost hygienic surveillance in this book, which includes pages designated for recording illnesses, injuries, responses to rhythm and music, creative tendencies, and special aptitudes during a child's first few years.

Such books emerged, particularly in the years following World War II, as modern life-style enablers: the underlying message was that you could wax sentimental and get things done at the same time—but only if you followed the rules. An entire chapter in the 1929 *Modern Baby Book and Development Record* is devoted to SUGGESTIONS FOR RECORD KEEPING in which "the parent is advised to examine the plan of the book carefully and familiarize herself with the

Only beginning the journey;
Many a mile to go—
Little feet, how they patter,
Wandering to and fro!
Father of All, oh, guide them,
The pattering little feet,
While they are treading the uphill road,
Braving the dust and heat!
Aid them when they grow weary,
Keep them in pathway blest
And when the journey is ended,
Savior, oh, give them rest!

The Modern Baby Book and Child Development Record
Parents Magazine and
W. W. Norton
1929

Baby's Kingdom
Lee and Shepard
1895

Baby's Kingdom, subtitled *Wherein May Be Chronicled as Memories for Grown-Up Days, The Mother's Story*, includes no shortage of illustrated verse, along with snippets of baby hair and copious diary entries marking a series of events during the summer of 1895. Most striking is the tiny flag the baby waved (*opposite*) while President McKinley presided over a July 4 parade that summer in Dorchester, Massachusetts.

contents of the various sections." With copious illustrations by Clara Elsene Peck, this book was published by the editors of the *Parents Magazine* as a compendium of child and baby care coupled with a journal for parents to keep track of their children's progress. Each chapter in this volume concludes with a single page earmarked for MISCELLANY intended for recording "any anecdotes or interesting events in the child's life." Readers were further advised to save mementos in the box file—the book came slipcased in a box, which included a set of graduated folders intended for use as a file—an odd recommendation, since there is hardly space for anything at all in the folders. Nevertheless, the writing in this book speaks volumes about the staunch, somewhat hygienic approach to child rearing that typified "modern" parenting practices in 1929.

Dee's Blessed Event Scrap Book, published in the early 1940s and touted "as new and modern as

tomorrow," includes a curious system of additional half-pages emblazoned by cartoon illustrations of Scoopy and Scrappy—two wizened toddlers who take on the roles of editor and art director, respectively, to help guide the new mother in the process of collecting materials. Periodic interruptions by Scoopy offer excruciatingly specific tips on what to include (the newspaper, the front page of the newspaper, the front page headline of the newspaper), while Scrappy advises on technique with such heightened perspicacity one is left wondering if the hormonal imbalances brought about by incipient motherhood have virtually annihilated all capacity for reason. "If the page is too big for your book," warns Scrappy, "fold it over."

The title page here is both poorly written and bizarrely organized. "This scrapbook with its many pages of news and views becomes increasingly interesting as child progresses," it begins, followed by the fragment "A lasting gift that is fun to make

in your leisure time." Finally, in case the reader is not yet persuaded, comes the hard sell: "On day of child's birth you clip news items or world events from newspapers and magazines, then paste in scrapbook as outlined in following instructions." Included, too, are pages to feature such things as appliances—important symbols of materiality and, indeed, modernity in the early 1940s.

This dumbing down would continue to erode the countenance of the memory book by insinuating extraneous thinking into what was, at its core, a personal vehicle for recording experience. But there would always be exceptions, and with the growth of the memory book industry as a whole, the visual variety and editorial mix grew apace: once children were of an age to assemble their own volumes, they had a plethora of options, many of which collapsed diary, scrap and autograph book into a playful volume that, more often than not, targeted the young teenage girl.

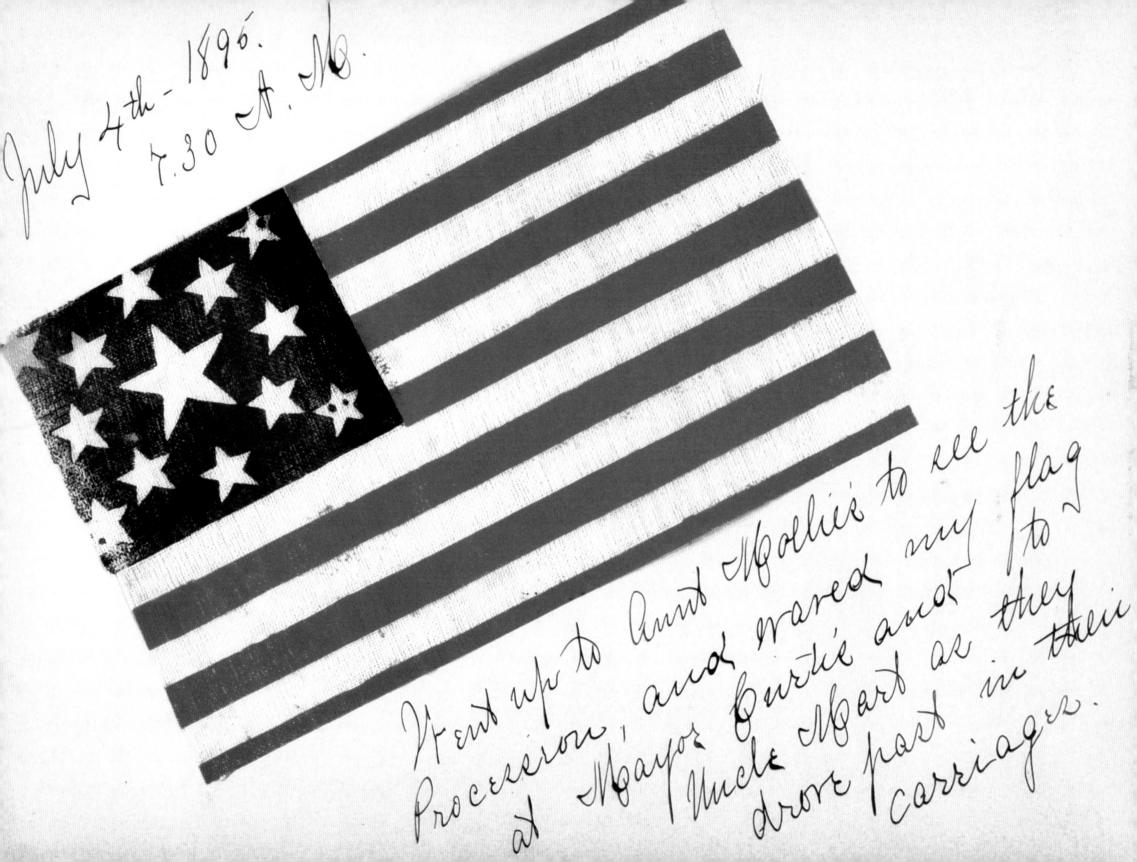

July 4th - 1895.
7.30 A. M.

Went up to Aunt Mollie's to see the
Procession, and waved my flag
at Mayor Curtie and to
Uncle Mart as they
drove past in their
carriages.

ANNOUNCING

ARRIVAL

NAME

ADDRESS

CITY   STATE

TIME OF BIRTH

WEATHER

WEIGHT

HEIGHT

COLOR OF EYES

BIRTHSTONE

DOCTOR ATTENDING

NURSE ATTENDING

PLACE OF BIRTH

My Family

"SCOOPY" SAYS —

WHEN YOU SEE THAT LONG-LEGGED
BIRD FLYING TO HIS DESTINATION THEN
IT IS TIME TO START YOUR BLESSED
EVENT SCRAP BOOK.

"SCRAPPY" SAYS —

BE SURE TO GET THE AUTHENTIC
TIME, DATE, ETC., ALSO NECESSARY
INFORMATION TO FILL IN THE
OPPOSITE PAGE - - 'CAUSE THIS INFORMA-
TION WILL BE OF REAL VALUE TO OUR
LITTLE FRIEND IN LATER YEARS.

IMAGINE LOOKING THROUGH THIS SCRAPBOOK
TWENTY YEARS FROM NOW!

DEE'S *Blessed Event* **SCRAP BOOK**

IS NEW AND MODERN AS TOMORROW

THIS SCRAPBOOK WITH ITS MANY PAGES OF NEWS
AND VIEWS BECOMES INCREASINGLY INTERESTING
AS CHILD PROGRESSES. A LASTING GIFT THAT IS
FUN TO MAKE IN YOUR LEISURE TIME.

ON DAY OF CHILDS BIRTH YOU CLIP NEWS ITEMS
OF WORLD EVENTS FROM NEWSPAPERS AND MAG-
AZINES, THEN PASTE IN SCRAPBOOK AS OUTLINED
IN FOLLOWING INSTRUCTIONS.

THIS SCRAPBOOK WHEN COMPLETE IS AN INTEREST-
ING AND EDUCATIONAL GIFT NEW ARRIVAL WILL
APPRECIATE AND ENJOY IN YEARS TO COME.

INSTRUCTIONS ON FOLLOWING PAGES

ARRANGE CLIPPINGS ON PAGE -LIKE THIS.

Dee's Blessed Event Scrap Book
Givens and Co.
1942

On a page earmarked for Appliances, Scoopy suggests, "With so many different streamlined appliances for household use, it will be easy to collect material for these pages."

The "Him" book was the prototypical data-base for the boy-crazy teenager, with blank name-and-address inventories provided for the aspiring stalker— accompanied, in at least one book, by a lyrical mantra: *From this day on I'll keep complete/ A record of all the boys I meet.* Another features bars of music on its cover (with boys' faces superimposed on the musical notes) and provides a comprehensive inventory for every possible "him" of note, including (but not limited to) SCHOOL HIMS (dreamboats and goons), SPECIAL HIMS (date bait, charmers, and gay deceivers), POPULAR HIMS, NATIONAL HIMS, MUSICAL HIMS, and finally, the "HIM OF HIMS." The last page in this book completes the gesture with a final observation of farcical worship: "AH, MEN!" Unabashedly gushing in their yearning for romantic attention, "Him" books enabled young girls to manage the documentation of numerous would-be male companions. Like them, *Date Data* gestured

to a young girl's need for privacy by providing envelopes in which to store any of a number of top-secret treasures. Mary Dorman's *Snip 'N Tuck* ("The Busy Gal's Scrapbook") consists of a series of blank pages interspersed with four oversized envelopes, pasted onto the page with the opening facing out and printed with handwritten sayings and editorial tips. In the spirit of playful insouciance that many books of this era seemed desperate to achieve, many of the tips here even rhyme: *Some things are bulky, and some things won't paste; so I'll shove 'em in here, and they won't go to waste;* or the equally saccharine *I come home with travel junk up to my ears, so here's where I'm parking my best souvenirs.*

Published the same year as Mary Dorman's *Snip 'N Tuck, My Graduation* includes rhyming directions for a REDUCING DIET, not for the owner but for the book itself, clearly based on the assumption that the book will overflow without some actionable suggestions for editorial control. Advice is given in verse: *Many pictures pasted in it (pictures of classmates, pictures of beaux) can fatten your book so it just won't close.* Perforated pages are thus included to allow for "thinning" the book and thereby avoiding this unseemly condition. It's a functional suggestion, although the tone here reads today as rather more patronizing than persuasive.

As the domestic mindset had dominated the purview of most Victorian-era women, memory books at midcentury often reflected the ideals of the aspiring homemaker. *My Graduation* is punctuated with detailed illustrations of flatware style, replacing the more classic scrapbook convention of inspirational quotes or ornamental flourishes. As if to further emphasize the exalted value of domestic achievement, the owner of one such book later reviewed and annotated the photographs in it, so that each classmate's marital status was duly recorded. Her own ambition is listed proudly, too: *Housewife.*

"HIM" BOOK

From this day on I'll keep complete
A record of all the boys I meet
Because among them there may be
The one who'll mean the world to me.

His PICTURE goes here

ABOVE AND RIGHT
Date Data
Mary Dorman
1949

FAR RIGHT
Snip 'N Tuck
Mary Dorman
1959

BELOW
My Him Book
C. R. Gibson and Co.
Undated

ABOVE AND LEFT
"Him" Book
Printed in Japan
Undated

Bound in wood and filled with preprinted pages of elegant silhouettes (intended as placeholders until the real thing came along), this understated book allowed for multiple listings—an editorial convention sure to have helped formalize the creepy art of stalking.

His name is
His nickname is
I met him at
He seems to be
He lives at

His name is
His nickname is
I met him at
He seems to be
He lives at

His name is
His nickname is
I met him at
He seems to be
He lives at

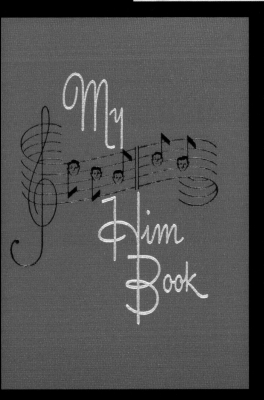

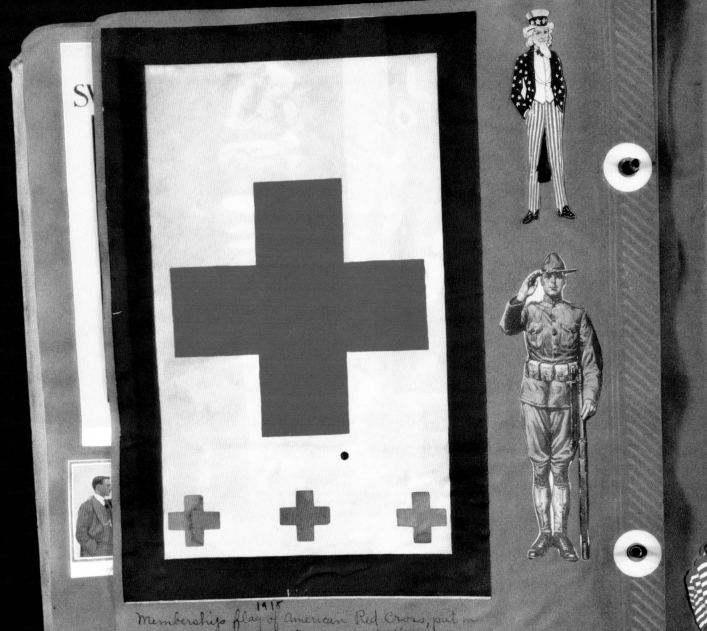

SW...

Membership flag of American Red Cross, put in
the window to show that parties living there were members.
Each small red cross for an individual subscription. *1918*

Wounds Bound Up *1923*

The departure of the Yankee detachment from Coblenz brought sadness to the community, not rejoicing. So far as concerned these soldiers and the Germans among whom they have lived since the beginning of the occupation, the war is over and its wounds are healed.

The experience is not unique in American history. Our youth are adaptive. They have a national gayety and carefree habit that break down sullenness and resentment and racial antipathies. Long ago, in the time that seems dim and shadowy to most of us, American soldiers left Mexico while folk they had but lately fought loaded them with gifts as sincere tokens of regard. The several armies of occupation in Cuba, whatever the politically minded Cubans may have thought of them, always won to the secret places of the hearts of the masses.

The great lesson of the stay at Coblenz is that if we would have it that way the bitterness of war lasts but a little hour. While the struggle continued, Germans and Americans hated one another with a passion equal to that of enmities among society women at Washington—which is saying a great deal if press correspondents tell their tales truthfully. The Germans felt we had invited ourselves into a fight which was not ours. Americans were stirred to violent anger against the submarine warfare, the inhumanities of militarism and the impudent assumptions of kaiserism. These feelings fade more and more as the months pass. They will become in years ahead of us as incapable of reawakening as those animosities which obtained between the United States and Spain nearly a generation ago.

The nations of the earth have to live together. They will live happily with one another only if they will have made some effort to forget the days they have quarreled and fought. It is a matter of congratulation for Americans that their force on the Rhine has done more than most of us thought possible to bind up the wounds of the war.

OLD GLORY'S ADIE... TO RHINE SPREA... CLOAK OF SAD...

BY WYTHE WILLIAMS.

Special Correspondence of The Toledo Blade and The Philadelphia Public Ledger.

Coblenz, Jan. 1?—The last time t... the Stars and Stripes on the Rhine ... will be solemnized this week when ... two men chosen from a Guard who fought at Chateau Thierry will lower the colors.

For more than four years the... Glory has been waving from a ... staff on the highest buttress of the ancient Ehrenbreitstein fortress over the head of the colossal statue of William I seated on his charger at the confluence of the Rhine and Moselle—facing the Rhine.

Only Replacing Flag

In a hundred years the American flag is the only one which has ever replaced the German banner on this historic spot. It has dominated the town and the country for miles around. Although the colors of conquerors the flag stands for something very different in the minds of the Rhine people. They have grown to look up to Old Glory on the bare staff as a symbol of what they have learned by experience stands for right and justice. They seem in no hurry to have it taken away from them.

THE WAR IS OVER

"The war is over!" so they said
When I recalled the days of pain,
The struggles and the blood they shed
That liberty might here remain.

"The war is over!" they replied,
"That happened four long years ago!"
Four years ago our brothers died,
Four years since we were cheering so!

But yesterday there passed along
A soldier with a missing limb.
The war is history for the throng,
But it's a lingering war with him.

The war is over! Now and then
I shudder when I hear the phrase,
Thinking of all the battered men
For whom it has no closing days.

Christmas of Peace; First in Nine Years
1922

London, Dec. 2?—Monday will be the first Christmas in nine years when war was not being waged in some part of the world. For four years the World War waged over Christmas time. Then came the war in Russia against the Bolsheviki and still later the war between Greece and Turkey.

SERVICE STAMPS

These stamps upon your letters ...
To all the world will say,
"I'm proud because my loved o...
Serves Uncle Sam today...

10-572   Patented November 6, 1917

Pershing Scrapbook
Toledo, OH
1917

Cover (*above*) and page
(*opposite*) from a large
scrapbook made by Jessie
Pershing for her uncle,
General John Pershing,
during World War I.

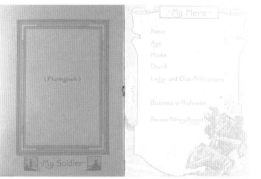

ABOVE AND LEFT
My Soldier
Magruder Bank Co.
Port Clinton, OH
1917

Given out as a promotional
item by a local bank in
Chicago, this blank book
was provided to soldiers
and their families during
World War I.

CHAPTER XIV
ARTICLES OF WAR

ticle of War provides:

'AIN ARTICLES TO BE READ AND EXPLAINED.'—Arti-
54 to 96, inclusive, and 104 to 109, inclusive, shall
ained to every soldier at the time of his enlist-
in, or within six days thereafter, and shall be
ed once every six months to the soldiers of
regiment, or company in the service of the

ticles of War of interest to Soldiers

FINITIONS.—The following words when used in
ll be construed in the sense indicated in this
e context shows that a different sense is in-

"officer" shall be construed to refer to a com-

ABOVE
Day Scrapbook
Staunton, VA
1921

Richard S. Day was a
young cadet at Staunton
Academy whose scrapbook
includes rescued bullets,
cartridges, and a piece
of belting from his dress
coat. Founded just before
the Civil War, Staunton
Academy closed in 1976.

Such books were not aimed so much at
graduates as at postgraduates, many of whom, in
the years after World War II, set their sights on
marriage as a career. But housewives weren't the
only scrapbook enthusiasts to make records of
their own, as well as their peers', achievements:
another key demographic target in this publishing market was the soldier.

The sobering palette for *My Soldier* is typical
of the kinds of scrapbooks that were produced
during World War I. Framed by an art nouveau
border that loosely recalls a scroll configuration,
each page is flanked by small illustrations of
heroic men in uniform. Distributed as a promotional item, it bears none of the jargon that would
emerge in many later advertising premiums, and
it is devoid of the kind of gimmickry, slapstick,
and buffoonery that characterized these later
books. And there's something chilling about it
as a result: both FIRST FIGHT and FIRST TIME
UNDER FIRE amplify the terrifying novelty of the
first-time soldier. Pages allocated for these events

suggest that the soldier managed to persevere
under attack, proceeding to record the date, if not
the attendant emotions that followed. Yet whereas
scrapbooks produced before and during World
War I manifest a distinct seriousness of purpose,
those made during World War II are for the most
part extraordinarily different in tone.

By the late 1930s, scrapbooks were more
commonplace both at home and abroad. Nevertheless, publishers provided extensive instructions
for producing a scrapbook: at once infantilizing

(use large picture to begin the story!) and ludicrous (fill book with cartoons if story runs short!), these sorts of didactic primer-style directives on graphic design persisted throughout the war and well beyond. Some publishers took the direct approach, providing humorless, no-nonsense instructions intended to facilitate the act of recording one's experience of military life. And at least one publisher appears to have engaged in some actual, if minimal, market research. "Snaps and Scraps has been developed in accordance with personal views and preferences of men in the services," notes one. "The most decided preference was for a pocket to file the clippings, photos, letters from home and miscellaneous material … the book was also purposely designed with a flexible cover to permit rolling of the book, if so desired." In a somewhat paradoxical, yet liberating, editorial intervention, the publishers of this volume "purposely omitted numerous sub-headings on the white sheets to enable you to enter your own data, as the occasion may require." How, after all, can one begin to anticipate—let alone design a memory book for—the kinds of unknowable eventualities awaiting the soldier?

Pressed for time, concerned for their future, worried about forgetting (or worse, about remembering), midcentury soldiers used a peculiar subgenre of memory books which are almost unbearably cheerful. Here, goofy headings (HIGH LIGHTS AND FURLOUGHS) mask what would likely have been much more complex, even turbulent recollections, resulting in what was, in retrospect, a virtual epidemic of nostalgic amnesia. Publishers thus reframed memory as fiction, trading veteran dysphoria for a kind of plucky optimism. Such books ultimately succeeded in

conjuring personal histories that were perhaps less pernicious than reality but probably palatable—even if they weren't, in the end, actually very personal at all.

The soldier was also handicapped by what would clearly have been a scarcity of materials—paste and scissors, for example—which further diminished any chance for artistic innovation. Even scrapbooks like *G-I've Been Around*, marketed to the soldier after his return home, imposed a kind of editorial shove in the right direction by including detailed maps and battle chronologies to assist in reconstructing one's tour of duty.

The inclusion of copious space for listing detailed activity in wartime did little to lessen the otherwise goofy spirit of many scrapbooks from this era. While overtly fawning in their praise of the steadfast soldier, these books were punctuated with cartoon spot illustrations and given comical titles to diminish an otherwise sober topic: memories of the war. For better or worse, cartoons of smiling soldiers dipping oversized brushes into gargantuan paste pots lend a happy-go-lucky tone to what is, otherwise, a potentially grim bit of human history.

His Service Record was an oversized, hardbound memory book that interspersed wartime chronologies with blank pages. Published in 1942, it was described as "a book for which many have long felt a need, a book that will become increasingly valuable with age." Rare was the soldier who filled everything in—and when entries were made, they were brief and perfunctory.

Francis "Pop" Johnson's copy of the *Service Record* includes a host of memorabilia—from his dog tags to his discharge papers—and only briefly hints at the actual human response to

ABOVE AND INSET
G-I've Been Around
C. S. Hammond and Co.
1945

My Buddy Book

ME THE GUY MY FRIENDS KNOW

Some of My NEW FRIENDS

JUST A FEW *Pleasant Memories*

My Dates

OFFICER'S *I know*

ENLISTED MEN I KNOW

Cadre MEN

GUYS ON MY "GOOD" LIST

GUYS ON MY *Other* LIST

Snaps

My Buddy Book
Stationers Specialty Corp.
1942

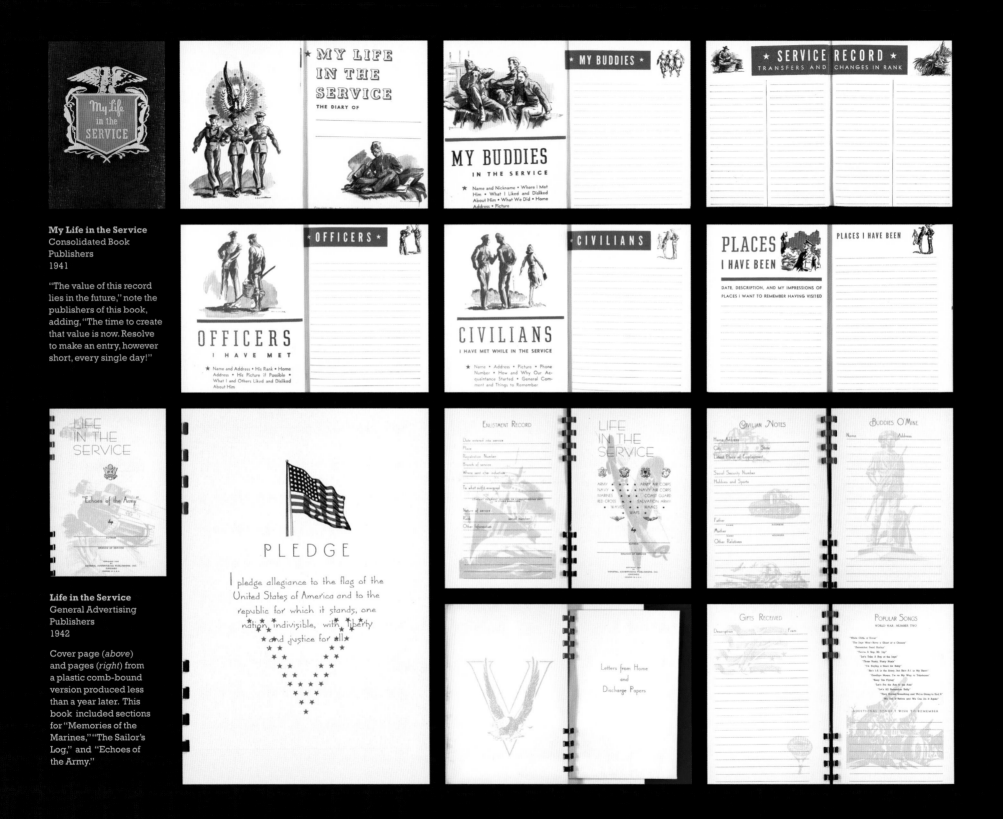

My Life in the Service
Consolidated Book
Publishers
1941

"The value of this record lies in the future," note the publishers of this book, adding, "The time to create that value is now. Resolve to make an entry, however short, every single day!"

Life in the Service
General Advertising
Publishers
1942

Cover page (*above*) and pages (*right*) from a plastic comb-bound version produced less than a year later. This book included sections for "Memories of the Marines," "The Sailor's Log," and "Echoes of the Army."

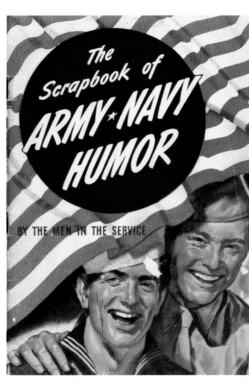

RIGHT
His Service Record
Stevens, Inc.
1942

USO Scrapbook
USO National Woman's
Committee
Undated

BELOW
Victory Scrapbook
Saalfield Publishing Co.
1942

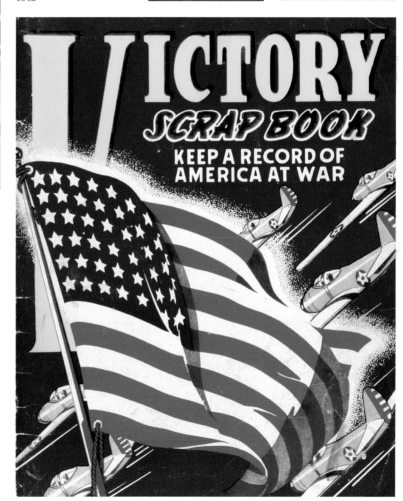

war. Noting the purpose of one furlough in 1943, Johnson writes: *Father died and I arrived home day after funeral — but father was held until I got here and seen him in the funeral parlor home.* Later, on a brief home leave, he notes: *Jack McSherry and I both home for 15 days. Perhaps, the last.* Was Johnson reflecting on his last furlough? Or did he assume that given the likelihood of battle, he might in fact lose his life prematurely?

As it happened, Johnson did indeed survive the war: he married, returned to his hometown of Waterbury, Connecticut, and worked for more than thirty years as a fireman before losing his battle with Parkinson's disease sometime in the early 1980s.[14] At the time of his death, he was in his early sixties, divorced and childless: little wonder, then, that his scrapbook went missing for nearly a quarter century, only to surface on the West Coast, whereupon it was sold online at auction.

His Service Record
Hickory Publishing Co.
1942

**The Scrapbook of Army
Navy Humor**
Texcel Tape Co.
1943

Snaps and Scraps
Feldco Loose Leaf Co.
1942

Designed in keeping with the needs of the itinerant soldier, *Snaps and Scraps* included an editorial disclaimer in its pages. Note the editors: "The size is not large enough to be cumbersome in the limited storage space available to service men."

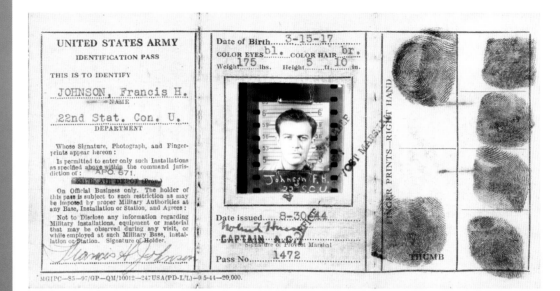

A small notice in the Waterbury newspaper soon yielded inquiries from Johnson's relatives, several of whom had no idea he ever kept a scrapbook. And here, a chronicle of his wartime odyssey—a journey that took him to China, India, and Burma in addition to multiple destinations throughout continental Europe—was soon rediscovered in the pages of his long-ago scrapbook.

Over the course of nearly a quarter of a century, memory books grew in steady popularity because they so radically simplified the process of self-reflection: they were graphic enablers, turning scrapbooks into prescriptive vessels for stockpiling our stuff. However subtly, they invoked an editorial upper hand through what eventually became a kind of generic paradigm for authentication, resulting in what were, in the end, much more controlled exercises in autobiography—and much less compelling explorations of the self. With more sophisticated packaging, easier access to picture taking, and more copious exposure to color printing, scrapbooks by the early 1960s began to mirror overtly the production values of printers and publishers. While they remained popu-

lar, they become less personal and idiosyncratic, less freewheeling and expository—and much less striking as visual artifacts. With the advent of television came a new age, unprecedented in its visual distractions—an era framed by the hyperreality of Technicolor movies, Madison Avenue packaging, and perhaps more than anything else, the incomparable visual grip of broadcast television. The outside world was brought inside, and our relationship with that world—with public figures, with politicians, and with purveyors of fashion, style, and news of all kinds—was no longer so distant as it had been when it existed only on the radio, in a black-and-white newspaper, or in our imaginations.[15]

By the 1970s, nostalgia was once again perceived as a negative cultural force, representing "collective ignorance and the manipulation of innocence."[16] Not surprisingly, scrapbooks produced after midcentury routinely aspired to the color-saturated, pop sensibilities of this new age. The golden age of the scrapbook, which had been for nearly half a century a vehicle for willful, formal self-expression, was over.

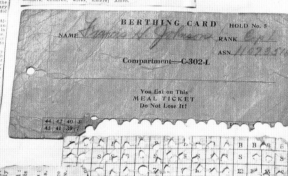

Yanks Back On Soil Of France

(By The Associated Press)

American troops again are fighting in western Europe—on the soil of France—in large numbers for the first time in nearly 26 years.

A few weeks ago, the American... raid, but only as adjunct to larger British and Canadian units.

In that other war, the so-called World war which since has had added to its title to distinguish it from the present greater conflict, the American war effort was, in a sense, just getting started when the shooting stopped.

There were two million Americans in France when the armistice was signed, but only about 750,000 served on the fighting front. Two million more were in preparation for early departure for France. Compared with those of the other major powers, American casualties were light: 37,000 killed; 12,000 mortally wounded, and 193,700 wounded who recovered. Other powers numbered their casualties in seven figures.

Historians of World war I have called the American contribution more moral, industrial and financial than military.

Yet, had that war continued as much as another year, the United States would have had in the field the greatest army of any nation.

As it was, the American contribution on the battlefields such as Chateau Thierry, the Meuse-Argonne, St. Mihiel and many others was a force to be reckoned with.

Allies Only On Small Part Of German Soil

The London Times history of the war called the American military effort "as incomplete but splendid fragment."

When the fighting ended, the Allies at no point were on German soil except for a small section in the southeast corner of Lorraine which then was part of Germany but which later was restored to France.

The final battle line ran roughly from the Dutch border south through Belgium to a point just west of Ghent, southeast to the French border of Roeren, southeast along the Meuse river east of Verdun to Thionville, then along the Lorraine border, taking in the Steinbach, Thann and Altkirch districts of Lorraine, and reaching the Swiss border directly south of Altkirch. The armistice provided for Allied occupation of Germany up to the left bank of the Rhine, with a "neutral zone" on the right bank excepting Mayence, Coblenz and Cologne on the right bank.

Except for this peaceable and comparatively brief postwar occupation of a small section of Germany, the Reich proper never felt the impact of an invading army. This time the story promises to be different.

President's Invasion Prayer

Washington, June 6—(AP)—This is the invasion prayer which President Roosevelt wrote while Allied troops were landing on the coast of France and which he will read to the nation by radio at 10 p. m. tonight:

My fellow Americans:

In this poignant hour, I ask you to join me in prayer.

Almighty God: Our sons, pride of our nation, this day have set upon a mighty endeavor, a struggle to preserve our republic, our religion, and our civilization, and to set free a suffering humanity.

Lead them straight and true; give strength to their arms, stoutness to their hearts, steadfastness in their faith.

They will need Thy blessings. Their road will be long and hard. For the enemy is strong. He may hurl back our forces. Success may not come with rushing speed, but we shall return again and again; and we know that by Thy grace, and by the righteousness of our cause, our sons will triumph.

They will be sore tried, by night and by day, without rest—till the victory is won. The darkness will be rent by noise and flame. Men's souls will be shaken with the violences of war.

These are men lately drawn from the ways of peace. They fight not for the lust of conquest. They fight to end conquest. They fight to liberate. They fight to let justice arise, and tolerance and goodwill among all Thy people. They yearn but for the end of battle, for their return to the havens of home.

Some will never return. Embrace these, Father, and receive them, Thy heroic servants, into Thy kingdom.

And for us at home — fathers, mothers, children, wives, sisters, and brothers of brave men overseas, whose thoughts and prayers are ever with them—help us, Almighty God, to rededicate ourselves in renewed faith in Thee in this hour of great sacrifice.

Many people have urged that I call the nation into a single day of special prayer. But because the road is long and the desire is great, I ask that our people devote themselves in a continuance of prayer. As we rise to each new day, and again when each day is spent, let words of prayer be on our lips, invoking Thy help to our efforts.

Give us strength, too—strength in our daily tasks, to redouble the contributions we make in the physical and material support of our armed forces.

And, O Lord, give us faith. Give us faith in Thee; faith in our sons; faith in each other; faith in our united crusade. Let not the keenness of our spirit ever be dulled. Let not the impacts of temporary events of temporal matters of but fleeting moment—let not these deter us in our unconquerable purpose.

With Thy blessing, we shall prevail over the unholy forces of our enemy. Help us to conquer the apostles of greed and racial arrogances. Lead us to the saving of our country, and with our sister nations into a world unity that will spell a sure peace—a peace invulnerable to the schemings of unworthy men. And a peace that will let all men live in freedom, reaping the just rewards of their honest toil.

Thy will be done, Almighty God. Amen.

BERTHING CARD HOLD No. 5

NAME *James A. Johnson* RANK *Cpl.*

ASN *11022576*

Compartment—C-302-L

You Eat on This
MEAL TICKET
Do Not Lose It!

OMP. NO. C-4

BOAT DRILL STA. NO. 12

Here is a list of "some of the information to make an orderly, permanent record of right now, before you are even in a year a..."
Separation Center ; Date.
(2) Army Serial Number.
Selective Service information. Local Board Number, Induction Place.
(3) Highest Rank attained.
(4) Date of entry into service. Place. Branch of service.
(5) Insurance information. Date and amount of policy. Amount of monthly premium.
(6) Army schools attended ; Place. Date. Subjects studied.
(7) Battles and Campaigns ; Decorations and citations ; Service Dates. Place.
Hospitalization ; Service wounds. Injuries. Place. Dates. Social Security Number.

Berneau

Gang in...

"Were I an American as I am an Englishman, while a foreign troop was landed in my country I never would lay down my arms, never! never! never!"
— WILLIAM PITT

Page Eleven

The memory book, beholden to its structure, has soldiered on nevertheless and remains popular even today. It is, however, perhaps fair to say that as a category, these books tend to read less as autobiographical narratives than as grab bags of achievement conveniently retrofitted into prefabricated rubrics. (Arguably—by virtue of the generic categories offered in these books—every bride is the same bride, every soldier is the same soldier, and every baby, measured by the barometer of memory-book milestones, is the same baby.) But in the hands of artists and poets, the scrapbook embraces new territory. Memories conflate, reposition themselves, diffuse and are recaptured, only to be brilliantly juxtaposed in some whimsical form on the page. In the case of scrapbooks kept by artists, the structure itself often becomes an integral part of the story. Saul Steinberg kept a scrapbook in an alphabetical ledger which he filled with recipes—beginning with A for APPETIZERS—and thereby initiating a system that, were logic to prevail, would be expected to play itself out: B for BREADS, C for CAKES, D for DESSERTS, and so on. Not so in Steinberg's case, where, having reeled the gullible reader into the promise of alphabetical fulfillment, he immediately violates the very system he imposed, proceeding methodically from APPETIZERS to SOUPS to LUNCH to SALADS to POTATOES to VEAL to CHICKEN to EGGS. It's a joyous, if jumbled, lexicon of saved material: just like Steinberg's visual wit, the organizational slippage here is just off-kilter enough to make you look twice. Memory, in this context, comes less from buying into the engineered system than from the discordant recollection: the less it fits in neatly, the more you remember it as a result.

Jane Collom, the first wife of experimental filmmaker Stan Brakhage, kept majestically dense scrapbooks in the 1950s and 1960s that are, in both content and structure, perhaps inversely proportional to the compartmentalized memory books of the same period. The couple's creative collaboration is reflected in pages overflowing with love letters, drawings by their children, notes, photographs, and an odd assemblage of extraneous objects (moth wings, blades of grass), densely interwoven into large, thick paperback volumes that more closely resemble telephone directories than personal albums. Fragments of film footage (Brakhage shot with Super-8, which was long and skinny, about half an inch thick) are taped in also: one of the hallmarks of his later work was that he drew right onto the film emulsion, etching into the actual surface of the celluloid. It is as if the making of the scrapbook is inextricably linked to life itself—to the family, to the garden, to work in the studio—and the book resonates with the textures of that rich and ultimately uneditable experience.[7] If nostalgia is a hypochondria of the

ABOVE
Saul Steinberg Papers
1953

A cryptic collage about Napoleon Bonaparte (and several insects) on top of a page of diagrams.

RIGHT AND OPPOSITE
Brakhage Family Scrapbook
Rollinsville, CO
1960s

Some forty years later, Collom described these scrapbooks as "a record of a dynamic moment in one generation of artists, a generation that dared to have families, even though many of the older artists warned against it."

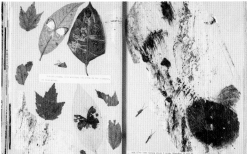

The mission of woman on earth !

to give birth

For the blessings

of a man

In act.

And more fair than the flowers, more fresh than the

First leaped into life,

Long enlighten'd

in his face

at my side ;

did the sun

Love   He

the children

and to your eyes

hands,

man

O Nature,

is power !

all things exist

At the sight

Life

Yes,

Of a land

on earth.

The mission of genius on earth !

the sight,

perceived,

A power

have need of for life.

Still the vision is there :

The mission of genius :

Hark ! the sight

the music,

beauty,

to look at her

may bring

that vision

a miracle !)—

eyes the pure

hand,

with wings

at least

rise

he found

In his hand,

the child

he bless'd

Of light

we see it at last,

love includes all loves,

we love.   We can

Spread your arms, O

To your eyes,

I come !

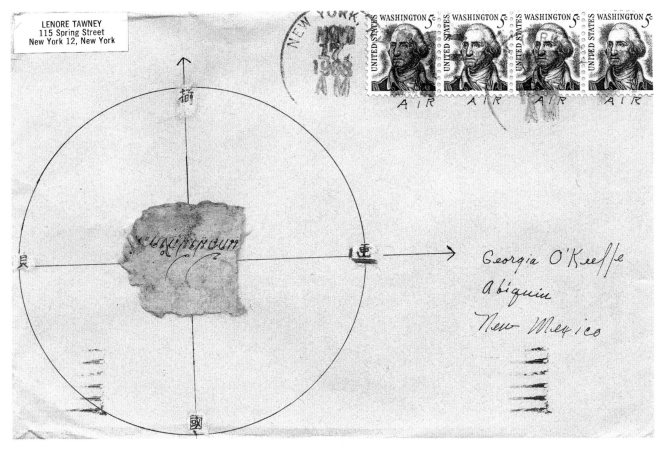

Letters to Georgia O'Keeffe
Lenore Tawney
1960s

heart, then it is the celebration of that affliction that resonates here, in these deeply layered pages produced during what were some of the filmmaker's most artistically fertile years. The relationship between a scrapbook and a filmmaker is a fascinating one, as both benefit from a kind of basic synesthesia, or at the very least, a curiosity and willingness to embrace the page of the scrapbook as one would a portion of a film—which is to say without preconceptions about rules, order, or chronology.

Here, another aspect of nostalgia becomes startlingly clear. The notion of challenging chronological time would become a fundamental hallmark of modernism, recasting the notion of material recollection as something decidedly more abstract. The experimental evidence of this new kind of thinking is magnificently demonstrated in scrapbooks kept by poets for whom the suggestion of memory was perhaps less a function of the duty-bound diarist and more a sort of chance operation produced from a kit of parts. William S. Burroughs used what he termed "cutups"—literally, word collages—as a kind of freeform poetry. (*Cut the word lines and you will hear their voices,* he once wrote.) He became obsessed with the subliminal, even supernatural meanings of his collages, but his attachment to words in general—and to newsprint in particular (cutting up the newspaper, he believed, mobilized form against content)—inspired densely crafted pages with great beauty and texture.[18] But the notion of reading and making sense of one's world while armed with scissors was not Burroughs' invention: "The habit of reading with a pair of scissors in my hand has stood me in good stead for much of my literary work," observed Louisa May Alcott.[19]

What is interesting about scrapbooks made by artists is that collaged recollections and composite messages rarely require a scrapbook to find form. Fiber artist Lenore Tawney's letters to Georgia O'Keeffe are compositions crafted from paper

debris, and while they might sooner be classified as mail art, they capture the kind of visual immediacy that characterizes the scrapbooks of Brakhage and others. Made from limited means, they are elusive snapshots of a moment preserved.

Even more unusual are the scrapbooks made by photographers, who crop, reposition, sequence, and amplify their visual observations through the addition of other materials. Rarer still is the photojournalist who chooses to document the world around him through such media, building a visual lexicon through layers of torn paper, fragments of masking tape, select pieces of political propaganda, and more. Created between 1985 and his untimely death in 1993, Dan Eldon's journals brilliantly interweave words and pictures (many, if not most taken by him) of his adventures throughout Africa. In a prescient gesture that seemed almost to anticipate the blurred boundaries of digital media, Eldon left behind a stunning body of work:

Eldon Journals
Mogadishu, Somalia
1985–1993

Filled with ephemera including assorted newspaper clippings, photographs, and even grains of rice, Dan Eldon's scrapbooks represent one person's remarkable journey across more than forty countries. Eldon, who kept these journals from the time he was a teenager, was killed in Mogadishu, Somalia, in the summer of 1993. He was twenty-three years old.

THE FABULOUS POODLES

Coffey Self Books
Various locations
1970s–1990s

Brian Coffey studied printing, establishing his own press, Advent Books, which published limited editions of poetry with a special emphasis on typography and cover design. His self books combine journal and scrapbook, and testify to one poet's enduring interest in word as image.

The Irish poet Brian Coffey, a robust chronicler of the everyday, began, on his seventy-first birthday, to compile what he called *Self Books*—which he saw not so much as repositories for recollection but as beginnings *for my wife, my children, my grandchildren and those who come after them in the succession—as much of what I see as can be reasonably expressed in words, if the time available—how long? allows.* Through the books themselves, which Coffey would keep until his death in 1995, he experimented with collecting, collaging, and a fractured narrative, created and annotated, redacted, painted, torn, captioned—and regrettably, unfinished.

These sorts of experimental constructions occasionally surface in the journals kept by poets, particularly for those who view language as highly visual, even tangible. Working piecemeal like H.D., Stan Brakhage, and others, he constructed makeshift collages from whatever means he had at his disposal. The resulting volumes are unedited and haphazard, with taped-over annotations and no shortage of impulsive, hand-scrawled opinion. The covers of his books are equally striking because they capture a lack of pretense that resonates throughout the self books themselves.

Such books remind us that the construction of memory owes perhaps more to randomness and chance than to reconstructed logic. Rather than bowing to the obligatory timeline favored by chronological time, or abiding by the dutiful rhythms imposed by episodic time, twentieth-century memory books came to thrive on the mercurial temperament and willful abstractions of their owners. Through war and recovery, amid chaos and change, one truth remained startlingly undisputed: however distant it might appear, death was, for all of us, an inevitable consequence. To this end, we would all continue to question who we were and where we might, ultimately, be headed.

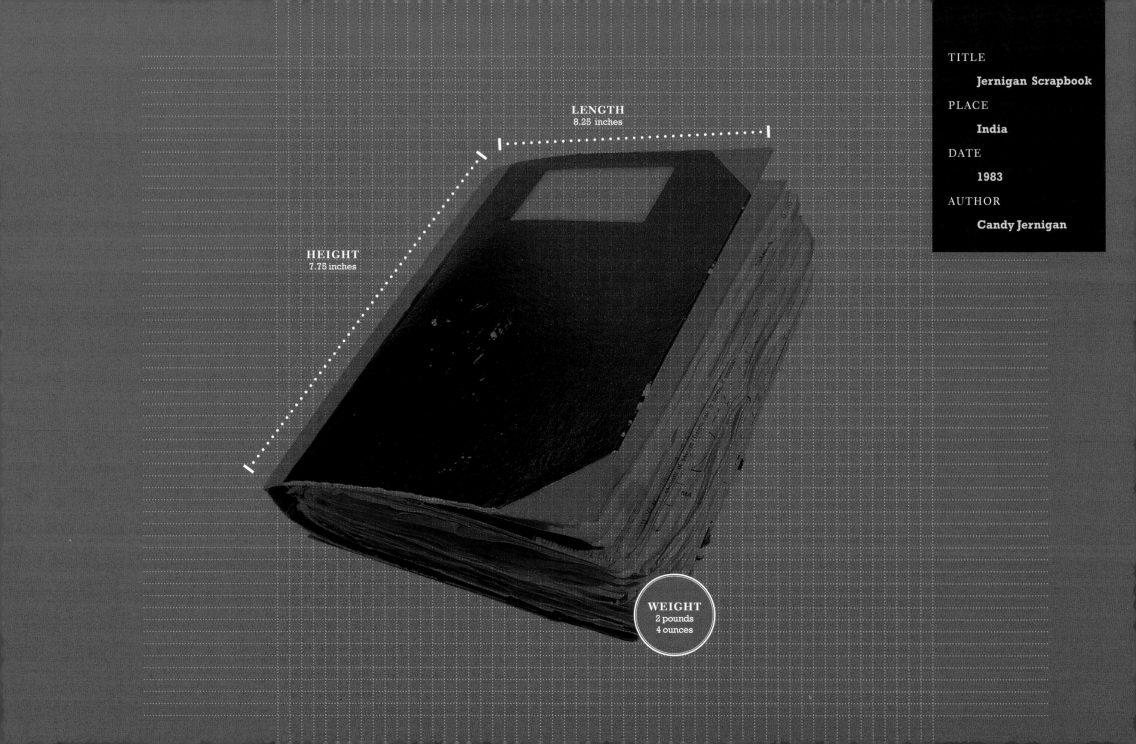

LENGTH
8.25 inches

HEIGHT
7.75 inches

WEIGHT
2 pounds
4 ounces

TITLE
Jernigan Scrapbook
PLACE
India
DATE
1983
AUTHOR
Candy Jernigan

JERNIGAN SCRAPBOOK

TRAVEL JOURNAL, INDIA, 1983

No 6

Cheruthuruthi

1 10 km It is situated at 3 km from Shoranur Railway
Junction on Trichur-Shoranur Road The famous poet
and scholar Vallathol set up Kerala Kalamandalam
here in 1930 for the revival of Kerala art forms.

Accommodation Govt Guest House Tariff Single
Rs 16 Double Rs 21 Reservations Manager.

PWD Rest House Tariff Single Rs 4 Double Rs 6
Reservations District Collector Trichur

Roof Thatch Kalamandalam School.

Flowers.
KATIKHALI

Beads
KATIKHALI

Beads.
Kalamandalam School.

From the fabulous KATIKHALI performance at the Kalamandalam School.

Max. Price Rs 0.71
Plus Local Taxes
Kerala
Sandalwood Soap
Made in India

Soap Package.
Government House
CHERUTHURUTHI.

Soap: Government House.

At the Gov't Guest House, we have an Indian-style shower which consists of a big bucket (for holding water), a small bucket (for pouring), and a wooden slab to squat on. After tea and "a wash" we are served a beautiful chicken in coconut with English style vegetables (over-boiled) + fresh fruit. Then on to the KATIKHALI.

Thatch.
Kalamandalam School.

Indian Airplane Glue.   Hibiscus.   Oleander.

The stewardesses
hand out pre-flight sweets.

A visiting dignitary
feted at the airport.

DEC 31 1983

8 AM – Breakfast

Puri Baji, Masala Dosai and
the wonderful South Indian
coffee... feeling better.

12:30 PM
Lunch near Mahabalipuram

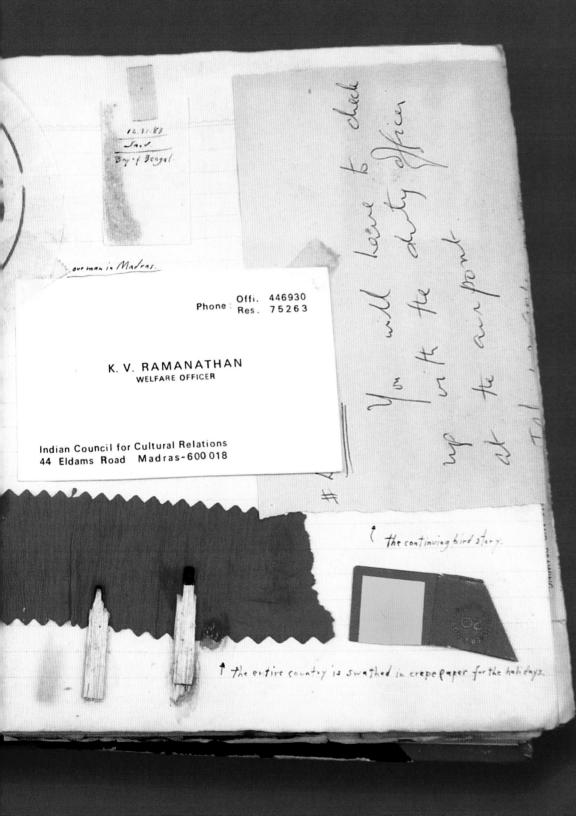

12.31.83
Sat.
Bay of Bengal.

our man in Madras.

Phone : Offi. 446930
        Res. 75263

K. V. RAMANATHAN
WELFARE OFFICER

Indian Council for Cultural Relations
44 Eldams Road   Madras-600 018

You will have to check
in to the duty officer
up at the airport
at Tel...

the continuing bird story.

↑ the entire country is swathed in crepe paper for the holidays.

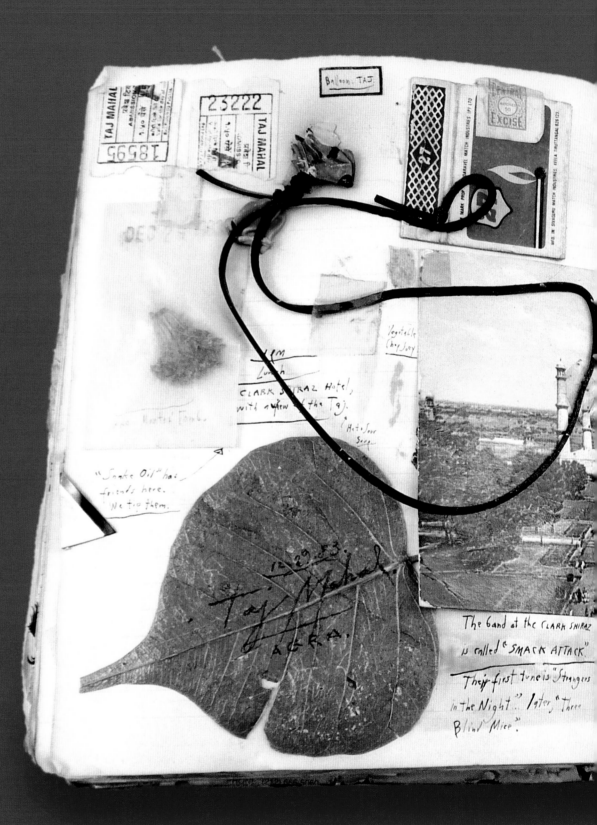

Once a magnificent Mughal capital, Agra is renowned for the Taj Mahal, one of the seven wonders of the world. This exquisite mausoleum stands eloquent witness to Emperor Shah Jahan's immortal love for his wife, Mumtaz Mahal.

Tameric tree outside the Taj.

DEC 29 1983

Model Fort
TAJ MAHAL.

Agra also has other historic monuments of great beauty—the tomb of Akbar at Sikandra, with its vaulted gateway and curious structural design; that jewel in stone, the mausoleum of Itmad-ud-Daulah; the massive Agra Fort; and nearby Fatehpur Sikri, the abandoned city of red sandstone.

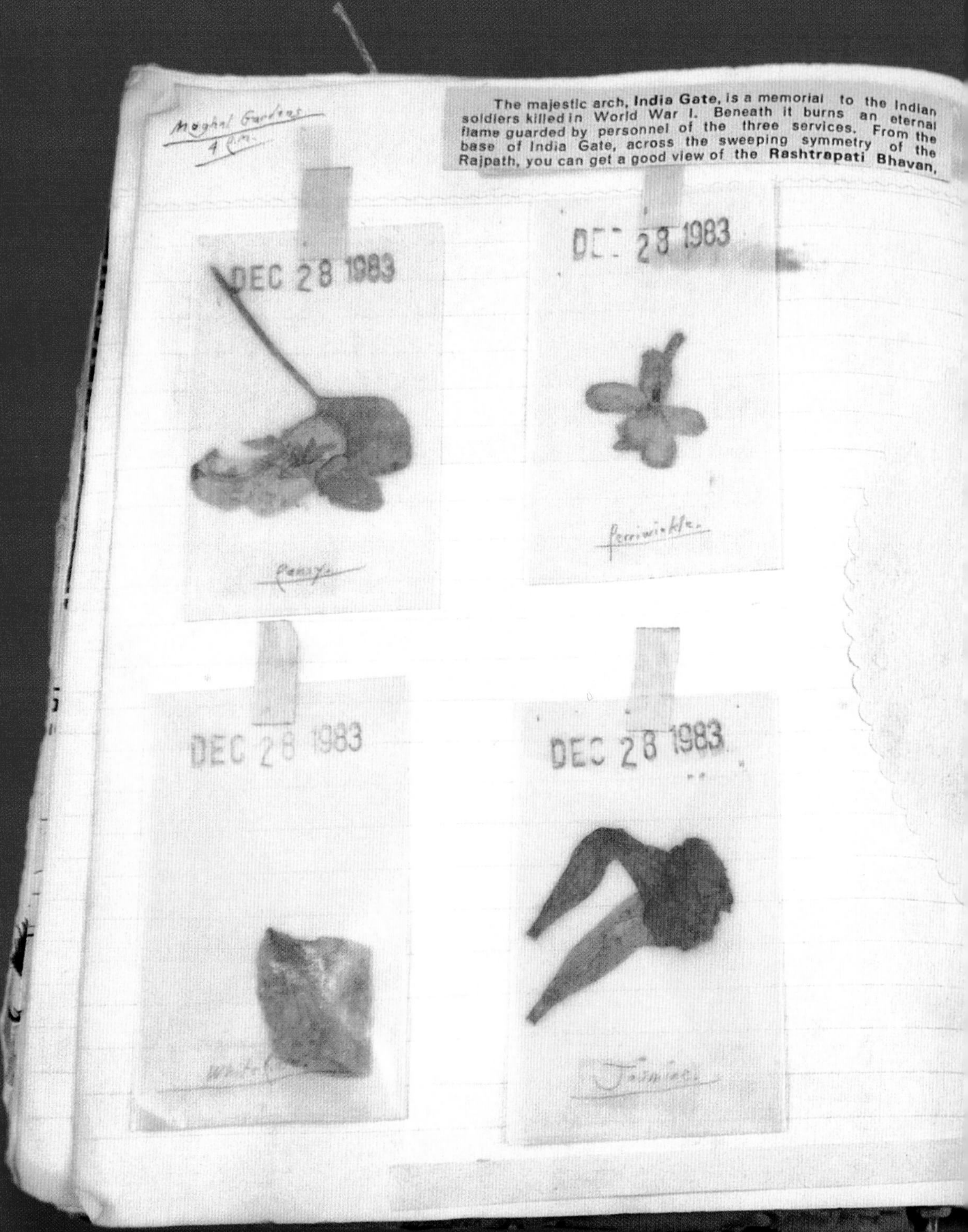

Moghul Gardens
4 cm.

DEC 28 1983

Pansy

DEC 28 1983

Perriwinkle

DEC 28 1983

White Rose

DEC 28 1983

Jasmine

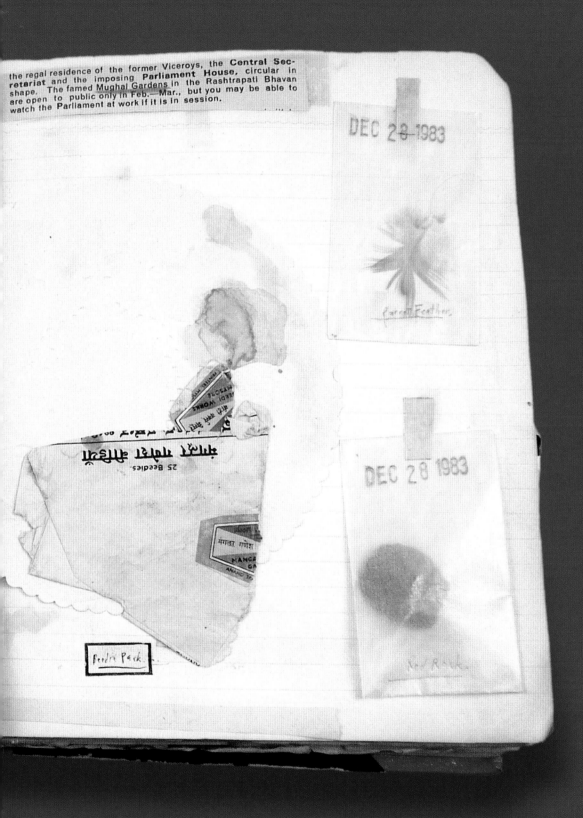

the regal residence of the former Viceroys, the **Central Sec-**
retariat and the imposing **Parliament House**, circular in
shape. The famed Mughal Gardens in the Rashtrapati Bhavan
are open to public only in Feb.—Mar., but you may be able to
watch the Parliament at work if it is in session.

DEC 28 1983

DEC 28 1983

25 Beedies

Parrot Feathers

Feedit Pack

Rat Rock

Settling the hotel bill.

$15=00
HH7-00
68.00

37848   4481
5428   7198
1416   5428
44692*   17107*

one half of a penny

प्रवेश पत्र
ए-300

BOARDING PASS
Airbus A-300

IC 402 26/12

Parry's

SPECIALLY WRAPPED FOR
Indian Airlines

Parry's

पीछे
Rear

सीट SEAT

35 A

अंडियन एयरलाइन्स
Indian Airlines

प्रवेश पत्र
एयरबस ए-300

BOARDING PASS
Airbus A-300

उड़ान/दिनांक
Flight/Date IC 402 26/12

प्रवेश
Entrance

पीछे
Rear

सीट SEAT

35 B

इंडियन एयरलाइन्स
Indian Airlines

Cotton
Wool

CALCUTTA → DELHI.

for the ears.

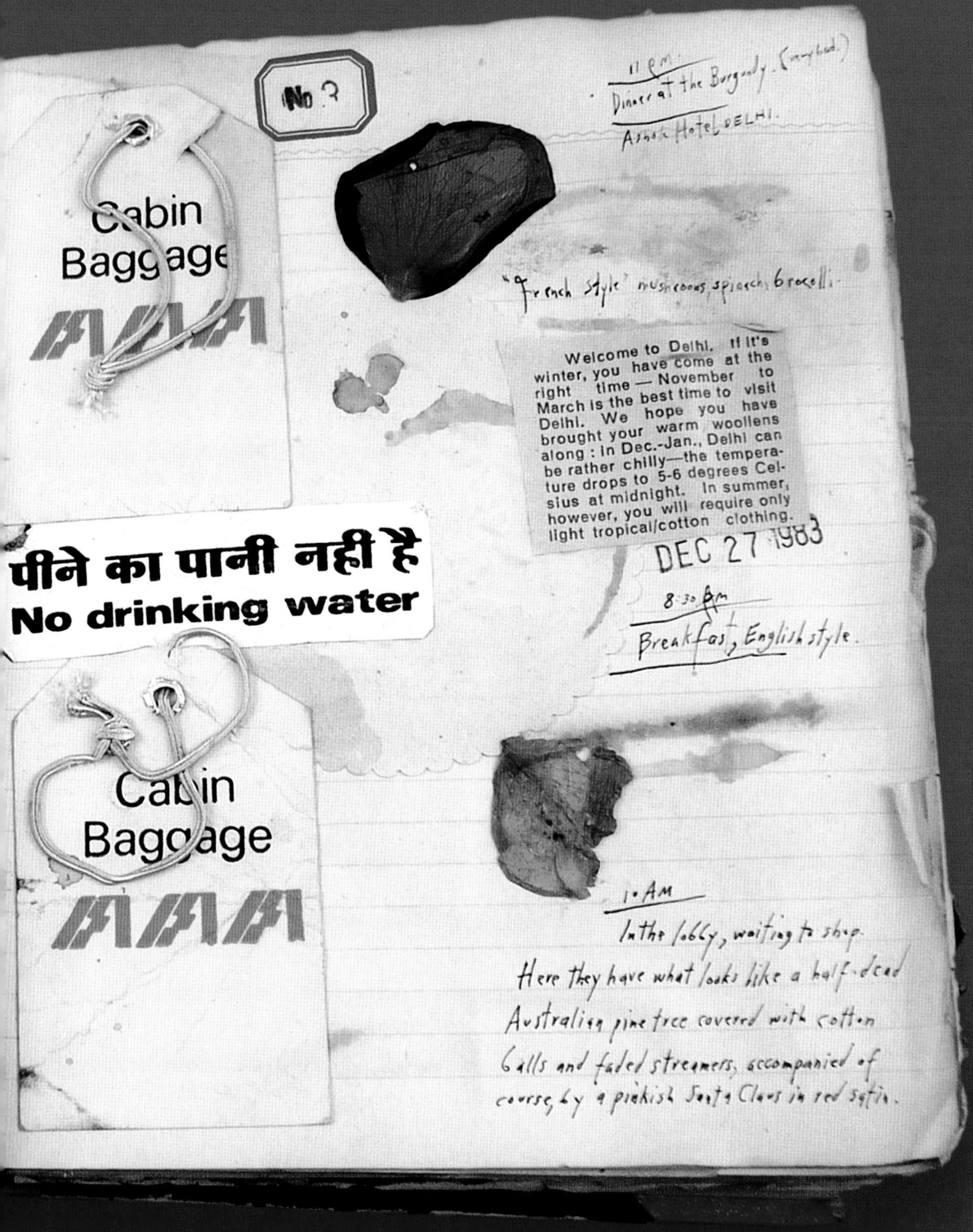

Cabin
Baggage

11 p.m.
Dinner at the Burgundy. (anyhow.)
Ashok Hotel DELHI.

"French Style" mushrooms, spinach, broccoli.

Welcome to Delhi. If It's
winter, you have come at the
right time — November to
March is the best time to visit
Delhi. We hope you have
brought your warm woollens
along : in Dec.-Jan., Delhi can
be rather chilly—the temperature drops to 5-6 degrees Cel-
sius at midnight. In summer,
however, you will require only
light tropical/cotton clothing.

DEC 27 1983

पीने का पानी नही है
No drinking water

8:30 am
Breakfast, English style.

Cabin
Baggage

10 AM
In the lobby, waiting to shop.
Here they have what looks like a half-dead
Australian pine tree covered with cotton
balls and faded streamers, accompanied of
course, by a pinkish Santa Claus in red satin.

5.30 pm
Taj Mahal Hotel
Bombay
Snacks after the
Prince of Wales Museum.

Our guide tells us
this is Indian junk food.

WE ARE HERE.

BACK BAY
RECLAMATION

BACK BAY

BOMBAY HARBOUR

from the Gandhi Museum in Bombay.

Where Gandhi worked
and slept.

Hanging Gardens
Bombay

12.23.83
Hanging Garden
Bombay.

bougainvillia

hibiscus

To be alive means to live in a world that preceded
one's own arrival and will survive one's departure.

Hannah Arendt

CHAPTER FIVE   POSTERITY

A CENTURY AGO, THE SCRAPBOOK OCCUPIED A central role in Americans' conception of leisure. Over time, personal narratives expanded in tandem with the scope and availability of printed matter, and as the books themselves evolved, so, too, did the kinds of stories we told. At the same time, our efforts reflected certain social, cultural, and economic changes: saving scraps was alternately considered a frugal ("waste not, want not") and educational endeavor; an expression of fidelity, piety, or patriotism; an artistic outlet and an organizational tool. Collage, montage, and assemblage all figured prominently in the scrapbooks of more experimental makers, while many simpler, more conservative chronicles revealed equally poignant, if less surprising, truths about everyday life. For more than a century, the genre brilliantly persisted, framed by the simple fact that scrapbooks were, first and foremost, works of autobiography.

In 1929, Helen Siebenthal, then sixteen years old, wrote about her favorite hobby for the *Los Angeles Times*: she called it scrapbooking. (Hers may be the first recorded use of the word as a gerund: she is also responsible for coining the term "scrapbookism.") "To the seeker, it leads him into new fields, new interest, new knowledge," wrote an enthusiastic Siebenthal. "It is the most interesting hobby there is, the most common, the most profitable."[1] Given that the article was published a mere four months before the stock market crash in October 1929, it is unlikely that her use of the word "profitable" had anything even remotely to do with the economics of her hobby—nor, for that matter, could she have foreseen the enormous commercial market that would emerge, a century later, to support the nation's fastest-growing hobby—but the activity Siebenthal once praised has seen an unprecedented revival in the past ten years.

OPPOSITE
Desk Clock
Hands stopped at 9:04

Acquired following the September 11, 2001 terrorist attacks by the World Trade Center Forensic Recovery Operation, Fresh Kills Landfill, Staten Island.

Martha Stewart Crafts
In-store display
2007

Combining utilitarian tools
(hole punches, scissors)
with eclectic materials,
Martha Stewart Craft's
supplies are in a class by
themselves: meticulously
designed, impeccably
manufactured, they are
also beautifully exhibited
in a variety of retail
environments in stores
nationwide, where they
compete for attention
with scores of other
embellishments (*opposite*)
for aspiring scrapbookers.

Target In-Store Display
2007

Even mainstream retail
environments and big
package stores like Target
sell scrapbook supplies.
Stationers and bookstores
have expanded their
offerings also, in an effort
to keep up with extreme
consumer demand.

Truth be told, today's volumes inhabit a radically different universe. Once personal, the scrapbook has resurfaced as something decidedly more group-oriented, social, and public. The prevalence of the digital photograph has both facilitated and devalued the act of visual documentation: there are more, though not necessarily better, photographs to be had. (Printing out and pasting pictures down rescues them from push-button deletion, but in general does little to ensure a more thoughtful editorial process.) In an age in which communication is routinely expedited by electronic means, memory itself becomes an endangered species: here, the material artifact in general (and the scrapbook in particular) takes on a kind of renewed value. Yet while today's scrapbooks share with their antecedents a profound interest in the visually recorded memory, the similarity ends there. Part creative fiction, part therapeutic contrivance, the twenty-first-century scrapbook has come to represent considerably different values.

And what does it mean, exactly, to "scrapbook"? What was once an allusion to something torn and ephemeral is today considered a craft—and more important, a verb ("to create compilations in albums"). With its own national holiday (May 7) and validated by a nearly $3 billion craft industry, scrapbooking today is a highly gendered activity: there's an almost tribal kind of pageantry to this phenomenon, which is often likened to a quilting bee in its celebration of motherhood, family, and community. Contemporary scrapbook enthusiasts are served by a robust industry of craft fairs, conventions, "scrap-and-spa" retreats, and "cropping cruises." With scrapbooking materials sanctioned by magazines, shared across Web sites, and sold through a dizzying array of merchandising efforts, scrapbook zeitgeist centers on "creating" keepsakes and on "making" memories—distinctive, personal, and unique ones.

Or are they? One of the principal features separating contemporary scrapbooks from those produced a century ago is the extraordinary emphasis placed on new rather than old materials—for whereas early twentieth-century scrapbooks were characterized by the chance vestigial artifact, today's scrapbookers opt for the store-bought one. Known as "embellishments" and including (but not limited to) brads, buttons, die cuts, frames, grommets, hinges, labels, stickers, and a host of specialty papers, such materials are believed to lend a tone of professional polish to the scrapbook, and in so doing, to liberate the maker from the ponderous responsibility of certain visual choices.

Yet while embellishments have come to dominate today's thriving multimillion-dollar scrapbook industry, they have also perhaps unwittingly encouraged the development of a meaningless visual grammar. This result represents a seismic shift in scrapbook culture and methodology: whereas such self-examination once took place in the private pages of a personal album, today's volumes are crafted in a decidedly more public realm. Modern-day scrapbookers enthusiastically share their materials and their time, making the act of scrapbooking a fundamentally social activity. Little wonder, then, that the resultant forms are focused more on embellishing the outside than on expressing what's inside. Indeed, the scrapbook today is served by an entire memory industry, founded on the implicit suggestion that what we saved from yesterday might not be as important as what we'll buy tomorrow.

And so, where we once preserved, we now purchase: tags and trinkets, stickers and glue, pompoms and die cuts are just a few of the millions of add-ons available at art, craft, and stationery supply stores nationwide. Some scrapbookers dislike their own handwriting, obliging them to seek alternative typographic options—disenfranchised words on tags and stickers, for instance—that unintentionally lend a coy, ransom-note style to their pages. Preprinted aphorisms free the scrapbook maker from having to actually write anything, a practice which occupies its own submarket in the scrapbooking universe, called journaling. Nontoxic, acid- and lignin-free adhesives boast surreal expiration dates: it is not uncommon for vendors to promise that their wares will last for the next two hundred years. And for those who yearn for instant history, here's the ultimate oxymoron: reproduction ephemera, in the form of acid-free daguerreotypes and artificially weathered billheads. Scrapbookers covet such materials because they conjure instant history—provenance be damned.

Contemporary scrapbook devotees are fueled by an ongoing fascination with their own personal narratives, stories made concrete in words and pictures—and stickers and ribbons. Yet in spite of such autobiographical intentions, an increasing reliance on extraneous decoration pulls the focus away from the personal artifact, making

ABOVE, LEFT, AND OPPOSITE
Delineator
June 1931

Created in the Depression, this anonymous scrapbook represents one woman's response to retail withdrawal. Dense with annotation, rich with detail, it is embellished to the hilt—but not with anything store-bought or new.

GENEALOGICAL TREE OF THE QUEEN AND HER DECENDANTS

"memories" into something at once formally homogenized and culturally neutral. And what will such polished portrayals of everyday life tell us a generation from now? That we watched too much television? That we lived for the weekends? That we deified our celebrities, our holidays, our pets? Will the books we keep today telegraph our fears or transmit our follies? Will future generations physically hold these books, experiencing the visceral sensation of what it was like to be alive in the twenty-first century—before everything was reduced to data and exiled to microfiche? Veiled by embellishments, drenched in die cuts and ribbons, won't scrapbooks all look alike?

Homogeny notwithstanding, there is an extraordinary spirit that binds these communities of like-minded makers together: scrapbookers are passionate, even evangelical, about what they do, and their efforts, while primitive by objective standards, may well deserve to be appreciated on their own merits. The makers of contemporary scrapbooks view themselves as the keepers of the genealogical flame.[2] They are the self-appointed historians of their own families, ancestral stewards whose efforts are reinforced by two critical—though not necessarily related—objectives. The first is an apparent urgency to document the fleeting memory, to seize the day in all its idiosyncratic, dissonant glory. And the second is to identify themselves as artistically worthy and capable of a creative act.[3] If the first quality links them, in intention, to the scrapbook makers of previous generations, it is the second condition that shifts the entire discussion, by introducing a new and arguably different visual basis for evaluating the current, and quite extraordinary, phenomenon of scrapbooking in America.

To keep a diary, journal, or scrapbook is one way to steel oneself against the inevitable tide of vulnerability that surges in the wake of any kind of tragedy—which may provide one explanation for the fact that sales of scrapbook supplies

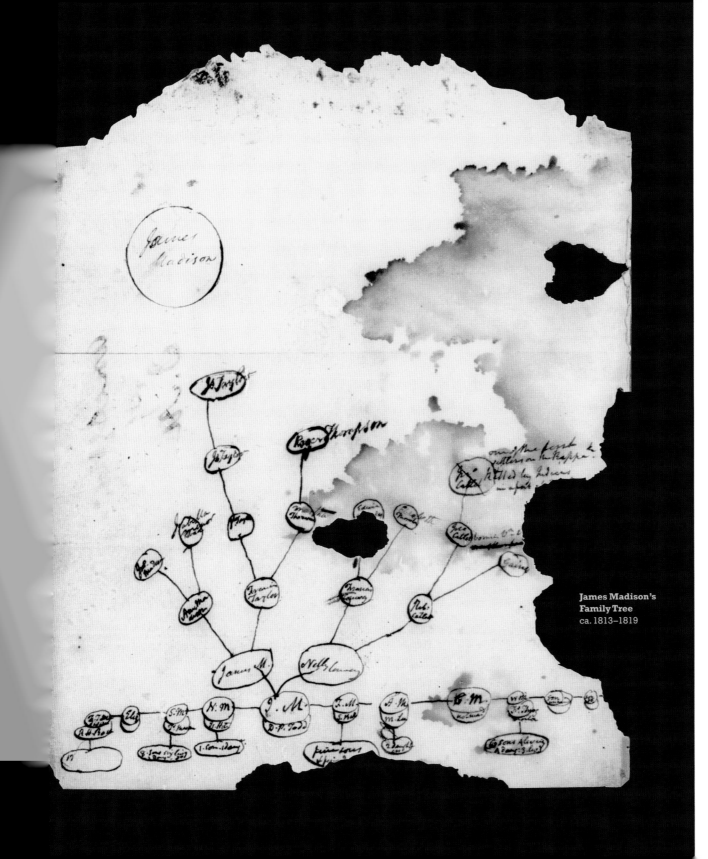

in America have essentially skyrocketed since September 11, 2001. In a climate of such widespread uncertainty, the concrete task of making a scrapbook becomes a reliable therapeutic outlet. It is also easier (and to some, more rewarding) to look back rather than to look forward, which may explain what has emerged as a parallel obsession with tracing ancestry.[4] In the first decade of the twenty-first century, an increase in the availability of Internet sites providing access to such things as historical census records has had a substantial impact on this rapidly growing hobby. As early as 1998, reports of robust research databases spawning comprehensive family histories made their way into the popular press—although certain historians have questioned the selective nature of these efforts.[5]

Where memory itself is concerned, the scrapbook has recently achieved additional status as a tool for recovery. Since the late 1990s, the act of making a scrapbook has been used in treatment for victims of posttraumatic stress, for foster children, for stepfamilies, and for anyone struggling with illness, aging, or bereavement. Scrapbook therapy is well documented in a variety of subspecialties, including gerontology, occupational therapy, and social work, where "therapeutic scrapbooking uses the art of displaying photographs, journaling and other memorabilia as a therapeutic approach to dealing with grief, loss and recovery."[6] Hospice social workers engage in scrapbooking exercises with their terminally ill patients who want to leave something of themselves and their stories behind for their grandchildren.

Family-tree enthusiasts embrace the scrapbook as a kind of expository roadmap, as do many fraternal, secular, and special-interest groups. The Church of Jesus Christ of Latter Day Saints champions scrapbooking (as it does genealogy) because it favors the practice of documenting one's family history as an indication of faith. (There is actually

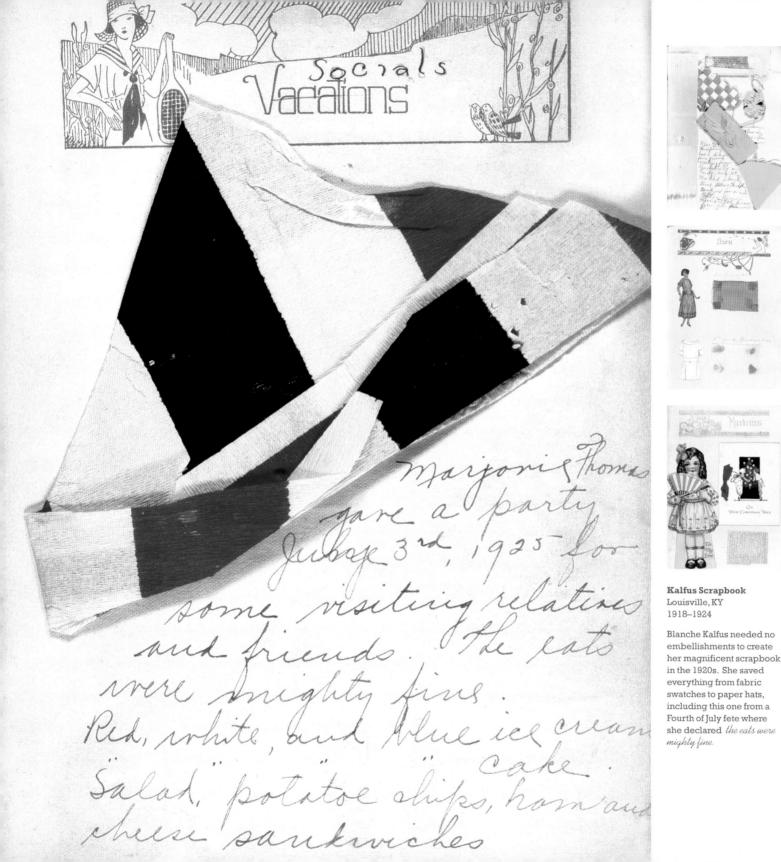

Kalfus Scrapbook
Louisville, KY
1918–1924

Blanche Kalfus needed no
embellishments to create
her magnificent scrapbook
in the 1920s. She saved
everything from fabric
swatches to paper hats,
including this one from a
Fourth of July fete where
she declared *the eats were
mighty fine.*

a subgenre of scrapbooking called *faithbooking*.)
Indeed, Mormons, who've been called the "genealogical gold standard" in matters of documenting ancestry, were among the earliest modern-day
adopters of scrapbooking. Today, they own and
operate many of the most successful scrapbook
businesses across the nation.

The birth of the modern-day scrapbook is
said to have occurred with an exhibit of fifty scrapbooks by Marielen Christiansen in 1980 at the
World Conference of Records in Salt Lake City.
A year after the exhibit, Christiansen and her
husband wrote the first "how-to" book on scrapbooking and opened the first scrapbooking supply
store in Spanish Fork, Utah. (By 1990, the Church
of Jesus Christ of Latter Day Saints had already put
its International Genealogical Index—with data
on more than 150 million names of Mormons and
ancestors—on CD-ROM for distribution in libraries
across the nation.) Over the next twenty years, their
company, Keeping Memories Alive (KMA), grew to
be a leader in the scrapbooking industry. KMA was
also the first company to launch a scrapbook Web
site, scrapbooks.com, which remains one of the
most visited retail sites on the Internet today.[7]

Meanwhile, many national consumer magazines publish human interest stories on the
value of scrapbooking with children as a method
for teaching empathy, and real estate companies include downloadable make-a-scrapbook
templates on their Web sites for children who
might be feeling apprehensive about a big move.
Even celebrities endorse product lines of season-
ally appropriate and color-coordinated supplies,
often tailored to key demographic groups. In 2004,
American television personality Leeza Gibbons
released a suite of software products dedicated to
helping others reclaim their memories. (Gibbons
was inspired by her mother's battle with Alzheim-
ers and is a staunch advocate of scrapbooking
as a therapeutic treatment for patients and their
families.) And Martha Stewart's strategic entry

into the scrapbooking market further extended her reach in the craft realm by introducing a more sophisticated product line. Among other things, Stewart hopes to enlarge her demographic to include men: "Any man in the advertising world is a scrapbooker, any guy involved in graphic arts is a crafter," noted Stewart in a 2006 interview. One year later to the day, *The Wall Street Journal* confirmed her suspicion. [8]

There is also, for many women, a palpable need to seek an outlet for personal expression. At least one historian has theorized a connection between memory and craft that rightly conflates these two obsessions, though it also raises important questions about their formal and critical parameters. [9] Another raises a similar tension in the critical evaluation of artist's books, a field lacking "a canon of artists—a critical terminology for

book arts aesthetics with a historical perspective … [and] a good, specific, descriptive vocabulary on which to form our assessment of book works." Speaking broadly of a genre that includes such subcategories as "altered books," scholars like Johanna Drucker are rightly concerned. She paraphrases her colleague Mark Dimunation, who observes: "ABs are the only field [he knows] where someone takes a weekend workshop, goes home, sits down with scissors, tape and paper, makes something in a few hours and then feels they have license to sell it as an artist's book." [10]

Scrapbookers in general tend to claim neither formal training (in graphic design, photography, or book arts) nor professional expertise. At the same time, scrapbook sharing tends to engender certain basic insecurities. What was initially considered a therapeutic outlet soon becomes

Kalfus Scrapbook
Louisville, KY
1918–1924

It is doubtful that Blanche Kalfus had any formal training in art or design, but her appreciation for the everyday—a napkin, a photobooth snapshot— is evident in her dense and colorful scrapbook.

a cause for concern over "getting it right," prompting increased attention to self-improvement. (This explains the significant demand for layout classes, online instruction, and tips for making "better pages.") In an interview with *Advance*, a magazine for occupational therapists, one owner of a scrapbooking store described the benefit of classes—as a kind of remedial scrapbook intervention. "It helps people overcome that initial hesitation when they perhaps don't feel that they are talented or creative; having someone there to show you how it is done is a way to take the intimidation out." [11]

Here, the tension between the rewards of individual expression and the rhetoric of public approval further distances contemporary scrapbooking from its earlier incarnation. Born out of sheer personal pleasures and interests, scrapbooking a generation ago was concerned with capturing

memories—not an audience for their memories. And while public scrutiny affects every artist's destiny, why must the scrapbook be subjected to such external approval? Once we hold scrapbooks to such professional standards, at what point are they subject to real criticism?

Such is the paradox of the modern scrapbook: it is at once playfully juvenile and strategically shrewd, steeped in memory yet inextricably bound to materiality, and seemingly devoid of any critical editorial conceit. Scrapbooks today tend to be overstuffed and all-inclusive—precisely the antithesis of what we have come to think of as modern. Just as the vernacular of the twenty-first century embraces the everyday with blind exuberance, so too does it unwittingly reinforce the value of just about everything. And yet, in a culture

that celebrates the everyman (think Reality TV) and glorifies the banal (think blogs), the scrapbook takes on renewed value: everyone's opinion matters, and everyone's every waking move is important. What better way to say I was here than to capture every fleeting thought on paper?

Or on screen. Web sites including MySpace, Facebook, and Friendster offer customizable databases of images and links that are philosophically related to scrapbooks in the sense that they permit—indeed, encourage—the sort of lateral browsing that has come to typify modern information retrieval. These sites appeal in particular to a generation of younger users, yet they raise certain fundamental questions about both the form and function of visual biography: on the Internet, it is easier to conceal one's motives than to reveal them, and doctoring photos is seen no longer as disingenuous but as inevitable.

The increasing bias toward screen-based venues also leads to more scrapbooks being produced entirely in this sphere. Though expedient, digital scrapbooking also drives a more significant wedge between human experience and the human hand, resulting in scrapbooks that quickly become formally neutral. Public, shared, and community reinforcing though they may be, such projects exist in their own separate orbit. And it's evident that they've had little, if any, noticeable impact on the work of scrapbooking afficionados, who prefer to take their cues not from artists but from each other.[12]

There is also an implicit contradiction between the speed that has come to characterize contemporary culture and the slowness demanded of the scrapbook-making process. Today, the modern scrapbook recasts memory as something not only fun, but fungible: not only can you create instant history, you can remove it, too. Digital enhancements—Photoshop filters, for instance—can eliminate everything from red-eye to a deadbeat dad, allowing the scrapbooker to rewrite history

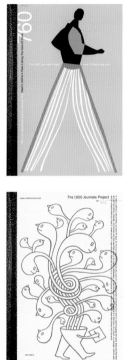

ABOVE, LEFT, AND OPPOSITE
1000 Journals Project
Various locations
2000–present

RIGHT
Post Secret
Various locations
2004–present

Broad and collaborative art experiments like these have occasionally been likened to a message in a bottle: their extensive geographic reach coupled with the randomness of the journey appeals to many participants. The content of these books is equally varied, combining art, wit, confession, observation, and no shortage of mystery.

and reframe the emotional content of a book in a nanosecond. In the event that such self-examination is too unpleasant, you can contract out to freelance scrapbookers: for the truly time pressed, there are scrapbook consultants who will come to your house and organize your memories for you. (Implausible though it may seem, there are also journaling ghostwriters.)

Such edited legacies are, of course, a casualty of any kind of scrapbook, and many artists and designers are drawn to precisely this notion of an externally edited self-narrative. Like all self-narratives, they are framed by the choices the author makes. The artist Candy Jernigan (1952–1991) created books composed of found materials that included the detritus of food she consumed and other odd, at times disturbing, discarded objects—roadkill, for example—engaging in a methodology perhaps closer to forensic pathology than to art. Her notebooks and journals recontextualize everyday items that amplify her daily peregrinations and observations with grace, humor, and an exquisite sense of balance. The French conceptual artist Annette Messager fragments images and language in assemblages that explore the dialogue between individual and collective identity.

While historians rightly doubt the veracity of collective memory, the notion of preserving memories in a public database is an idea that may benefit from the erratic, though devoted, efforts of scrapbook and genealogy enthusiasts. In Great Britain, the social networking so prevalent among the digitally literate embraces a different kind of online scrapbooking. Nations' Memory Bank is an online resource created as a collaborative repository: "The internet has democratized the pursuit of history by bringing research tools and resources to the disposal of millions of people…. What about the physical archives that we all generate daily? We no longer write to one another on paper, but use email, SMS message,

Jernigan Scrapbooks
Various locations
Early 1990s

Candy Jernigan saved everything from empty crack vials to soda can tops. Laurie Dolphin, who published a posthumous biography of Jernigan in 1999, characterized her friend's approach as the "glorification of the insignificant."

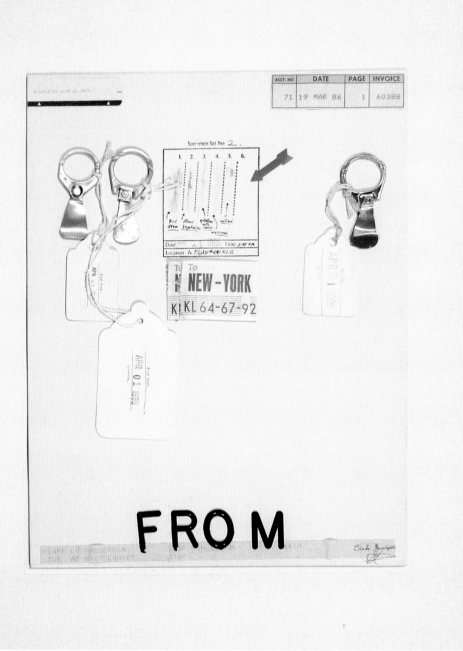

Wandering Moleskine Project
2004–present

A page by Brooklyn-based artist Emily Gerz uses a photograph, tape, and cut paper. Other pages consist of typography, collage, and even more radical elements—sewing, embroidery, and more.

phonecalls—none of which leave a personal trace unless we make a conscious decision to preserve them."[13]

Using a kind of modern spin on the classic surrealist game of the Exquisite Corpse, some artists have even begun to experiment with producing collaborative scrapbooks, many of them spread across far-flung geographic borders.[14] Like a relay race, the 1000 Journals Project grows over time as a series of notebooks traverse the planet and individual artists add their own imprimatur, one page at a time. PostSecret is an ongoing community art project in which people anonymously divest themselves of their innermost thoughts by putting them on a postcard, which is then mailed, and later uploaded to a public Internet archive. The Wandering Moleskine Project hybridizes the sketchbook model from 1000 Journals with the anonymity of PostSecret to create a series of globe-trotting scrapbooks that are collectively produced by a series of unknown makers. Like scrapbooks they are personal and idiosyncratic, but their trajectory follows a decidedly more social, even viral, path.

FROM 1915 TO 1983, BUCKMINSTER FULLER documented something going on in his life every fifteen minutes. The result—later christened the Dymaxion Chronofile—was an enormous scrapbook that included correspondence, newspaper clippings, notes, and sketches and bills. By the end of his life, the file amounted to 270 linear feet of paper and is believed to be the most exhaustive record of one person's life.

Fuller's records will likely be of more interest to future scholars than, say, the scrapbooks of Robert Shields, identified in his 2007 *New York Times* obituary as a "wordy diarist" who spent four to five hours a day similarly devoted to a kind of extreme documentation. (In addition to noting his basal body temperature and the cost of everything he bought, he also taped samples of nasal hair into his diary.) And while it is easy to mock such gestures, one thing seems clear, and that is that the simple need to document remains, for so many people, a critical human activity. Who are we to judge the content, let alone the form such documentation may take?

Perhaps in the end, it doesn't matter what scrapbooks look like or what, for that matter, they behold: for in a culture marked by vulnerability, there's something remarkably gratifying about simply pasting something in a book and calling it your own. That basic act endures because it mirrors our own human frailties, our own endearing, perpetual, and timeless incompleteness. The study of scrapbooks in America reveals that rich or poor, male or female, young or old, black or white—we kept scrapbooks to try to capture those few mesmerizing years when we were here, alive and alert and, in a million small ways, bearing witness. Perhaps this is why we love our scrapbooks so—why we cling to them, bury ourselves in them, hide in and behind them. Their odyssey is but a reflection of our own crooked path: raw, triumphant, fearless, or bereft, we make scrapbooks as gestures of permanence in a world we can only temporarily inhabit. And there we remain, forever cocooned in their fragile pages. Such volumes implore us to remember who we were, and why it mattered.

If you're hung up on nostalgia, pretend today is yesterday
and just go out and have one hell of a time.

Art Buchwald

EPILOGUE

OTHER PEOPLE'S STORIES

I AM SITTING IN THE READING ROOM OF THE American Antiquarian Association in Worcester, Massachusetts, reading a scrapbook. It is pristine and orderly, undistinguished as a visual artifact but diligent in its record keeping—an album compiled by a man whose professional activities led him, on more than one occcasion, to dine at the White House during the Cleveland administration. Interspersed between the many engraved invitations are copious records of the social worlds of Manhattan and Washington, the dances and parties at which his only child, a daughter, was a privileged guest.

A chronology of life events soon emerges: there are numerous parties leading in turn to an engagement, a marriage. Soon the daughter is sailing off to England with her new husband.

I turn a few more pages and browse the many letters sent by the daughter, whose penmanship I now recognize. *He's four months old now,* she writes to her father, *and he's just darling.* Logical inference suggests that the new bride has proceeded to the next evolutionary step. She's produced an heir.

I read on and soon discover that nothing could be further from the truth. She's divorced. She's back in New York. The letter, it turns out, is about her new puppy.

TO READ ANOTHER PERSON'S SCRAPBOOK is to acquire a body of knowledge about an entirely different time and place. But one also becomes an accidental biographer, making astonishing discoveries about other people's lives—and consequently, developing new awareness about our own. Such practices require both compassion and curiosity, for while the story of scrapbooks is the story of social and material

OPPOSITE
Assorted Scrapbooks
Winterhouse
2008

A few of the more than 200 scrapbooks acquired over the course of researching this book.

PAGE 172
Snow Cap Sisters
1913

Very likely a cast photo from a school play, and probably based on the 1901 play by Ruth McEnery Stuart, *The Snow-Cap Sisters,* which took a farcical look at the impact of suffrage on femininity.

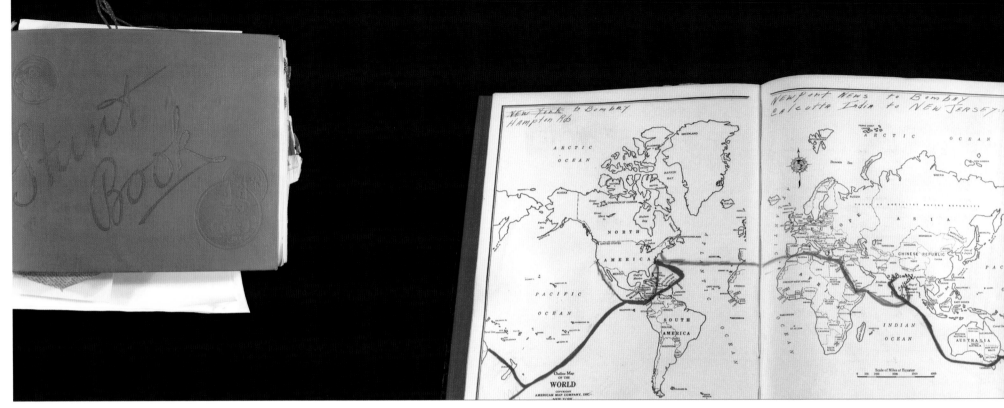

culture, it is also the story of family dynamics—conflicting, mysterious, and highly subjective as they are. To interpolate is to miss the point: rather, one is better advised to look for cues, because other people's stories rarely follow any kind of prescribed pattern. There's no map, and as you muddle through, the hints themselves are often murky, at best. Identifying the principals is the easy part—but who were these people, really, and how can we tell? Everywhere there are puzzling gestures, including (but not limited to) political overtones, psychological undertones, sexual innuendo, and an extraordinary amount of interpersonal nuance. There are odd acronyms, loopy synonyms, and no shortage of regional and cultural colloquialisms. Some scrapbooks are tapestries. Others are minefields. Most are somewhere in between, and the more you familiarize yourself with the stories, the more you want to know—sometimes forging a path that takes you beyond the scrapbook itself.

CONSIDER THE STORY OF *Elinor Moses,* the California debutante whose 1927 engagement was featured in the society pages of the *Los Angeles Times.* I dig a bit and find the couple later moved to Paris, where they had a daughter, whose own nuptials were reported in the spring of 1956.

Elinor Moses died in 1998. Her daughter, in her early seventies when I track her down, had no idea her mother ever kept a scrapbook.

She fills me in on the many missing details of her mother's life—comical ones, like the tale of the cousin who dyed his hair pink in the 1950s, and more serious ones, like her feelings when their family left Paris in 1940. Our correspondence continues by telephone and mail. Some months later, scrapbook in hand, I fly to see her and record our conversation.

OR THE STORY OF ONE *Francis "Pop" Johnson,* whose big scrapbook went along with him to Europe and on to Asia, where he charted his many wartime adventures. Johnson's life was mostly a quiet one, and the only record of his distinguished military service is in the album's yellowing pages.

Approached by an interested reporter, I agree to share the scrapbook, which is featured several days later in the Waterbury, Connecticut, newspaper. Almost immediately, I am flooded with phone calls from tearful relatives, former friends, and nostalgic co-workers. Everyone has stories to add. Some want the scrapbook, a few of them rather desperately. Their reactions to it, and to him, amplify the narratives of one soldier's life. Details emerge and coalesce, and Johnson's story grows richer and deeper because of it.

FAR LEFT
Moses "Stunt" Book
Los Angeles, CA
1920–1922

The scrapbook kept by Elinor Moses will be donated to her alma mater, the Marlborough School for Girls, in Los Angeles.

ABOVE
Johnson Scrapbook
Waterbury, CT
1942–1945

Pop Johnson's scrapbook includes a great deal of army memorabilia and will be returned to his family upon publication of this book.

FINALLY, THERE IS THE densely captivating story of *Lydia Blanchard*, the skillful young artist from Natchitoches, Louisiana, whose scrapbook surfaces one day in an online auction. Within minutes  of my winning bid, I am contacted by a woman whose mother is featured in its pages. She and her daughter help me resurrect the stories by identifying the people, the school, the details in the book. I enthusiastically design a Web site, LYDIABLANCHARD.NET, to which I hope they will eagerly contribute.

With great expectation, I wait for the wealth of input to help me complete Blanchard's story. But whereas a flurry of excitement followed the discovery of her scrapbook, the Web site is greeted with trepidation, and visitor traffic is nonexistent. Instantly, the uncertain boundary between public archive and private journal is made patently evident, and it seems that even if the site brings Blanchard's story to a wider audience, it can't replace the intimacy of the real thing.

Nor should it. Squirreled away in drawers or captive in private collections, scrapbooks today are as vivid a reflection of their long-lost authors as they ever were, yet they remain a fragile enterprise, an endangered species. Librarians struggle with how to preserve them. Scholars are puzzled by how to analyze them. As unpublished sources, are they legitimate as historical texts? And to the extent that so many of them are driven by image rather than language, how do we even begin to understand their logic, their purpose, their role?

Understanding them is precisely the point, and in some cases, returning the scrapbooks to their righful descendants seems to complete an unspoken yet highly necessary gesture. For Elinor Moses, Pop Johnson, and Lydia Blanchard, that cycle is now complete.

The study of scrapbooks is complicated and messy and far from complete: as material artifacts, they're basically an untamed species. Yet there will always be exceptions: from the books by Buckminster Fuller (who saved things with an almost militant regimentation) to those by Candy Jernigan (for whom the detritus of everyday life—she called it *rejectimenta*—demanded an equally vigilant approach) to the countless albums by generations of unknown people, scrapbooks constitute an eclectic, yet inclusive genre that spans everything from decoupage to diaries, indexical systems to artful compilations. Each a unique portrait, together they provide a cross section of the range and pluralism of more than a century of modern American experience—and an astonishing experience it is. To spend any time at all with these scrapbooks is to fall a little bit in love with the people who created them. They remind us who we are, where we're going—and perhaps why, in the end, it might actually matter.

NOTES

INTRODUCTION

1 Quoted in Stephen Railton, "Mark Twain in His Times," The Electronic Text Center, University of Virginia, http://etext.lib.virginia.edu/railton/marketin/scrpbook.html. See also Jim McWilliams, *Mark Twain in the St. Louis Post-Dispatch, 1874–1891* (Troy, NY: Whitston Publishing Company, 1997), and R. Kent Rasmussen, *Mark Twain A to Z: The Essential Reference to his Life and Writings* (New York: Oxford University Press, 1996).

2 Mark Twain to Daniel Slote, September 1876. Clemens invented his self-pasting scrapbook in August 1872 and received a patent on it in June 1873. A version of this letter appeared in the column "Literary Chit Chat," *New York Herald*, December 11, 1976.

CHAPTER ONE: TIME

1 After her divorce was final in 1872, Mrs. Vielé fled to Paris with her youngest son, Egbert. Later renamed Francis Vielé-Griffin, he went on to become a leading Symbolist poet. Teresa herself spent the remainder of her life living in self-imposed exile in France until her death in October 1906. http://www.tshaonline.org/handbook/online/articles/VV/fvi18.html.

2 Katherine Ott, *The Scrapbook in American Life* (Philadelphia: Temple University Press, 2006), p. 16.

3 "A Family Scrapbook." *Boston Daily Globe*, April 25, 1895, p. 6

4 "A Family Scrapbook," *Boston Daily Globe*, April 25, 1895; Johnny Mack, "Our Boys and Girls," *Boston Daily Globe*, July 24, 1903; "Women and Society," *Atlanta Constitution*, March 3, 1897; "Philbrick's

Poems," *Hartford Courant*, December 26, 1904; "Mrs. Fillmore's Scrapbook," *New York Times*, December 6, 1885; Abbie M. Worstell, "Home World," *New York Observer and Chronicle*, June 28, 1900; "Scrap-Books and Scrap-Screens," *Saturday Evening Post*, February 13, 1875; Nellie Burns, "Mothers' Department," *Arthur's Home Magazine*, May 1884, p. 52; "Scrapbooks Give Pleasure," *Christian Science Monitor*, September 12, 1911, p. 6; "A Sunday Scrap-Book," *Ladies' Home Journal*, May 1891, p. 16.

5 Hjalmar Hjorth Boyesen, "The New Womanhood," *Lippincott's Monthly Magazine*, July 1895.

6 *Chicago Daily Tribune*, June 10, 1894.

7 E. Richard McKinstry, "Papered Dream Houses Offer Clues to Imagined Lives," *Ephemera News* 22, no. 3 (Spring 2004): 1. Many fine examples of scrapbook houses can be found at the Strong Museum at the University of Rochester and at the library of the Winterthur Museum in Delaware. For more about scrapbook houses, see Deborah Smith, "Consuming Passions: Scrapbooks and American Play" *Ephemera Journal* 6 (1993): 73–74; Rodris Roth, "Scrapbook Houses: A Late-Nineteenth-Century Children's View of the American Home," in *The American Home: Material Culture, Domestic Space, and Family Life* (Hanover, NH: University Press of New England, 1998), and Beverly Gordon, *The Saturated World: Aesthetic Meaning, Intimate Objects, Women's Lives, 1890–1940* (Knoxville: University of Tennessee Press, 2006), pp. 37–61.

8 A more thorough discussion of the psychology of episodic time can be found in Tamar Katriel and Thomas Farrell, "Scrapbooks as Cultural Texts: An American Art of Memory," *Text and Performance Quarterly* 11:1 (January 1991): 1–17.

9 Alice Richtor, "Memory Books: Souvenirs Enshrined by Girl Collectors," *Boston Daily Globe*, July 4, 1920.

10 Ibid.

11 Leppert observes that modernity may be considered "marked and defined by an obsession with 'evidence,'" visuality, and visibility. See Richard Leppert, "The Social Discipline of Listening," in *Aural Cultures*, ed. Jim Drobnick (Toronto: YYZ Books, 2004), p. 19.

12 For more on the scrapbooks of Teresa Vielé, Jessie Southard Parker, and Grace Walsh, see L. Rebecca Johnson Melvin, *Self Works: Diaries, Scrapbooks, and Other Autobiographical Efforts.* Catalogue from the exhibition August 19–December 18, 1997, Hugh M. Morris Library, University of Delaware Library, Newark, p. 27.

13 Isadore Twersky, "Harry Austryn Wolfson, 1887–1974," *Journal of the American Oriental Society* 95, no. 2: 181–183.

14 The custom of confessional books took an oddly social turn in Victorian England, where they were used as a companion to autograph books, intended as repositories for interviewing one's friends. (They may well have been the precursors to "Slam" books, a later twentieth-century kind of group confession in book form.) For more on the culture of confession books, see Samantha Matthews, "Psychological Crystal Palace? Late Victorian Confession Albums," *Book History* 3 (2000): 125–154.

15 Fatherless Children of France (FCF) was formed to aid an estimated twenty thousand French children left fatherless by World War I. Based in New York, the organization operated from 1916 through the end of 1920 and sold subscriptions through local committees to aid individual French children.

CHAPTER TWO: SPACE

1 The Quaker migration west from the states of Virginia, North and South Carolina, and Georgia after 1795 led to Quaker enclaves in parts of Ohio

and Michigan in the nineteenth century. For more on the history of their eighteenth-century migration, see Rebecca Goodman, "Quakers Found Home in Waynesville Village," *Cincinnati Enquirer*, February 3, 2003, online edition.

2 For more on the patois of the autograph in midcentury schoolbooks, see Marguerite Ivins Wilson, "Yours Till—: A Study of Children's Autograph Rhymes in Utah," *Utah Humanities Review 1*, no. 3 (July 1947): 245–260.

3 Lucy Peltz, "The Pleasure of the Book: Extra-Illustration, an Eighteenth-Century Fashion," *Things 8* (Summer 1998): 6–31; and Robert Shaddy, "Grangerizing: One of the Unfortunate Stages in Bibliomania," *The Book Collector* (Winter 2000): 535–546.

4 That spring, the American press shared reports of the newly emancipated murderer: "Aboard the steamship Roma, Mrs. Charlotte Nash Nixon-Nirdlinger returned to the U.S. from Nice, where a court had justified her killing her wealthy, elderly husband," reported *Time* in June 1931. "Said she: 'Sometimes I'm sorry that I am beautiful, considering all the trouble I've had over it.' During the interview Baby Charlotte screamed and Son Fred, 4, beat Grandmother Nash on the head with a paper horn." "Names Make News," *Time Magazine*, June 1931.

5 Curator L. Rebecca Johnson Melvin notes that Ruck's journals are "a mix of diary, workbook, and scrapbook." There are six volumes, covering a decade of work, family, vacations, and travel throughout Europe and the United Kingdom. See L. Rebecca Johnson Melvin, *Self Works: Diaries, Scrapbooks, and Other Autobiographic Efforts*, catalogue from the exhibition August 19–December 18, 1997, Hugh M. Morris Library, University of Delaware Library, Newark.

6 *The Great War and the Shaping of the Twentieth Century*, PBS documentary, 1996.

7 For more on the pathologies surrounding Zelda Fitzgerald's prodigious creative output, see Elizabeth Waites, "The Princess in the Tower: Zelda Fitzgerald's Creative Impasse," *Journal of the American Psychoanalytic Association 34* (1986): 637–662.

8 This essay first appeared in the *New York Tribune* on April 2, 1922, under the headline "Mrs. F. Scott Fitzgerald Reviews 'The Beautiful and Damned,' Friend Husband's latest." Reprinted in Matthew J. Bruccoli, *The Collected Writings of Zelda Fitzgerald* (Tuscaloosa: University of Alabama Press, 1991), pp. 387–389.

9 Colin Wells, "Thomas Jefferson's Scrapbooks: Poems of Nation, Family, and Romantic Love Collected by America's Third President," *Early American Literature 42*, no. 3 (2007): 626–629. Notes Wells: "Unlike his political views, which sometimes veered toward the radical, Jefferson's domestic values tend to reflect the common verities of eighteenth-century literature and life: there are poems praising moderation and temperance, the benefits of matrimony and conjugal love, and the importance of choosing a spouse based on virtue rather than physical beauty" (p. 627).

10 Zelda Fitzgerald's autobiographical novel *Save Me the Waltz*, reprinted in Bruccoli, *Collected Writings of Zelda Fitzgerald*, p. 69.

11 In January 1913, H.D. published "Three Poems" in *Poetry Magazine*, a moment that is generally acknowledged to mark the birth of the imagist movement.

12 For more on the Camp Fire Girls, see Jennifer H. Helgren, "Inventing American Girlhood: Gender and Citizenship in the Twentieth-Century Camp Fire Girls," PhD diss., Claremont Graduate University, 2005.

CHAPTER THREE: SENTIMENT

1 Eva Grant Marshall, "The Post Impressionist," *Washington Post*, September 17, 1942.

2 For more on the typographic customs of nineteenth- and twentieth-century calling cards, see John H. A. Young, *Guide to the Manners, Etiquette, and Deportment of the Most Refined Society* (Reprint, New York: Lyons Press, 2001), pp. 75–83. Originally published by John H. Young and Lillie M. Spaulding. *Our deportment: or, The manners, conduct, and dress of the most refined society, including forms of letters, invitations, etc., etc., also, valuable suggestions on home culture and training*, comp. from the latest reliable authorities. Detroit: F. B. Dickerson & Co., 1882.

3 Marilyn F. Motz, "Visual Autobiography: Photograph Albums of Turn-of-the-Century Midwestern Women," *American Quarterly 41*, no. 1 (March 1989): 63–92. Motz notes how this new kind of photography led to a new kind of album: whereas nineteenth-century albums were slotted, enabling the strict placement of stiff-backed cardboard photographs, "the creator of this new type of album could arrange photographs symmetrically or asymmetrically, could overlap photographs, could place photographs at any angle, could cut the photographs into any shape desired, and could combine the photographs with anything flat enough to fit into an album" (p. 64).

4 The Rare Book and Special Collections Division at the Library of Congress includes a significant cache of suffrage scrapbooks that "offer a unique look at a slice of social history, documenting the gradual evolution of public sentiment and the changing strategies of several generations of activists as they struggled to win the vote for women."

5 "Star Compiling Memory Book," *Los Angeles Times*, September 23, 1935.

6 "Defense of Diaries," *Washington Post*, January 31, 1943; "Huge Scrapbook a Work of Years," *New York Times*, February 3, 1929; "Thirty Five Scrapbooks to Show Marriage Is a Success," *Chicago Daily Tribune*, October 29, 1905; "A Scrapbook Chariot," *Christian Science Monitor*, July 13, 1931, p. 8.

7 "Scrapbooks Show America to England," *Washington Post*, July 18, 1943. Warde's program proved hugely popular: several years later, one New York publisher sponsored a prize for the best original school scrapbook. The idea of scrapbooks as emissaries of goodwill caught on quickly. See also "Scrapbooks as Ambassadors," *Christian Science Monitor*, December 29, 1945, p. 8; "Women Collecting Scrapbooks for USO," *New York Times*, January 5, 1943; "Scrapbooks National Chief Details Compilation Here," *Los Angeles Times*, September 9, 1944.

8 Originally published in French as *L'invention du quotidien*, vol. 1, *Arts de faire* (1980). The English translation is published as *The Practice of Everyday Life*, trans. Steven Rendall (Berkeley: University of California Press, 1984).

9 Mrs. Harry A. Burnham, "Excavating the Commonplace," *Christian Science Monitor*, March 6, 1936, p. 7.

10 A 1918 advertisement in the *Hartford Courant* offers a robust series of "Record Books" for sale, including *My School Life*, *The Commencement Memory Book*, *My Graduation*, and *My School Days*, priced between $.95 and $2.25 per copy. *Hartford Courant*, June 6, 1918.

CHAPTER FOUR: NOSTALGIA

1 Svetlana Boym, *The Future of Nostalgia* (New York: Basic Books, 2001), p. 5.

2 "A Girl's Memory Book," Women and Society Page, *Atlanta Constitution*, March 3, 1897.

3 Marion C. Sheridan, "Scrapbooks: An Experiment," *The English Journal* 13, no. 4 (April 1924): 279–281; and "Colby Junior Girls Compile Textbooks," *New York Times*, October 31, 1937.

4 *New York Times*, April 12, 1900.

5 Marianne Hirsch, *Family Frames: Photography, Narrative, and Postmemory* (Cambridge: Harvard University Press, 1997).

6 Boym, *Future of Nostalgia*, p. 13.

7 The impressive list of illustrators whose work was featured in early twentieth-century memory books includes Erna Anderson, J. T. Armbrust, L. J. Bridgeman, Victor de Kubinyi, Milo G. Denlinger, Melcena Burns Denny, Elise E. Edwards, M. Farini, Elizabeth Furlong, Meta Morris Grimbali, Bernice Hunt, Dulab Evans Krebbiel, E. V. Lodron, Harry B. Matthews, H. E. McDonald, Elizabeth M. Owen, Marion L. Peabody, Clara Elsene Peck, Cornelia M. Weyburn, Randall Wheelan, Florence White Williams, Claire Powers Wilson, Amelia Winter, and Gaye Woodring.

8 As early as the 1840s, preformatted pocket diaries allowed Americans to actively manage the myriad complexities of daily record keeping. For more on the social history of the diary, see Molly McCarthy, "A Page, a Day: A History of the Daily Diary in America," PhD diss., Brandeis University, 2004.

9 For more on the complexity of collective memory, see Susan Engel, *Context Is Everything: The Nature of Memory* (New York: W. H. Freeman, 1999). Of particular relevance to the study of scrapbooks as cultural artifacts is Engel's discussion of autobiography in Chapter 5: "Autobiographies are the forms of remembering where the deeply personal and the concretely public meet" (p. 145).

10 For more on do-it-yourself instructions featured in the popular press, see Johnny Mack, "Our Boys and Girls," *Boston Daily Globe*, July 24, 1903; Madeline Marston, "A Mother's Memory Book," *Ladies' Home Journal*, May 1905, p. 56; "Bride's Book in Original Form," *Christian Science Monitor*, October 15, 1913, p. 6; "This Easily Made Memory Book Will Be a Fine Record of Vacation Pleasures," *Atlanta Constitution*, June 3, 1928; "Vera's Winter Memory Book," *Christian Science Monitor*, February 2, 1929, p. 17. See also Lina and Adelia Beard, *American Girls Handy Book: How to Amuse Yourself and Others* (New York: Charles Scribner & Sons, 1898), pp. 395-402.

11 Matthew J. Bruccoli, with Scottie Fitzgerald Smith and Joan Paterson Kerr, *The Romantic Egoists: A Pictorial Autobiography from the Scrapbooks and Albums of F. Scott and Zelda Fitzgerald* (Columbia: University of South Carolina Press, 1974), pp. 6 and 8.

12 Katherine Ott's excellent anthology with Susan Tucker and Patricia P. Buckler, *The Scrapbook in American Life* (Philadelphia: Temple University Press, 2006), includes further discussion of the social, psychological, and cultural merits of women's friendship books before the twentieth century. See also Starr Ockenga, *On Women and Friendship: A Collection of Victorian Keepsakes and Traditions* (New York: Stewart, Tabori, and Chang, 1993), pp. 20-31.

13 Josephine Gear, "The Baby's Picture: Woman as Image Maker in Small-Town America," *Feminist Studies* 13, no. 2 (Summer 1987): 419–442. The culture of baby worship was a particular turn-of-the-century notion that further enshrined the mother-baby relationship through the use of staged portraits.

14 My thanks to Brigitte Ruthman at the *Waterbury Republican-American* for her research on Johnson.

15 Erik Barnouw, *A History of Broadcasting in the United States*, vol. 2, *The Golden Web*, 1933–1953 (New York: Oxford University Press, 1968); Michael Ritchie,

Please Stand By: A Prehistory of Television (New York: Overlook Press, 1994); David Halberstam, *The Fifties* (New York: Villard Books, 1993). Erik Barnouw and Michael Ritchie, among others, have written at length about the history of television in America and the evolution from an audio medium to an audiovisual medium. But it is the American journalist David Halberstam who most poignantly describes the impact of television on American domestic life at midcentury, particularly with regard to the way we came to perceive our politicians, our nation, and ourselves.

16 Eleanor Foa, "The Past Is Prologue—and a Growth Industry," *New York Times*, February 20, 1980. Looking back at the recycled sensibilities that pervaded the 1970s, Foa attacks nostalgia because, in her view, it makes us feel good for the wrong reasons: it is "so often [an] excuse for bad taste, derivative thinking and sentimentality for a 'reality' that never existed."

17 D. W. Griffiths kept scrapbooks to help coordinate the complex elements of many of his grander films: while less visually free-form than the albums compiled by Brakhage, they point nevertheless to the idea of the scrapbook as a narrative tool. See Bernard Hanson, "D.W. Griffith: Some Sources," *The Art Bulletin* 54, no. 4 (December 1972): 493–515; and Floyd W. Martin, "D. W. Griffith's 'Intolerance': A Note on Additional Visual Sources," *Art Journal* 43, no. 3, *Art History and the Study of Film* (Autumn 1983): 231–233.

18 For more on the scrapbooks of William S. Burroughs, see David Banash, "From Advertising to the Avant-Garde: Rethinking the Invention of Collage," *Postmodern Culture* 14, no. 2 (January 2004): 1–53. On how making collages transformed Burroughs as a writer, see Morgan Falconer, "Cut and Paste," *Guardian*, August 24, 2005.

19 Deschler Welch, "Profitable Scrap-Book Making," *Writer* 27, no. 8 (August 1915): 113–115. Quoted in Ellen Gruber Garvey, "Scissorizing and Scrapbooks: Nineteenth Century Reading, Remaking and Remodeling," in *New Media, 1740–1915*, ed. Lisa Gitelman and Geoffrey B. Pingree (Cambridge: MIT Press, 2003), pp. 207–227. Garvey makes an excellent argument for the way scrapbooks were physically used, and compares our reliance on them to the way we manage modern-day systems like Internet bookmarks.

CHAPTER FIVE: POSTERITY

1 Helen Siebenthal, "What's Your Hobby?" *Los Angeles Times*, June 9, 1929.

2 Nancy Shute, "New Routes to Old Roots," *Smithsonian* 32, no. 12 (March 2002): 76–83. There is some research to suggest that Americans' interest in family history originated with the enormous success of the miniseries *Roots*, based on the novel by Alex Haley and initially broadcast in the United States in 1977.

3 Pam Matthews, "Evoking the Muse," *Library Journal* 126, no. 13 (August 2001). Although there is a rich history of writing on the subject of art making and its spiritual benefits—by authors from Ralph Waldo Emerson to John Dewey to Carl Jung—the general public is perhaps not the intended audience for such thinking. More recently, creativity has become a synonym for self-help. "To create simply means to make something out of nothing," notes Matthews. "So in theory anyone—from sanitation workers to CEOs—can boast of being imaginative."

4 Patricia Ward Biederman, "Hobby Brings Family Trees into Full Flower," *Los Angeles Times*, June 9, 2000, Valley edition; Nathan Cobb, "Cyber Roots Transforming an Age-Old Hobby, the 'Net Has Become Tool of Choice for Those Who Seek to Unearth Their Family Trees," *Boston Globe*, March 9, 1998.

5 A more skeptical perspective on the surge of interest in family trees appears in Richard Conniff, "The Family Tree, Pruned," *Smithsonian* 38, no. 4 (July 2007): 90–97.

6 Nancy Duncan, "Why We Remember," *Memory Makers Magazine*, September 2006.

7 "Mormon Lineages on Disk," *USA Today*, August 16, 1990, p. 4D.

8 Kelly Crow, *Los Angeles Times*, April 6, 2006; "Wanted: A Few Good Men (With Scissors)," *Wall Street Journal*, April 6, 2007: W1.

9 See Tammy J. L. Powley, "Memory-Craft: The Role of Domestic Technology in Women's Journals," PhD diss., University of Central Florida, 2006.

10 Johanna Drucker, "Critical Issues/ Exemplary Works," *The Bonefolder* 1, no. 2 (Spring 2005): 3.

11 "Crafts Are Back!" *Advance Magazine for Occupational Therapy Practitioners* 21, No. 1, January 10, 2005, p. 15.

12 Lisa Kocian, "Artists Are Judging Books in a New Way," *Boston Globe*, December 30, 2004. Altered books are palimpsests—manipulated works of collage created on top of existing books, inspired as much by the verbal deconstructions of William Burroughs as by the more visually experimental work of Tom Phillips. Within the context of scrapbooking workshops, such historical sources are seldom, if ever, cited.

13 Nick Barratt, "Nation's Memorybank," *History Today*, May 2007, p. 5.

14 Stephanie Rosenbloom, "Internet Updates Message in a Bottle," *Chicago Tribune*, November 3, 2005. See also Maria Aspan, "Thousands of Words and Now Pictures, Too," *New York Times*, January 30, 2006; and Tara Bahrampour, "Today's Diarists Now Lay It Online; the Days of Scribbling Innermost Thoughts in a Little Lockable Tome Are Long Gone. Web Journals Are Now an Open Book," *Los Angeles Times*, January 5, 2007.

BIBLIOGRAPHY

Allen, Alistair, and Joan Hoverstadt. *The History of Printed Scraps.* London: New Cavendish Books, 1983.

Banash, David. "From Advertising to the Avant-Garde: Rethinking the Invention of Collage." *Postmodern Culture* 14, no. 2 (January 2004). pp. 1-53.

Batchen, Geoffrey. *Forget Me Not.* New York: Princeton Architectural Press, 2004.

Batchen, Geoffrey. "Vernacular Photographies." *History of Photography* 24, no. 3 (Autumn 2000): 262–271.

Block, Diane W. "Books and Company: Mid-Victorian Photocollage Albums and the Feminine Imagination." PhD diss., University of New Mexico, 1995.

Boym, Svetlana. *The Future of Nostalgia.* New York: Basic Books, 2001.

Bruccoli, Matthew J. *The Collected Writings of Zelda Fitzgerald.* Tuscaloosa: University of Alabama Press, 1991.

Bruccoli, Matthew J. *The Romantic Egoists: Scott and Zelda Fitzgerald.* New York: Scribner and Sons, 1974.

Buckler, Patricia Prandini. "A Silent Woman Speaks: The Poetry in a Woman's Scrapbook of the 1840s." *Prospects* 16 (1991): 149–169.

Certeau, Michel de. *The Practice of Everyday Life.* Trans. Steven Rendall. Berkeley: University of California Press, 1984.

Collins, Douglas. *The Story of Kodak.* New York: Abrams, 1990.

Conniff, Richard. "The Family Tree, Pruned." *Smithsonian* 38, no. 4 (July 2007): 90–97.

Demos, Elizabeth J. "Scrapbooking: Women Making 'Me' Time and Doing Family through Making Memories." PhD diss., Loyola University, 2006.

Di Bello, Patrizia. "The 'Eyes of Affection' and Fashionable Femininity: Representations of Photography in Nineteenth-Century Magazines and Victorian 'Society' Albums." In *Phototextualities: Intersections of Photography and Narrative*, ed. Alex Hughes and Andrea Noble, pp. 254–271. Albuquerque: University of New Mexico Press, 2003.

Dolphin, Laurie, ed. *Evidence: The Art of Candy Jernigan.* San Francisco: Chronicle Books, 1999.

Downs, Heather Ann. "Crafting Culture: Scrapbooking and the Lives of Women." PhD diss., University of Illinois at Urbana-Champaign Graduate College, 2006.

Drucker, Johanna. *The Visible Word: Experimental Typography and Modern Art, 1909–1923.* Chicago: University of Chicago Press, 1994.

Engel, Susan. *Context Is Everything: The Nature of Memory.* New York: W. H. Freeman, 1999.

Fleishman, John. "The Labyrinthine World of the Scrapbook King." *Smithsonian* 22 (February 1992): 79–87.

Ford, Colin, and Karl Steinorth, eds. *You Press The Button. We Do The Rest.* London: Dirk Nishen Publishing, 1988.

Garvey, Ellen Gruber. *The Adman in the Parlor: Magazines and the Gendering of Consumer Culture, 1880s to 1910s.* New York: Oxford University Press, 1996.

Gernes, Todd. "Recasting the Culture of Ephemera." In *Popular Literacy: Studies in Cultural Practices and Poetics*, ed. John Trimbur, pp. 107–127. Pittsburgh: University of Pittsburgh Press, 2001.

Gernes, Todd. "Recasting the Culture of Ephemera: Young Women's Literary Culture in Nineteenth Century America." PhD diss., Brown University, 1992.

Hall, Peter. "Souvenirs of a Life." *Print* 54, no. 3 (May–June 2000): 82–89, 122–123.

Hartigan, Linda Roscoe. "The House That Collage Built." *American Art* 7, no. 3 (Summer 1993): 88–91.

Hines, Babette. *Love Letters Lost.* New York: Princeton Architectural Press, 2005.

Hirsch, Marianne, ed. *The Familial Gaze.* Hanover, NH: Dartmouth College Press, 1999.

Hirsch, Marianne. *Family Frames: Photography, Narrative, and Postmemory.* Cambridge: Harvard University Press, 1997.

Huyssen, Andreas. *Twilight Memories: Marking Time in a Culture of Amnesia.* New York: Routledge, 1995.

Ivins Wilson, Marguerite. "Yours Till—: A Study of Children's Autograph Rhymes in Utah." *Utah Humanities Review* 1, no. 3 (July 1947): 245–260.

Johnson Melvin, L. Rebecca. *Self Works: Diaries, Scrapbooks, and Other Autobiographical Efforts.* Catalogue from the exhibition August 19– December 18, 1997. Hugh M. Morris Library, University of Delaware Library, Newark.

Katriel, Tamar, and Thomas Farrell. "Scrapbooks as Cultural Texts: An American Art of Memory." *Text and Performance Quarterly* 11, no. 1 (January 1991): 1–17.

Kotkin, Amy. "The Family Album as Folklore." *Exposure* 16 (March 1978): 4–8.

Langford, Martha. *Suspended Conversations: The Afterlife of Memory in Photographic Albums.* Montreal: McGill-Queen's University Press, 2001.

Lesy, Michael. *Time Frames: The Meaning of Family Pictures.* New York: Pantheon Books, 1980.

Levine, Barbara. *Snapshot Chronicles: Inventing the American Photo Album.* New York: Princeton Architectural Press, 2005.

Lyttle, B. "Memories: Page by Page." *Martha Stewart Living,* no. 146 (January 2006), pp. 128–135.

Matthews, Samantha. "Psychological Crystal Palace? Late Victorian Confession Albums." *Book History* 3 (2000): 125–154.

McCarthy, Molly. "A Page, a Day: A History of the Daily Diary in America." PhD diss., Brandeis University, 2004.

McKinstry, E. Richard. "Papered Dream Houses Offer Clues to Imagined Lives." *Ephemera News* 22, no. 3 (Spring 2004): 1, 13–16.

Miller, Nancy K. *But Enough about Me: Why We Read Other People's Lives.* New York: Columbia University Press, 2002.

Motz, Marilyn. "Visual Autobiography: Photograph Albums of Turn-of-the-Century Midwestern Women." *American Quarterly* 41 (March 1989): 63–92.

Ott, Katherine, with Susan Tucker and Patricia P. Buckler. *The Scrapbook in American Life.* Philadelphia: Temple University Press, 2006.

Pascali, Lara. "Baby Books and Childhood Narratives: Writing the Self through Material Culture." PhD diss., University of Delaware, 2007.

Perloff, Marjorie. "The Invention of Collage." *New York Literary Forum* 10–11 (1983): 5–47.

Powley, Tammy J. L. *Memory-Craft: The Role of Domestic Technology in Women's Journals.* PhD diss., University of Central Florida, 2006.

Poynor, Rick. "True Stories." *Print Magazine* 60, no. 2 (March–April 2006): 33–34.

Sheridan, Marion C. "Scrapbooks: An Experiment." *The English Journal* 13, no 4 (April 1924): 279–281.

Shute, Nancy. "New Routes to Old Routes." *Smithsonian* 32, no. 12 (March 2002): 76–83.

Slater, David J. "The American Girl, Her Life and Times: An Ideal and Its Creators, 1890–1930." PhD diss., University of Minnesota, 2005.

Smith, Deborah. "Consuming Passions: Scrapbooks and American Play." *Ephemera Journal* 6 (1993): 63–76.

Spraggs, Melita. "To Change the Subject: Scrapbooks across the Sea." *Christian Science Monitor,* May 19, 1943, p. 13.

Stansell, Christine. *American Moderns: Bohemian New York and the Creation of a New Century.* New York: Henry Holt, 2005.

Tucker, Susan. "Within a Scrapbook's Pages." *Historic New Orleans Collection Quarterly* 15, no. 1 (Winter 1997): 6–7.

Updike, John. "Visual Trophies: The Art of Snapshots." *New Yorker,* December 24 and 31, 2007, pp. 144–148.

Vosmeier, Sarah M. "The Family Album: Photography and American Family Life since 1860." PhD diss., Indiana University, 2003.

Waites, Elizabeth. "The Princess in the Tower: Zelda Fitzgerald's Creative Impasse." *Journal of the American Psychoanalytic Association* 34 (1986): 637–662.

Watts, Margaret L. *Visiting Cards in Correct Social Usage: A Course of Instruction in Good Form, Style and Deportment.* New York: Society of Self-Culture, 1903.

Whalen, Catherine. "Finding Me." *Afterimage* 29, no. 6 (May–June 2002): 16–17.

Williams, Val. "Cutural Sniping: The Art of Transgression and Family Secrets." *Creative Camera* 335 (August–September 1995): 37–38.

INDEX

Ball Scrapbook
Bridgeton, IN
1926

CREDITS

Hair Book. Northwestern State University of Louisiana, Watson Memorial Library, Cammie G. Henry Research Center. [PAGE X] *Anne Sexton Scrapbook.* Anne Sexton Papers, Harry Ransom Center, University of Texas at Austin. [PAGES XII, XIV, XVI, XVII] *Letterbook.* Sir Francis Castillion, ca. 1590–1638. James Marshall and Marie-Louise Osborn Collection, Beinecke Rare Book and Manuscript Library, Yale University. [PAGE XVIII] *Self-Pasting Scrapbook.* Mark Twain House and Museum, Hartford, Connecticut. *Scraps and Sketches.* George Cruikshank, 1829. The Lewis Walpole Library, Yale University. [PAGE XIX] *Teresa Vielé Scrapbooks.* Special Collections, University of Delaware Library. [PAGES 2, 3] *Victorian Scrapbook.* Courtesy David Freund Collection. [PAGE 4] *Making the Scrapbook.* Juliana Oakley. Graphic Arts Collection, Smithsonian Institution. [PAGE 5] *Scrapbook Volunteers.* Courtesy of the Chicago Historical Society. [PAGE 6] Albert George Morrow poster for *The New Woman*, a play by Sydney Grundy, 1894. Mark Samuels Lasner Collection, on loan to the University of Delaware Library. [PAGE 8] *Scrapbook Houses.* Courtesy of the Winterthur Library, Joseph Downs Collection of Manuscripts and Printed Ephemera. [PAGE 9] *Jessie Southard Parker Scrapbook.* Special Collections, University of Delaware Library. [PAGES 16, 17] *Harry Wolfson Scrapbook.* Harvard University Archives, Pusey Library, Cambridge, Massachusetts. [PAGE 18] *Grace Lloyd Walsh Scrapbook.* Grace Lloyd Walsh Papers, Special Collections, University of Delaware Library. [PAGE 19] *Frederick Nixon-Nirdlinger Scrapbook.* Special Collections, University of Delaware Library. [PAGES 44, 45] *Berta Ruck Scrapbook.* Special Collections, University of Delaware Library. [PAGES 46, 47] *Minnie Reed Scrapbook.* Photography: Jason Brownrigg. [PAGE 48] *Effie Davis Putnam Scrapbook.* Elizabeth Yates Papers, Sophia Smith Collection, Smith College Library. [PAGE 49] *Zelda Fitzgerald Scrapbook.* F. Scott Fitzgerald Papers, Manuscripts Division, Department of Rare Books and Special Collections, Princeton University Library. [PAGES 52, 53] *Hilda Doolittle (H.D.) Scrapbook.* Yale Collection of American Literature, Beinecke Rare Book and Manuscript Library, Yale University. Reprinted by permission of New Directions

Publishing Corp. [PAGES 54, 55] *Agnes Medill Scrapbook.* Agnes Medill Papers, Special Collections, University of Delaware Library. [PAGE 56] *Carl Van Vechten Scrapbook.* Carl Van Vechten Papers, Yale Collection of American Literature, Beinecke Rare Book and Manuscript Library, Yale University. Courtesy of the Carl Van Vechten Trust. [PAGE 88] *Lillian Hellman Scrapbook.* Lillian Hellman Papers, Harry Ransom Center, University of Texas at Austin. [PAGES 91, 92] *F. Scott Fitzgerald Baby Book.* F. Scott Fitzgerald Papers, Manuscripts Division, Department of Rare Books and Special Collections, Princeton University Library. [PAGE 119] *Saul Steinberg Scrapbook.* Saul Steinberg Papers, Beinecke Rare Book and Manuscript Library, Yale University. ©2008 The Saul Steinberg Foundation/Artists Rights Society (ARS), New York. [PAGE 136] *Jane Collum Scrapbooks.* Stan Brakhage Papers, Beinecke Rare Book and Manuscript Library, Yale University. [PAGES 136, 137] *Lenore Tawney Envelopes.* Georgia O'Keeffe Papers, Beinecke Rare Book and Manuscript Library, Yale University. [PAGE 138] *Dan Eldon Journals.* Courtesy Creative Visions Foundation and Candela / Decker Gallery. [PAGE 139] *Brian Coffey Self Books.* Brian Coffey Papers, Special Collections, University of Delaware Library. [PAGES 140, 141] *"Desk Clock, Hands Stopped at 9:04."* Collection of the New-York Historical Society. [PAGE 158] *Family Tree, Victorian Photocollage Album.* Mary and Leigh Block Endowment, Art Institute of Chicago. Photography: Robert Lifson. [PAGE 164] *James Madison Family Tree.* James Madison Papers, Manuscript Division, Library of Congress. [PAGE 165] *The 1000 Journals Project.* Courtesy of SomeGuy. [PAGES 168, 169] *PostSecret.* Permission Courtesy of HarperCollins, Publishers. [PAGE 169] *Candy Jernigan Travel Journals.* Photography: Jeri Coppola. Used with Permission of the Candy Jernigan Foundation for the Arts. [PAGES 142–156 and 170] *"The Wandering Moleskine Project."* Collage by Emily Gerz. Photography: Armand B. Frasco. [PAGE 171] Featured Scrapbooks. Photography by Carl Kaufman, Yale Media Services. [PAGES XXII–XXXI, 10; 24–33, 60–69, 85, 96–105, 132, 133] All other photography: Winterhouse.

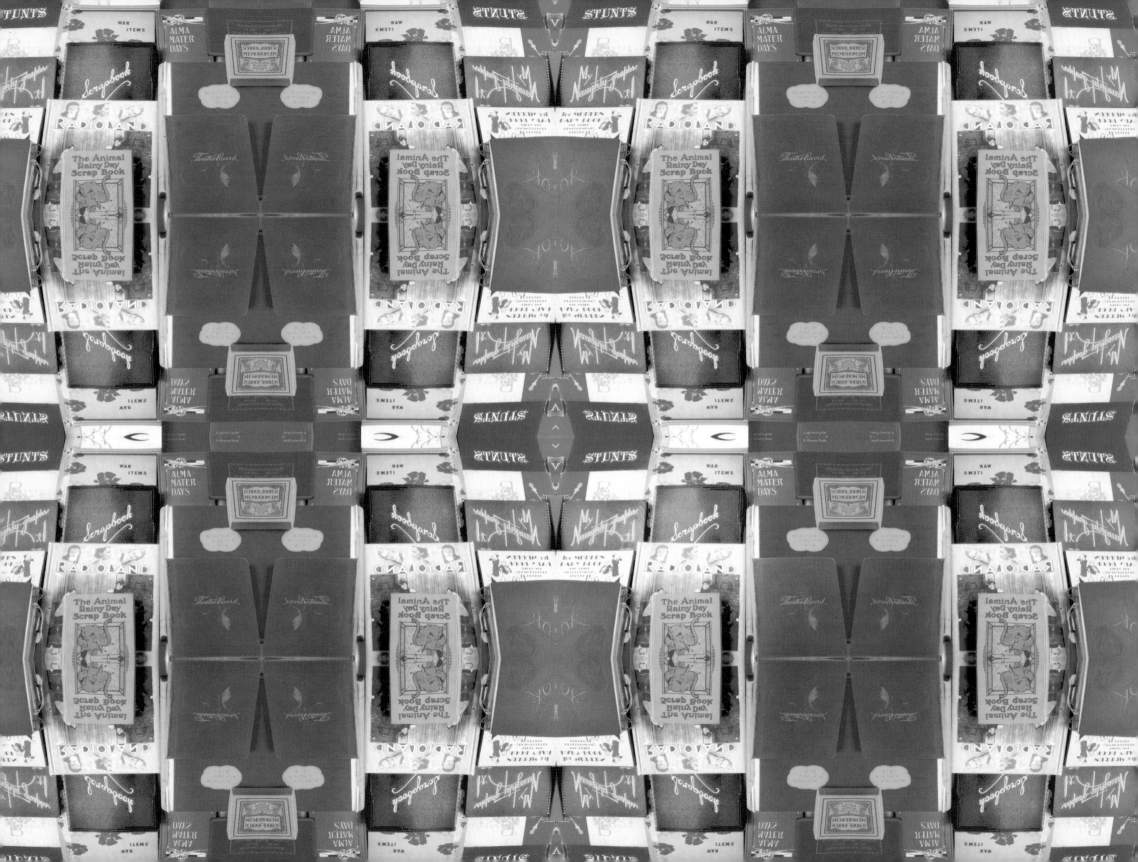